# Seed's Sketchy Relationship Theories - A Guide to the Perils of Dating

# (How Not To Become A Bar Regular)

By

Penned By: The Seed & German Seed

authorHOUSE

*1663 LIBERTY DRIVE, SUITE 200*
*BLOOMINGTON, INDIANA 47403*
*(800) 839-8640*
*WWW.AUTHORHOUSE.COM*

© 2004 Penned By: The Seed & German Seed
All Rights Reserved.

No part of this book may be reproduced, stored in a retrieval system, or transmitted by any means without the written permission of the author.

First published by AuthorHouse 09/24/04

ISBN: 1-4208-0030-2 (sc)

Printed in the United States of America
Bloomington, Indiana

This book is printed on acid-free paper.

# WHAT THE FIRST READERS ARE SAYING:

(Disclaimer: Once this book reaches #1 Status. Please Burn It.)

"It is like all of these thoughts fell out of my head and right onto the pages."

- the seed.

"This is one of the greatest literary works of the century. I believe it will save a lot of troubled relationships. I know if I had only received this wealth of information sooner, I would still be alive on the inside."

- Bill (a broken bar regular in Chicago)

"It is a funny thing, sometimes when you take a bunch of words and throw them together in the right order, they seem to form sentences."

- the seed.

"I read this book cover to cover several times and each and every time I was actually riveted by the sheer passion and intensity. Every time I would rush home and give Harry a little something, something to show how I really feel about him. I knew Seed was gifted when I read his early work and actually I believe I am responsible for a great deal of the success he is receiving now. I made him who he is today."

- Mrs. Grant (Seed's grade 5 English teacher)


"Who's Harry?"

- Tom (Mrs. Grant's husband)


"I love pork. I could eat it every meal of the day. Wait, I do eat it every meal of the day. Thank God, that I like it so much."

- German Seed


"I have read *War and Peace*. This is nothing like it."

- Carl (some guy who read *War and Peace*)


"Fuuuuucckk!!!"

- Mary (Head of Mothers Against the Use of Profanity in America)


"Just because I am your mother, doesn't give you the right to know my name."

- Seed's mother


"I really enjoyed the way he numbered the pages: 1, 2, 3, 4... I found it to be quite convenient and logical."

- Mr. Carlyle (Seed's grade 7 math teacher)

"Hey!!! You cut me off jerk."

- Dick (an angry motorist)


"Thank You Seed. You basically made me who I am today. I think my star will be shining brightly, thanks to you."

-Johnny


"Did you call me an *Attention* ——-?"

- Chastity


"Well it took me a while but I finally was given the time to read it and it is <u>**GOOD!**</u> An entertaining read with realistic, useful information. My favorite line is: **They have their own bars... why can't they have their own book?** You have a winner here and now is time to unleash it on the world whether they can handle it or not."

- W


"It is a great honor to be accepting this award. I had some stiff competition from such words as *fuck, a, and, attention, girl, boy, woman* and *period,* along with thousands of other words that were in the running. As for the words *on* and *in* ... you came close! At this time I would also like to thank.................."

- The word "This" (accepting an achievement award)


"I have had a fantastic time reading this book. Some parts were totally hilarious, others made me think, which I feel is the point of the book in the first place. I love the raw energy and passion that Seed exudes in his writing. It is nice to see someone has the balls to tell it how it is. At least from his perspective. I think this Seed fellow is onto something big. I look forward to future works from him."

- Greg (some guy in Germany, one of the first people to read the book)

"Hello!!!"

- the seed. (answering the telephone)

"Yes, we accept MasterCard, Visa, American Express, Cash, Money Orders and Certified Cheques. So how many Bobble Heads would you like?"

- Velvet (a clerk at Seed's Succulent Boutique and a true Hollywood 10)

"Ohh My!!! Ohh My!!!! Not only does German Seed know how to touch the G spot, but he knows where the H, I, J and K spots are as well. Can I just say he is some sort of Sexual Dynamo!!! And by the way the book is kicking."

- Angela (past lover of German Seed)

"I really like the paper."

- Pepe (a blind panhandler)

"I must commend Seed. He has tackled a very tough subject matter and spared the fluff that most books on relationships inflict upon us. He has shared big parts of his life to give the reader an understanding of where a lot of his knowledge comes from. It is very refreshing to see that he never held back on his opinions. He seems to say what everyone else seems to be afraid of saying and he talks from the heart. The book is laced with deep thoughts and yet it is filled with original comedy to keep it light and fresh to read. If you read it with an open heart and an open mind, Seed provides a very powerful positive message. I highly recommend this book to anyone trying to sort out their personal relationships or for those who simply want a good laugh. It is rare but Seed provides us with both. I wish him great success."

- David (typesetter for a large printing company)


"I am not lying Marge. I am just writing fiction with my mouth."

- Homer Simpson


"What a fucking laugh I got from your book. I cannot wait to read more!!!! Awesome job buddy. Finally at 40-something years old, you have found your calling. Great job. I am proud of you!!!"

- Rick Gillis


"As the great philosopher of our time, Yogi Berra, once said: *If you don't know where you are going, you will wind up somewhere else.* Deep, very deep.

Judging by your book cover and birth certificate, you seem to know where you are going! Love the birth certificate."

- YT


"Do you realize what you have here? What you have is worth several million dollars and I would like to be part of bringing that to fruition."

- Wade (discussing the possibilities of representing Seed)

"Welcome to The Burger Barn. Can I take your order?"

- the seed.

# DEDICATION:

This book is dedicated to both my late Grandparents who raised me despite some trying conditions. It is also dedicated to my late Great Aunt Priscilla who without your love and kindness I may have not found the strength to complete this project. You are dearly missed.

It is also dedicated to all of my friends both new and old who have stood by me all of these years. You have all helped to make the trials and tribulations of life a wicked ride and I look forward to many more years with you on this journey.

# TABLE OF CONTENTS

WHAT THE FIRST READERS ARE SAYING: ........................ v

DEDICATION: ................................................................ xi

CHAPTER 1 Opening Rant ............................................ 1

CHAPTER 2 What Is............? ........................................ 8

CHAPTER 3 Why.............? ........................................... 13

CHAPTER 4 Love & Relationships: What the Fuck Are They?. 21

**SECTION 1 The Formative Years** ................................. 33

CHAPTER 5 Man ......................................................... 36

CHAPTER 6 Woman .................................................... 48

CHAPTER 7 Theory: Your Mother Is Probably Lying To You.... 53

**SECTION 2 Getting In The Game** ................................ 63

CHAPTER 8 Theory: How to Get Dates Or Pickup Lines Don't Work .................................................................. 66

CHAPTER 9 Theory: Don't Listen to The Pressure to Hook Up. Stay Single. Have Fun. Sleep Around If You Must At Least Till You're 25. ............................................................ 72

CHAPTER 10 Theory: We Attract What We Can Afford Beginnings (Finding and Keeping Dates) How not to get Fucked ................................................................. 75

CHAPTER 11 Theory: If You Are Not Hot! Find Something to Excel At ............................................................... 83

CHAPTER 12 Theory: Though Early on in Life For Guys Looks May Attract Women. As We Age It is Power, Money and Fame That Attracts ........................................................ 88

CHAPTER 13 Theory: To Have a Chance You Must Learn How to Be Alone ............................................................. 97

CHAPTER 14 Theory: If You Want To Keep Her Interested Don't Be A Nice Guy (The Girls Want The Bad Boy Theory) . 102

CHAPTER 15 Theory: Beauty is a Consistent Thing ........... 108

CHAPTER 16 Theory: If You Want To Date Babes You Must Surround Yourself With Babes ..................................... 112

CHAPTER 17 Theory: Most Attractive Women are Attention Whores ............................................................. 115

CHAPTER 18 Theory: Hot Girls May Fuck The Bartender But They Are Not Staying For The Long Term ..................... 122

**SECTION 3 You Have Someone You Think You Want To Keep Now What?** ................................................................. 129

CHAPTER 19 Theory: Never, Never, Never, Never, Never, Never Absolutely for No Reason Did I say Never Settle No Matter What ................................................................ 132

CHAPTER 20 Theory: Life's Troubles Don't Build Character They Reveal it ....................................................... 137

CHAPTER 21 Theory: There Is No Such Thing as Security ... 145

Chapter 22 Theory: Women May Fall for the Present But They Stay For The Future ................................................. 148

CHAPTER 23 Looks & Currency ................................... 151

CHAPTER 24 The Role of Friends (Who Can and Who Can't Be in Your Relationship if You Want it to Succeed) ............... 158

CHAPTER 25 Understanding the Roles of Age How The Age Thing Works Between The Sexes. As We Age We Become More Valuable. As They Age Arghh... Run for your life.... ........... 167

CHAPTER 26 Connections: Is It Love or Just a Rash .......... 172

CHAPTER 27 Is It Working: The Red Flags? ..................... 176

**SECTION 4 It's Not Working: Picking Up the Pieces of You ... 181**

CHAPTER 28 I Just Want To Be Friends "We Have Been Through So Much Together"........................................ 183

CHAPTER 29 But I Love Her.............Him............ ................ 187

CHAPTER 30 "We Have To Talk?" Run, Run, Run. The Myth That You Can Change Someone. We Are Who We Are. ....... 190

CHAPTER 31 The Girlfriend With A Lot Of Male Friends ..... 194

CHAPTER 32 The Only Way Men & Women Can Be Friends.. 198

CHAPTER 33 Infidelity: Dating or Being Married To Liar & Cheater ............................................................................201

**SECTION 5 For Better Or Worse You're Staying................. 211**

CHAPTER 34 Call It Serious Call It Dead ....................... 215

CHAPTER 35 Honey We're Going To Have a Baby.... Procreation ........................................................... 217

CHAPTER 36 We All Force It Don't We?........................ 224

CHAPTER 37 After All We Are All Human ..................... 227

CHAPTER 38 Should You Stay Or Should You Go? More Red Flags ................................................................... 229

CHAPTER 39 Finally: The Simple Formula To How It Should Work ...................................................................... 235

CHAPTER 40 Throw Away The Fucking Formula.............. 243

**SECTION 6 Other Realms ..................................................249**

CHAPTER 41 Roommates ............................................ 252

CHAPTER 42 The Gay World......................................... 255

CHAPTER 43 Closing Rant ........................................... 265

CHAPTER 44 Seed's Wonderful Magnificent Brilliant Succulent Tasty Boutique www.seedenterprises.com .................... 277

CHAPTER 45 Who Is Seed................?............................. 284

CHAPTER 46 Gravy ................................................... 288

CHAPTER 47 Outtakes:................................................316

ACKNOWLEDGEMENTS............................................. 349

# Seed's Sketchy Relationship Theories
## A Guide to the Perils of Dating

**Welcome!!!**

Hop on. Enjoy the ride. It is going to be wild

the seed.

Page 1 — Seed Productions 2004

# CHAPTER 1
# Opening Rant

*"Promise Yourself:*
*To be so strong that nothing can disturb your peace of mind.*
*To talk health, happiness and prosperity to every person you meet.*
*To make all of your friends feel that there is something special in them.*
*To look at the sunny side of everything and let your optimism come true.*
*To think only of the best, to work only for the best and expect only the best.*
*To be just as enthusiastic about the success of others as you are about your own.*
*To forget the mistakes of the past and press on to greater achievements of the future*
*To wear a cheerful countenance at all times and give every living creature you meet a smile.*
*To give so much time to the improvement of yourself that you have no time to criticize others.*
*To be too large for worry, too noble for anger, too strong for fear, and too happy to permit the presence of trouble!"*

-Christian D. Larson

*Penned By: The Seed & German Seed*

*"What will we find at the other end of the tunnel?"*

    The World is a fucked up place. At the time that I started writing this (early 2003) the globe was spinning out of control and fuck it is not necessarily in a positive spiral. We currently have a global population of over six billion people. Wait, six billion and one thousand more. Wait, six billion and two thousand more. I can't count fast enough. Just think in the beginning, which is really not all that long ago, we started with two. Hell, the USA is less than 200 years old and it has a population of over 290 million. Never has there been a time in the short history of modern mankind where there has been so much uncertainty. We have maybe one madman threatening world peace and who knows it may actually be several madmen who are in charge of our current destiny. We have had a man who most would call less than the brightest bulb in the pack, just lead the Western world and our only true superpower into war (perhaps World War 3), even though the majority of people are not certain if this was the right thing to do. Every day that passes, every bombing or ambush in Iraq and every soldier that gets killed

## Seed's Sketchy Relationship Theories - A Guide to the Perils of Dating

in a country that was supposed to be liberated and not occupied, only emphasizes this point. However it appears to be this man's agenda and what he needs to do to save his administration. Let us all hope and if you are a spiritual person pray that he is doing the right thing.

In a way the world is like NCAA College Football. The USA is sort of like Nebraska and during the regular season they get to play Gopher State and Helen Keller University, with the end result being annihilation. This is all in preparation for one of their only meaningful games of the year: the big moneymaking bowl game at the end of the season. Now just think about it for a moment – the USA is looking out at the world and comes to the conclusion that, on one hand, Iraq is run by a maniacal dictator who oppresses and tortures his own citizens. On the other, China is in a similar situation, with the atrocities against its own people being perhaps even greater than that of Iraq. However, if the USA was to challenge China there is a chance they just might lose that game so instead they attack Iraq, which in terms of its military strength does resemble the football prowess of Butthead State and the outcome is quite predictable. The USA quickly annihilates them, sending a message to every other challenger. Let's just hope their actions and policies don't lead to a bowl game (vs. North Korea?).

At the present time the world media is controlled by a few people resulting in a situation where you have to ask: Can we really trust the information that we are being fed? If you turn on the news, it is just one tragedy after another, most of the stories create a scenario where leaving your own home seems like a risky venture. Just think about it. On any particular day you can read about Snipers, Al Qaeda, Aids, SARS, the West Nile Virus, Ebola, Mad Cow Disease, the Avian Flu and major cities in the Eastern US and Canada being shut down by the blackout of 2003 along with countless other things that are threatening humankind as we know it.

Technology is rapidly going out of control. No one can keep up with the daily advances that are taking place. It was not that long ago when the party line was still in use in rural communities. These advances are causing the gap between the rich and poor

*Penned By: The Seed & German Seed*

to become even greater with the middle class quickly becoming eroded.

Never has there been a time when huge companies are failing overnight with the ramifications to the stock markets being so extreme. Big-time managers, however, though their companies are broke, still keep their villas and "earn" enormous bonuses. The investors are left holding the bag.

Our weather appears to be changing dramatically. We have global warming caused supposedly by the greenhouse effect. There is El Nino, La Nina and whatever other supposed phenomena affecting the Earth's climate. One must ask if this is naturally caused or controlled by man. Or is man simply too fucking stupid to see that acre after acre of rainforest is not worth obliterating in order to raise cattle for fast food chains. Have you noticed that the "flood of the century" seems to come every few years? Hurricanes, typhoons and tornados are commonplace. Droughts, mild winters no big surprise. Have you ever stopped to think why this is so? Interesting things to ponder...

If one is to believe the Mayan calendar, this is all starting to happen for a reason and on December 21, 2012 things will become clear. There are different theories on what may happen on this day. Standard thought is that the world is starting to go through a transformation of sorts – or one big correction as we start to go into the next cycle in the history and evolution of mankind. The dramatic events that are taking place now are sort of a weeding out of evil. When this above-mentioned date comes along, those of us who adjust or transform (basically get it), will have a chance to move forward into a better, more evolved earth. We are not promoting this belief but just saying that it is definitely food for thought.

On the one hand, you can have a world filled with war, hatred, fear, tragedy, racism and crime. No wonder relationships are struggling and the divorce rate is so high. We are living in a world of "me" time. Everyone seems to have stopped thinking of others and just looks at what is best for themselves. Fuck, how many different types of rage have been diagnosed over the last few years – the world needs really to slow down. Life is moving too fast. Everything is not that fucking important. We need to

## Seed's Sketchy Relationship Theories - A Guide to the Perils of Dating

get back to a day where we say "Hi" to our neighbors instead of fearing them. We are all in the same ball game together.

On the other hand we can turn off the news and start looking at things positively. As hard as it may be, we can all try to be aware of our emotions and no matter how hard it is, only be positive about things. We are all in a way being controlled or at least influenced by the media. So shut off the TV for a minute and think. A shuttle tragedy, though a horrific event, does not warrant a lot of discussion by the average person, unless you have family members involved or you work at NASA. It can only create more despair, fear and negativity in the average man. A 100-car pileup on the Interstate does not need to be discussed, though tragic it is not positive, it does not warrant much time unless you are directly affected or on the safety committees that help to design highways. We know this sounds cold and our hearts go out to those who have lost loved ones, but the world is challenging enough just caring and looking out for those who are in our lives. If we are also being filled with the pain of people we don't know and have nothing to do with, how are we ever going to find peace and happiness? Come on people.

We all have at one time or another mourned the loss of a celebrity, athlete or a politician. We don't need to worship these people. We need to worship those around us that matter to us. Period. Celebrities, athletes and politicians have their own loved ones. Sure we can appreciate what they have added to our lives in the form of entertainment or policy changes, but that is it. What we are saying here is, maybe more so than at any other time in history, it may be in our best interest to start looking at ourselves and the people in our lives who matter, and to try to encourage, nurture, love and, most important, be positive around them. We know that if you appear to be happy all the time and not consumed with some sort of despair in these trying times, people may start looking at you like you are crazy. Well the choice is yours. Would you not rather be happy and fucking crazy, than immersed in all of the troubles of this big fucked up world. If you believe the message of the Mayans, those who remain positive, remove negative thoughts and love others have a chance of evolving. Whereas those who are negative and filled with despair - well, your world as you know it may be coming to an end. In fact, if you are this way your world has probably been over for a while anyway.

Unfortunately for me during the writing of this book I became a case study in how important it is to care and nurture those whom you love. The people who are really important to you in your life. In a one-month period of time, the following events occurred in my own personal life. My relationship, which I deeply cherished, suddenly and unexpectedly came to an end for no understandable reason. A friend of mine, 28 years old, came to me to tell me that he has cancer and does not have much time to live. Another friend told me one Friday afternoon that his life sucked. I tried to encourage him, but on Sunday he took his own life. My closest Aunt called to tell me she was changing her will and, oh by the way, that she might be sick and dying. Less than one month later she died and, finally, after that you'd think it would be enough, an uncle of mine died unexpectedly. At that moment I realized I was kind of fucked up, as I could not even drum up an emotion when hearing about the loss of my uncle. Unless numbness is considered an emotion. To top it all off, I started thinking about the loss of my parents, which happened when I was in my early 20's. I watched both them take their last breaths a year apart. I thought I had dealt with those emotions, however, they came rushing back. I am not revealing this for sympathy or to have anyone feel sorry for me, I am just revealing this because it illustrates how important it is, not to spend too much time or emotions on the other tragedies of the world, that honestly, do not directly impact our lives. It is hard enough to process things in one's own life and at the same time to be concerned with tornados in Oklahoma. OK, if you live in Oklahoma or one of the neighboring states, then fine, worry about it. If you live in Alaska, then you probably have other, more pressing issues (we hope).

Another thing I learned during this time is that most of the people in this world are so fucking self-absorbed that they forget to be kind to strangers. Due to their trivial shit (John was supposed to pick me up at 6 and he was 5 minutes late), which they think is actually important, they treat strangers rudely without knowing, or caring, what is happening in that person's world. The message here is this and I don't care where the fuck you are – at the counter at McDonald's, your Mechanic's or even

## Seed's Sketchy Relationship Theories - A Guide to the Perils of Dating

your Doctor's office, just because your illegitimate son neglected one of his chores don't take it out on a stranger. These people are human as well and are just trying to get through their day-to-day challenges and who knows – maybe they just lost a loved one in a tragedy. The last thing they need is to take crap from you. Sorry if that sounds harsh, but believe me, if we all listen to this advice it would definitely be a kinder world.

You may all be thinking by now that this Seed guy is a jaded cynical bastard. Well, he is not. He is basically just another guy who is mostly happy, loves those important to him and would do anything for them without conditions. He likes to try to be brutally honest: Take that for what it is worth. Hell, I am not asking you all to agree with me. It is just one man's opinion and takes on the current state of affairs in the world.

Hey, this book is supposed to be a light-hearted look at relationships. However, I believed it was necessary to comment on the way things presently are, to give you an understanding on why relationships are taking such a beating in this current version of the world. With all of the uncertainty and fear that is present how can it be any other way. It has become "me" time and it doesn't have to be. Everyone needs to slow down a bit, take a big deep breath and stop letting the outside world affect them so much. If you can do this you may actually have a chance of making it through this mess. That is not to say that people in general are not good hearted and caring. Unfortunately the fact is a lot of people are actually egotistical, shallow, conniving and fucked in the brain. The point is: I am just asking people to stop acting like sheep and live their own lives. Is that too much to ask? Well is it? Now having said all of this I am sure you are confused as to what this book is about. Well, it couldn't all be light, there had to be a reason that relationships are in a confusing, beat up mess. I think the above rant gives you some insight into our view of what has happened to our world, and why, just like our world, relationships have spun out of control. They are evolving as well, once again not necessarily in a positive way.... So to help you wind your way through all of this mess and understand what is happening, here it is: *Seed's Sketchy Relationship Theories*. So let us lighten up a bit and start looking at things from a different perspective. And while you are at it, have some fun. I insist.

# CHAPTER 2
# What Is..........?

*"The eyes of other people are the eyes that ruin us.
If all but myself were blind, I should want neither fine clothes,
fine houses nor fine furniture."*

-Ben Franklin

First off *Seed's Sketchy Guide* is "real" and in no way intended to be politically correct. It was never meant to be a social, political or religious commentary on how the world works. But at the same time it would be inappropriate if it did not touch on the way the world is operating at the current time. Without a bit of a commentary on what is going on in the world we would have no understanding of why relationships are the way they are currently. Fuck we don't live in a bubble now do we?

This book is a practical and humorous guide to the perils of dating and relationships. It could quite easily be placed in the *Relationship, Self Help, Comedy* or *Bargain Bin Sections* of your favorite bookstore. It draws from years of relationship adventures (mistakes) and a lot of fun and confusion (drunken lonely nights). It also uses "most of the time" generalizations which can be confrontational, but if you have the balls to admit it, tough skin and aren't a sensitive wuss, it will help you make big strides both in

## Seed's Sketchy Relationship Theories - A Guide to the Perils of Dating

your dating and personal lives. Don't "most Asians eat rice"? Fuck, aren't we all just a little too sensitive these days? This guide will be confrontational and will probably get a lot of people to despise me but if you really read it, you will understand that it is just calling the kettle black and what is wrong with being honest.

*Seed's Sketchy Guide* is ultimately a series of essays on the different aspects of relationships, dating and the world. It represents opinions on the current state of these topics and the chapters may pertain to certain aspects of your life and may be used individually or as a whole to help you gain perspective. It is not necessarily a picture of how I would like the world to be, but more so a reflection of how it is.

*Seed's Sketchy Guide* was not initially meant to have an autobiographical feel to it. However, as mentioned in the Opening Rant, some strange things happened during the writing of it and it would be amiss if I did not share some of the experiences with you. After all, the reason Seed has some expertise on the subject is because he shares his life experiences and is constantly striving to get it right, or at least marginally better. This project even became therapy for a lot of different aspects of his life. When it was started, life was good. And then WHAM! Everything changed. So for those of you out there who find yourself going through some traumatic situations, I highly recommend writing as therapy. Hell, who knows maybe you can write a book. Just don't write this one it has already been done and plagiarism is a bad thing. As for some of the traumatic life experiences that started taking place, man, when Seed is faced with life challenges they are monumental!

*Seed's Sketchy Relationship Theories: A Guide to the Perils of Dating* may not be for everyone ... fuck that, it is for EVERYONE!!!!!!!!! It will help some people wind their way through the often scary and evil world of dating, relationships, breaking up, starting over again, and most importantly being as happy as you can be with what you are given. It is an honest "most of the time" perspective of how the world works. It is filled with different scenarios, which help simplify what is and what could happen in one's dating and relationship life. It is written from the heart and it should work for most people. But as in everything in life there are exceptions to the rules, so if you are an "exception" you will know it. I am going to let you in on a little secret here.

*Penned By: The Seed & German Seed*

Are you paying attention? This is vitally important, ready? No I don't think you are. Put down the phone, turn off the TV, stereo or computer. I said this is important now take it seriously, ok. Here we go. If you want to live an exciting fulfilling life: *STRIVE TO BE THE EXCEPTION!* You will be the one with the smile on your face, not the one who is desperately trying to prove that they are the *EXCEPTION!*

*Seed's Sketchy Guide* will help you navigate your way through all of the steps of relationships, from the first date to "I do" and everything in between. It will help you to decide whether you should stay, leave, or just stick around for the sex. It will help you to put the fun back into dating and relationships. Fuck the things-are-complicated attitude. Dating should be your retreat, not your nightmare. *Seed's Guide* will try to give you the tools to understand the differences between the sexes and where you are in the pecking order of things. Most of the time love really is not enough. The divorce rate is somewhere between 40% and 60%, depending on where you live. Do you want to be in that group? If you already have experienced divorce, do you really want to go there again?

It will also help you to notice some of the danger signs, the red flags. Why are we staying in so many fucked up relationships? Is it so we can have a bunch of screwed up children to continue the fucked up legacy? If it is, enough already, let us all take a deep breath and realize that it is time to break the cycle. Let's give our kids a chance. Single parenthood is not an achievement and staying together for the kid's sake may even be less of an accomplishment. It's simple: if you do not want to raise your own children, then don't have any. It is a travesty that the television stars or overpaid prima-Donna athletes are the role models of today. Parents should be the role models. Trust me on this one, I know from experience. I was actually raised by some imaginary people I created myself. So I want you all now to repeat after me.... *WE ARE NOT ALL MEANT TO PROCREATE.*

Finally *Seed's Sketchy Guide* is truly a love story. It is filled with passion and a positive message of the ideal world, sort of a utopia. You just need to read between the lines to find the positive message. Though it seems to be intended for a male audience, it is not, it can be equally useful to the fairer sex as well. So find a

## Seed's Sketchy Relationship Theories - A Guide to the Perils of Dating

comfortable chair, maybe a beer or a gin & tonic and let the fun, conversation, debate and fighting begin. For those of you who use your brain, enjoy the wisdom and power you are about to receive.

By the way I might as well get this out of the way now. The word "fuck" is used a lot in this book. Actually for those of you who like to keep stats, our statistician informed us that it was used in some form or other 290 times. Which represents roughly once in every 408 words. It is not used to offend or due a lack of vocabulary. It is used because of its power to illustrate and because it simply popped into my head at the time I was writing. I do not encourage or use the word very often in my day-to-day conversations. For those of you concerned about its use, the following is how I answered some close friends when they suggested the word was being used too fucking often: I would like to thank all of you for your tremendous feedback. Thus far it has been very, very positive. However one thing keeps being mentioned and that is the use of the word FUCK. Some of you even suggested maybe toning it down a bit. Well NO! I do not think there is a word that so aptly describes just about all emotions, whether they are happiness, sadness, anger etc. And also I do not really think of it as a swear word anymore. So you all can FUCK OFF! Just kidding. Instead be happy I don't use the word c_ _t. My advice to those of you who are really offended by the word FUCK, don't read it out loud."

Also at this time we feel it is necessary to address one other common occurrence throughout the book. At times the book is written in first person, sometimes third person and at others it is written in eighth (is that actually a writing style or did I just make it up?) and sometimes well who the hell knows what person Seed used. The reason for this sometimes confusing writing technique is that The Seed and I (who really is The Seed) along with the German Seed (who really is German Seed) had many heated debates over whether or not it would be best to write in one style (actually we had zero debates over this and we got along rather swimmingly. It was our editor's suggestion to explain our style to you). However, we realized that there were two of us collaborating on the theories along with our several alter-egos and we were not really sure how to reflect that - so after some

*Penned By: The Seed & German Seed*

discussion *I* decided for **Seed** that *we* should continue to write in the various styles. After all as we worked our way through the writing process we came to realize that though The Seed is my nickname - "Seed" actually was transforming into a state of being, or a way of thinking and anyone could be "Seed". It simply illustrates becoming an exception.

Oh yeah - it was also fun to confuse our editor. Anyway regardless of style we feel the positive message of the book is far more important than style - so just sit back, relax and enjoy. Seed concurs!

# CHAPTER 3
# Why..............?

*"For love to survive the tests of time, one must have reached a comfortable point in their own life or the daily stresses of life will tear it apart."*

- the seed.

Why? The answer to this question is paramount to the reason this whole project began in the first place. Why is a difficult question to answer definitively, so in an effort to simplify things I decided that the best way to explain "why" was to break it down into point form. Here goes:

1. **To share personal relationship experiences in order to gain an understanding of how relationships actually work.**

During the course of his life, Seed has experienced and failed at many, many relationships. Hell, maybe failed is too strong of a term for the outcomes. Some of these relationships were tremendous learning experiences, a way of learning how to love and share with another human being. Some of them were purely sexual pit stops, the course of which was filled with hot steamy passion without much else to sustain the relationship.

And some of them were deep and meaningful experiences to truly be cherished. The latter were the relationships that caused the greatest pain and anguish. Most of us have been there at some point in time, finding the one person who makes us glow at the thought of a lifetime together. The person whose imperfections make them even more perfect. In a sense we have found our own personal bliss. The one place where we feel safe. Then with no warning it ends, leaving you reeling and trying to understand what went wrong. These are the relationships that cause us to make the greatest mistakes, yet they also give us the greatest opportunities for personal growth.

Part of the healing and self discovery process is to make the mistakes, to get out your hurt as long as you do not cross certain lines, to do whatever you think you need to do. You may embarrass yourself and actually do things that drive your love farther away from you. But remember this, if you truly loved someone and they have hurt you badly, sometimes even if no one is listening, you need to vent your emotions. Sure, you could play games to try to win them back, but even if you succeed at those games without expressing your deep pain in some way, playing games will only be a short-term solution. Like I said earlier, some of my relationships have been tremendous journeys of self-discovery, some have been short and purely sexual, and some have been torture. The one common thing they all provided was tremendous insight into the way the sexes work.

2. **Demand. Both friends and acquaintances were constantly asking Seed to share experiences with them. Primarily my dear friend Fiona.**

Some people believe in the battle of the sexes. Let me assure you, it is not a battle: it is a war. It has not been until recently, after many discussions with friends and acquaintances both married and single on their relationships and the pain and pleasure that they have gained from these experiences, coupled with my own personal experiences that I have started to realize the brutal and beautiful truth of how the world of dating and relationships truly works. It is not difficult to understand, however, that it requires being honest with yourself. Honesty will help you to understand what is possible and how to discover and achieve the most happiness with what you have been given to work with.

*Seed's Sketchy Relationship Theories - A Guide to the Perils of Dating*

Thanks must be extended to my dear friend Fiona, who put a lot of pressure on me to come up with theories. It became a weekly event on the social calendar. A note on Fiona here. I met her several years ago in a line-up to a club and somehow through my ability to interact with strangers we struck up a conversation. I must make this perfectly clear, this ability to have conversations with strangers is a gift and in no way was I making the moves on her at the time that I met her. I was not making the 140K necessary to keep her, so it was primarily a friendly discussion. However, my somewhat of an understudy, Wayne, was enthralled. His eyes lit up at the sight of Fiona and his heart started pounding a bit faster because thanks to his dear friend, the Seed, he found the love of his life by accident. Over the next several years their bond grew and they finally married at the end of 2002.

### 3. Experience.

For several years, I found myself being constantly asked by friends and acquaintances to share my theories. These experiences led to a lot of heated debate and discussion, a bit of drunkenness, but never ever a dull moment. It also produced a lot of temporary hatred (ok, so some of the hatred wasn't temporary, those are the chances you take when you have an opinion!). Essentially the more sensitive the theory, the more heated the nights became. The Seed was starting to be in demand at social events, primarily by women (due to his rapier-like good looks and charm) and surprisingly some of the most confrontational topics brought about future comments that went sort of like: I hate to admit it, but what we talked about the other day, fuck you were right! Even the women were starting to say "fuck" and that *before* they read this book!

If I happened to be out with a couple, it seemed like they were taking notes on what I was saying, especially the women. On many occasions, the Seed would hit a nerve. Some found the theories to be a negative look at the world and relationships. It is funny how when one hits a chord and does not just take the same stance as the majority, people think you are being negative. The world views honesty as negative and as a whole we have a responsibility to stop fucking accepting it! Face reality, people, we will all be better off instead of expecting the impossible.

*Penned By: The Seed & German Seed*

### 4. Seed is an individual and he has a positive message to deliver.

Seed is an individual. He does not fit in or belong to any social, political, union, club or association. He does not run with the majority. He strongly believes in original thought. He believes that people need to use their own brainpower to be the best person that they can be. He believes in the brutal and honest truth, which sometimes leads to sadness because a lot of people cannot or will not accept honesty.

He believes in not playing games. He believes that if you are truly in love, express it, there is no purer gift. It does not lose meaning. If those around you are playing games and they leave your life, they were not worth it to begin with. This may be a hard lesson or a jagged pill to swallow, but it is necessary from time to time to purge or do an inventory on the people in your life. Be confident my friends. Love is meant to be cherished. It has tremendous value and is not to be taken away on a whim.

The Seed is an individual who does his own thinking and formulates his own opinions. He has stayed away from the opinions of relationship experts and avoids radio and television shows on the subject. He wanted his message to be primarily that: his message. The only research he has done on this subject has been life and observation. He is not saying that his outlook is the only one, but come on people, start using your brains and take what you learn and come up with some thoughts and idea's of your own. Or save yourself the time - the Seed is right (ha ha)!!!!

### 5. I want relationships to succeed.

Finally, the biggest why of all! Seed wants relationships to succeed. Of course, not the really dysfunctional ones. As said before, never has there been a time in the evolution of the Earth where we need to be kind to each other and have a little bit of fun. We need to slow down and love, nurture, hold and care for one another. There is too much fucking uncertainty in this world and we need a retreat from all of the fear and despair. So people, turn off the news. It is time to focus on the positive things in your life and to treat others with a little respect and kindness. I know as you progress through this book you may call the Seed a

*Seed's Sketchy Relationship Theories - A Guide to the Perils of Dating*

hypocrite, but he is just letting you know how things are in the evolution of life as he sees it.

Let's face it fellows; it is fucking confusing out there. We don't know how to talk to women, nor do they know how to talk to us. We don't know what women really want and usually by the time we figure it out, we are fucked, but not in the sticky sheets sort of way. So the "why" is really just to simplify this big confusing world so we can have the most enjoyment possible out of the fun part of our lives, our intimate relationships.

You know everything in our lives is based upon relationships. We have relationships from the day we are born till the day we die and let's face it, the world is a big, scary fucked-up place. Whether you come from the most loving, caring and nurturing environment, or the most screwed-up trailer park existence, it is our relationships that over time mould and create who we are. To have a chance at living the happiest day-to-day existence, I decided it was time for me to simplify my life and my relationships. To me, the first step of this was to realize that it is not me, my family, my bosses, my friends, my acquaintances or anyone else that is screwed up or dysfunctional. This is a very key point. The whole world is dysfunctional and to survive in a dysfunctional world, one must first understand that even though you may be well adjusted and a great person, you are going to have to learn to deal with other people and their drama daily and that is what will eventually help to reveal your character and dictate who and what you become. One does not need to look far to realize that this is reality. For example, as mentioned before, the divorce rate is between 40-60% and people still hate other due to such things as race, economic background and sexual orientation.

What is the point of this book? First of all, we should maybe point out what this book is not. *Seed's Sketchy Guide to Relationships* is not intended to be a self-help book. We are not here to counsel, analyze or to relieve you of making your own decisions. We did not study psychology and cannot provide you with any psychological help. If you require such help then please, please go to a professional.

The point of this book is to make you think. And to make you laugh! You should think about your relationships, your job and your life. You should give some thought to your abilities, your standard of life and whether or not you're happy with what you're doing and who you're doing it with.

If over the course of reading this book, should you choose to read any further (congratulations if you do, you are on the road to becoming an *"exception"*), you may think Seed is an arrogant idiot. Who does he think he is with his generalizations? That's your opinion. The generalizations serve to illustrate the theories put forth in the book. Naturally, there are *"exceptions"* to every rule. Maybe you think the theories don't apply to you, however, chances are they do. Seed is a living example of his theories and on occasion has hoped and even prayed that he was the *exception to the rule* or at least that his relationships were. But time after time, he was met with bitter misery and sadness and found that there are very few exceptions. On numerous occasions Seed believed love would get him through anything and that ambition and desire to be successful in life would be enough to keep important relationships strong. Unfortunately it was not. My goal is to pass on my experience gained through good and bad relationships, trial and error, and situations that have occurred amongst my family and friends. Most important, my goal is to speak the hard beautiful truth.

In our families and society, honesty has fallen by the wayside. Do you really think that your colleagues, acquaintances and family only want the best for you? Do you really think that everyone likes you? People want what's best for themselves. It is one big self-absorbed world and let's face it, if you're successful you'll have more "friends" than you know what to do with.

The Roman playwright *Plautus* made the following observation: **Homo homini lupus est**. That is, "Man is a wolf to another man" or in other words, humans are out for themselves. Today, if we're honest, human nature has not changed and this saying still reflects the character of people in our society. If the Romans were wise enough to recognize this, why don't we, in the year 2004, finally get it?

The message is simple. Don't rely on other people to make you happy. Expect the best from yourself and never settle for anything less. Treat those who are important to you like gold. We are lucky if we go through our lives with a handful of good friends. You may meet a lot of quality individuals along the way that at any moment can provide you with insight and perhaps enhance your life, remember though, it is only in the moment, and these moments should never be at the expense of the ones that really matter.

As author *David Rakoff* illustrates in an interview when he was asked: When you meet new friends, do you think they're as good as your old friends?

> "New friends are really, really, really exciting. Cause it's like falling in love. You can be with a new friend, and all you want do is be with that new friend, and your oldest friend in the world could come in with a knife in their side and you would turn to them and you would go (sighs),"What is it?" And it's harder to have old friends because it's like a relationship. It takes work and you know them well and they know you well and they're not gonna put up with your shit. I love having new friends, but I think that's the mark of a coward. I mean it's easier to have new friends 'cause it's the romance of friendship with almost none of the work."

Once again, the point of this book is not to provide advice or to claim any psychological competence. We can't tell you what to do or how to live your life. The point of this book is to make you think about your life. Seed is a big fan of relationships - he actually would like to see them succeed. He is also a very positive individual and as he reveals small parts of his own experience you will come to realize this. Life is a big challenge and winning is a never-ending proposition.

So there you have it, the answers to "why". One last thought on the topic. I started to realize that my massive brain (LOL) was full of theories and that there is an audience for what I have to say. I am not claiming to be an expert in the world of relationships, but in the world of *"most of the time"* I have definitely hit a chord, and though my thoughts may be controversial, I believe it is about time someone had the guts to step up to the plate and tell people

*Penned By: The Seed & German Seed*

how it really is. Or at least, to give people some material that will help them to have some interesting conversation.... By the way I am an expert, so forget what I said seven lines ago.

# CHAPTER 4
# Love & Relationships: What the Fuck Are They?

*"I believe that imagination is
stronger than knowledge.
That myth is more potent than facts
That dreams are more powerful than history.
That hope always triumphs over experience.
That laughter is the only cure for grief.
And I believe that Love
is stronger than death."*

-Robert Fullgham

Now that you had to endure my enlightening, earth-shattering *Opening Rant,* and in the process you discovered the reason why this project came to be, as well as what qualifies me to write on this intense and controversial subject matter, I am certain that you have an understanding of what this book is all about. The objective is to show you how the theories are to be used to assist you in working your way through your intimate life. Above all, it is my goal to simplify it for you.

*Penned By: The Seed & German Seed*

So let's get to the real meat of the book, what you opened it for in the first place. This is perhaps one of the most important sections. It will help you to understand the scope of everything else in the book and for that matter the whole fucked-up world.

It is now time to try to understand, if that is at all possible, the inner workings of the two most important things in life: Love and Relationships. If you can get a handle on these topics, then you will be living a life that is prosperous, fulfilling and deeply satisfying. At the end of the day, isn't that what we are all striving for? That warm feeling of contentment you get at the start or end of your day. That everything is ok. If you are lucky enough to experience it in your love life, cherish it and hold on to it as tightly as possible. I don't believe it is something that we experience very often in this hectic day and age. For those of you who have not experienced it in your relationship life, the closest thing that I can compare it to is a tropical vacation. It is that feeling that you get when you get off of the plane, when all of your cares just seem to slip away and even though the humidity may be 190%, it does not matter because for the next period of time nothing in the world matters: everything is going to be ok. As the Jamaicans say: *"No Problem, Mon"*. I know that by comparison to the world of intimate relationships this may be a very vague explanation. The point is, if you ever experience true love there is nothing that can come close to it. To know that you have found it, is like knowing that despite of all your shortcomings and the characteristics that make you – you – you have been fortunate enough to find the one person who will accept you for who you are and regardless of how you fuck up or what you say it is going to take something horrifically egregiously major for that person not to see the beauty in you and leave you. At this moment in time I would like to share with you a simple observation, in the last sentence the word "you" was used 10 times, including 3 times in succession. That, my friends, is some fancy writing. Back to the topic at hand, it is a very happy place where insecurities go to die. Does it exist? The jury is out. Being the positive person that I am, I must believe that it does.

To simplify the world of love and relationships, I have decided to include the MSN Encarta Dictionary definitions of the words "Relationship" and "Love". I figured that this would simplify the whole thing and end the confusion that we all may be having on the subject.

### Relationship

*Noun*

1. Connection: a significant connection or similarity between two or more things, or the state of being related to something else

2. Behavior or feelings towards somebody else: the connection between two or more people or groups and their involvement with each other, especially as regards how they behave and feel toward each other and communicate or cooperate

3. Friendship: an emotionally close friendship, especially one involving sexual relations

4. Connection by family: the way in which two or more people are related by birth, adoption or marriage, or the fact of being related by birth, adoption or marriage

### Love [luv]

*Noun (plural loves)*

1. Very strong affection: a tender feeling of tender affection and passion Young children need unconditional love.

2. Passionate attraction and desire: a passionate feeling of romantic desire and sexual attraction

3. Somebody much loved: somebody who is loved romantically - He was her first real love.

4. Romantic affair: a romantic affair, possibly sexual

5. 5. Strong liking: strong liking or pleasure gained from something - His love of music.

6. Something eliciting enthusiasm: something that elicits deep interest or enthusiasm in somebody

*Penned By: The Seed & German Seed*

7. Music was his greatest love but he also liked ballet.

8. Beloved: used as an affectionate word to somebody loved

9. U.K. term of friendly address: used as a friendly term of address, usually to a woman (informal)

10. Here's your change, love.

11. CHRISTIANITY God's love for humanity: the mercy, grace and charity shown by God to humanity

12. CHRISTIANITY worship of God: the worship and adoration of God

13. SPORTS GAME zero of score: a score of zero in sports and games, for example tennis, squash and whist

Verb (past loved, past participle loved, present participle lov-ing, 3rd person present singular loves)

1. Transitive and intransitive verb feel tender affection for: to feel tender affection for somebody, for example a close relative or friend, or for something such as a place, and ideal or an animal

2. Transitive and intransitive verb feel desire for: to feel romantic and sexual desire and longing for somebody

3. Transitive verb like very much: to like something or like doing something very much

4. Transitive verb show kindness to: to feel and show kindness or charity to somebody

5. Transitive verb have sexual intercourse with: to have sexual intercourse with somebody (dated)

Well that did a couple of things. First of all it filled a couple of pages of the book, which is excellent, something our publisher likes to see. Secondly, it has illustrated how confusing the whole subject is. Not only is there a whole list of possibilities when we talk about Love and Relationships, but it is very difficult to understand how they intertwine. Because Seed is such a Saint,

## Seed's Sketchy Relationship Theories - A Guide to the Perils of Dating

he has decided to simplify it even further by digging deeper into the subject and coming up with his own definitions.

There are several different kinds of relationships. If you think back over the course of your life, the term "relationship" is probably a bit too vague. You've most likely had "physical relationships", "practical relationships", "long-term relationships", "one-night relationships", "long-distance relationships", "holiday relationships", maybe even "abusive or psycho relationships", which quite often are a result of "family relationships." Hell, where do you think dysfunction comes from. Primarily, it is a product of your upbringing and the candy-assed parents who went ahead and had children for selfish reasons without any intent of raising them. Many parents failed to instill in their children strong values and morals, and omitted teaching them how to behave and treat others. Instead, some parents choose to blame society for their kids being fucked up instead of blaming themselves. I am asking you, stop it. Not only are you screwing with your own lives, but that of every other person that your offspring comes in contact with. For once I am in agreement with George W. Bush, we have a responsibility to stop the actions of the "evil doers", so let us have some input in our children's lives so they, as well as society, can have a chance.

In fact every encounter that you have with other people is in a sense a relationship. Actually, the one positive by-product of parents fucking up their offspring is that it creates a tremendous need for mental health professionals to try to put the lives of these shattered individuals back together. It also has a positive effect on the pharmaceutical corporations, which have made a large fortune in the manufacturing of the various anti-depressant medications on the market. Oh yeah, I almost forgot the street-level drug merchants that sell these individuals an escape from the day-to-day grinds, only to fuck up society to a level that can not yet be determined. Oh well, so much for the positives.

A relationship should be a partnership. It is the main goal of our society to be "in a relationship" and therefore, not to be alone. Two people working together can assert and protect their interests and fulfill their psychological, physical and, above all, their material needs.

*Penned By: The Seed & German Seed*

That said, this fulfillment of needs should be mutual. However, depending on the type of relationship (see above) and the type of person you are (look in the mirror), it is more often than not one-sided. If, as far as you can remember, you have only had relationships where you're doing the giving or you're fulfilling the needs of your partner, then it's time to start thinking about what you want, what you're capable of and getting your ass in gear in order to bring about some change in your life before you're old and bitter. If you're the one who's always giving, then it's a pretty good indication that your partner doesn't respect you and will keep on walking all over you as long as you let him or her. As much as it can be a wonderful experience caring for another human being, it is a fine line between being taken advantage of and being abused. If you find yourself always giving until you can give no more, it can be very easy to fall into the trap that your sweetie needs you and without you they will not be able to survive, so you convince yourself that is why you must stay. Trust me, your sweetie will survive and as soon as they use you up emotionally, financially etc, there will be another sucker waiting to take your place and to fill your role. I know it bites the big one, but that is the way the world works some times and I just want to you to realize that, so you can make better, healthier choices in the future. Don't get me wrong. I am not saying that relationships in which one of the partners takes on more of a nurturing or a providing role is not a good relationship, as long as your partner is giving to you in other ways, sexually or otherwise.

In relationships, the idea of "love" plays a decisive role. Unfortunately in the current state of the world, love is not enough. In major cities such as New York, San Francisco, Los Angeles, Vancouver and London to name a few, people are hooking up just for the simple reason that rents and mortgages are almost impossible to afford because real estate prices are skyrocketing. Now if ever there was a wrong reason to get married or get into a relationship this illustrates it.

A lot of people mistake love for infatuation. They believe that "true love" means meeting the "one person on Earth meant for you" and it can only be accompanied by the following symptoms, namely: butterflies and a weak-in-the-knees feeling. You meet a new person and fall in love with them. Everything they do is wonderful. You count the seconds and minutes until you can finally see them again. You do things you wouldn't normally do: write poems, buy flowers, even drive hundreds of miles to see them every weekend. You smile at the mere mention of your true love's name. That's fantastic. Only, the question is: how long will this bliss last? Maybe I am cynical. Yet, I believe that one of society's biggest problems now is the use of the word *"Love"*. Are we all that fucking insecure that we need to use this word as if it has no meaning? Just about everyone in this world is constantly craving love, they search everywhere for it. They want their friends, families and mates to express it to them constantly. People use it daily. They meet someone a few times and they tell them that they love them. Just because someone likes the same song, sports team or same designer does not mean they have enough qualities to be loved by you. That is not to say that you should not treat the people you meet with the same kindness you would expect to be treated with, nor is it saying that you cannot periodically meet someone and have this amazing connection and know that you love them and want them to be a part of your life.

But come on people. Let us quit using the word so freely. I know a lot of people think that they are loved. Also, that they are loved by a lot of people, maybe even hundreds of people. I am telling you, that is impossible. A person is only capable of sharing his or her love with a small number of people. For each individual that number is going to be different. You are lucky if it is only a handful of people in your lifetime and that includes family members. Love is not something that is to be taken lightly. When you tell someone you love them – that is, barring horrific events – it should be a permanent thing, something that will exist for a lifetime. Think about it for a second, if this was the way people were to look at love, then the divorce rate would not be so high and people would also not constantly be changing friends. It should be something that if you say it, you mean it, and those to whom you express it should cherish this love. Period. No conditions. No insecurities. Sure, things might not work out with someone you love, but even when they don't, the love needs to be permanent and if it is not or you don't think that it can be then don't fucking say it. If you do, you are just lying. And the damage you are causing to another individual is sometimes insurmountable. So my friends, I hope you realize the positive sentiment here. And, by the way, since you

*Penned By: The Seed & German Seed*

have read this far you probably have bought the book and *I love you for that!!!!!*

But seriously, we've all been "in love" before. We know how it feels. The problem is that one day this love, or in all honesty, infatuation, is simply gone. Unfortunately, life has little to do with the stereotypes presented today in films and TV. "And they lived happily ever after", as shown by the high divorce rates, is the *exception* for today's relationships. As your relationship gets longer and you both get older, you'll have to come to realize that you're probably not Brad Pitt and your partner most likely does not resemble Jennifer Aniston. You have to assess the situation and not just the girth of the ass. Is this person (your "true love") going to stand by you ("till death does us part"), support you, help you raise the children and not run off with your best friend? Do you want to spend the rest of your life with this person? Do the positive character traits of your sweetie outweigh the other, less positive aspects that drive you up the wall? Or are you just killing time and waiting for something better to come along? If you are just killing time, have some decency and be honest with yourself and your date. We don't need any more broken lost souls on our streets, in our bars, restaurants and Internet chat rooms. Let them know where they stand so they can just rock the bed with you and so they don't have any grand plans of a magical life together.

Love is what remains after the infatuation is gone and does not result from hormones. Love is based on mutual trust, responsibility, honor and respect. If your relationship is not based on these factors, then for God's sake it's time to stop using your interpretation of "love" as an excuse for not living your life.

Love is such a complicated thing, how does one really know if they are in love or have ever been in love. Is it just a chemical reaction that makes you feel a high that cannot be sustained and as soon as the reaction diminishes it is time to get another fix? I feel that unfortunately for most people in this self-gratification seeking society, that is the norm and therefore, not really love.

My definition of love is much simpler than that. Allow me to digress for a moment (it will become a bit corny). I believe that when someone is born their soul is cut in two, and they spend their whole lives looking for the person who has the other half of

*Seed's Sketchy Relationship Theories - A Guide to the Perils of Dating*

their soul – or *"Soul Mate"*. Now for the most part, people miss the point here and spend their time looking for themselves. They want to find someone that has a lot of things in common with them and when they do find someone that fits the "in common" criterion they find out that they are actually boring. Now imagine that, you have found your perfect match, someone so like you that it is scary (Mick and Bianca Jagger), and then "bang" you realize that not only are they dull, but that they are also a reflection of yourself arggghhhhhhh!!!

What I am saying is cherish the differences, as they are what truly will keep your life fresh and exciting. Sure, in the beginning, loving the exact same music, food, sport or whatever might seem great, but if that is the case, date yourself, because once you've discovered all you need to know about each other, then what? Go out and try to develop some more similar interests to spice it up? The trick is to be open to the unfamiliar. As important as it is to have some things to talk about, embrace the differences if you are lucky enough to discover someone you find interesting and that you care about. Think about all the new stuff you can learn and become involved in. Life can become exciting.

Another point to consider: you don't have to do all the same activities. The time apart doing things you like is extremely important in a relationship. Fuck, if you work together, ski together, golf together, always eat together and so on and so on... good luck! You may have a great relationship but once again unless you are the exception to the rule you are not likely to stay together, you will eventually get bored of each other.

So does true love and unconditional love really exist in the world of adult relationships? My views of this have changed over the years. I never thought that these kinds of love existed until I experienced them myself. I know you may be thinking that I'm a wuss. Well, I do believe these types of love rarely ever occur and it is impossible sometimes to know if the feelings are real. After all, love is not just an emotion, it is also a chemical reaction, a high. I tell you, when you experience it, you will know and it is something to cherish and to be very grateful for. The type of love I am describing is something like this, say you have been dating someone for an extended period of time and during that time every single time you touched, hugged or kissed that person you got chills up and down your spine, and every time you were on your way to meet them you felt an unexplainable warmth in your heart, and when you gave it some thought you had no conditions or expectations on the relationship. That, my friend, is true love. Unfortunately, like mentioned before, love is rarely enough. Remember, everyone has something dysfunctional in their lives and since we are all individuals, if we don't have this feeling at the same time in a relationship, great relationships fail as well. Remember also, your sweetie may be one who freely uses the term love, their insecurities and dysfunctions may not allow them to cherish what they have, but instead like a drug addict, go searching for the next high. The point they are missing is simply that the grass is not always greener elsewhere. It is just different and different is not necessarily better.

If you find you are in a relationship that is nurturing, caring and non abusive. Where neither of you are chemically or alcohol dependent. Where neither of you is a slug nor have let yourself go emotionally or physically. Where the sex is great. Don't throw it away, just because you think there might be more out there for you. Because there very likely isn't, and at some point of time you have to stop looking for something better. Sure, you may find someone who makes more money, who is slightly more attractive, funnier, smarter or whatever. But it is the whole package that really matters. So work at it, we don't have that much time on this planet to get it right.

Finally, more than anything on Earth, love is something that should be sacred, it needs to be cherished. No word can cause so much joy and happiness and so much despair and anguish at the same time. It is the one thing that every human being craves and quite frankly, cannot live without. It gives us hope, encouragement and security. It creates an illusion where we believe everything is going to be all right. But if it is used prematurely or with questionable motives, it can destroy and cause great psychological damage and hardship. So if you are to use it, please make sure you mean it. Sure you may deeply love someone one day and that may for whatever reason change suddenly, but the love should never be taken away. Just imagine if you love someone and their core, their essence does not change. They are still the wonderful person that you decided you loved in the first place, maybe even better.

*Seed's Sketchy Relationship Theories - A Guide to the Perils of Dating*

Then one day you decide you don't want them anymore, so you tell them you no longer love them. Now just imagine the damage that causes. Likely years of therapy. They will ask themselves: What happened? You said you loved me?

Please, don't inflict that pain on anyone. It is not fair and it is fucking selfish. So if you are ever going to tell someone that you love them, make sure you mean it. Because it is forever, if you don't feel that it can be, don't say it. And for that matter, they will probably sleep with you still if you just tell them you like them. Quit listening to your idiot friends. Be your own person. Evolve!!!!!!

So here they are, after all of that, Seed's simple definitions of Relationships and Love (in this instance the focus is on intimate relationships).

***Relationship*** — The emotional, spiritual, financial bond that two people who cherish each other and care for each other develop so that they can tackle this big world as a team. That bond truly makes them better together as opposed to the individual. They become a finely tuned romantic corporation.

***Love*** — Initially a chemical reaction to another human being. However, when carefully cultivated and nurtured, it is an amazing bond that two individuals share which helps make this world a better place. The powerful feelings that make you put another person's life and well being ahead of your own. To know that on this big fucked-up scary planet, you no longer have to keep looking, you have found the one person who puts you at ease. To put in the simplest form imaginable, love is when you no longer put yourself first and you can do that with ease. Love when it is pure, truly completes you.

*"'I love you' means that I hold you in high enough regard that I endeavor to burden you with the responsibility of maintaining my happiness."*
*-David Slater*

*Penned By: The Seed & German Seed*

# SECTION 1
# The Formative Years

*"We've Got These Chains
Hanging Around Our Necks
People Try To Strangle Us With Them
Before We Take Our First Breath"*

*-The Barenaked Ladies (What A Good Boy)*

     Section 1 is to help us get focused and to set the structure of the book. It is to help establish the flow and make this an easy read. It may not be in the book, but it likely will be. Actually you're reading it, so it is in the book. Sometimes the intelligent ones seem so stupid, don't we?

     To establish the structure I feel we must first understand the differences between men and women and what to expect as we go through this journey we call life. As mentioned one of the reasons for this guide is to be brutally honest and to help people to realize that we are constantly being lied to and conditioned to strive for things out of our grasp. Things that may work in the corporate world, have some severe limitations in your relationship life. Growing up, mothers are mainly responsible for a lot of this misinformation. I know you may be thinking, "here we go, this guy is against women". You've probably just branded the Seed as

*Penned By: The Seed & German Seed*

a misogynist. Well, on the contrary, the exact opposite is true. I strive to understand women, both genders for that matter. Ultimately, they are not the weaker sex: women actually hold all of the cards. Men use power, money and strength to control and get what they want from life. Whereas women, use beauty, manipulation and the heart. As a rule, they make or more appropriately, let, men think that they're calling the shots. Yet, women are in charge of everything emotional in life; fuck - what could be more emotional than carrying a child for 9 months, having it grow inside of you until it is somewhere between 6 to 10 lbs and then arghhhhhhhhhhh: child birth. There is not one guy on the planet that could understand what that must actually be like. We have no reference for it.

Following that, while the men are out slugging their way through their careers or trying to find themselves, they are compelled to suppress most of their emotions. They must bring home the proverbial bacon as they have several mouths to feed along with providing clothes and shelter. While all of this is taking place, the role of care giver for the new born is and should rest mostly on the shoulders of the mother, unless you want some strangers to raise your children and instill their morals and values upon "YOUR" children.

Thanks again to my friend Fiona. Fiona conveniently got pregnant during the writing of this book and since I am a close friend of both Wayne (husband) and Fiona, I now have first-hand knowledge of what pregnancy can be like. It is not pretty! The hormonal mood swings, which must be a complete hell for the woman to endure, and the emotional toll it takes on the man must be quite significant as well. It is not a one sided thing. We know that no two pregnancies are alike and some are easier than others. In dear Fiona's case, the first eight months had been hell.

The theories that will be discussed in this book are not always correct but you will be doing yourself a big favor if you realize that most of the time they are. So let us begin with an outline of what it is like to be a man and what it is like to be a woman growing up. By the way, Seed has expert knowledge on this subject, because in a previous life he was a call girl.

*Seed's Sketchy Relationship Theories - A Guide to the Perils of Dating*

At this time, I feel it is very appropriate to let you know how much it is appreciated that you have decided to come along for this fun, highly-informative and educational ride. I am sure you will gain some valuable insight as you have stepped into a path that will lead you to the land of the *"exception."* Maybe you already are one and this is just reconfirming that point. Anyway, welcome aboard for the wonderful roller coaster ride of life. And when you take a minute to get out of the roller coaster, I think now would be an excellent time to head to the website <u>www.seedenterprises.com</u> where you will find a wealth of informative and interactive information. You may ask Seed a relationship question. Perhaps share some of your personal experiences and insight. While you are there, it is highly encouraged that you take a step or click into **Seed's Highly Fashionable Boutique** where you will find some incredible products, that will not only help you through the relationship quagmire, but they will help your friends and of course your children develop during their formative years. Seriously the products will help. You will not be disappointed. You can be a trailblazer in your community.

# CHAPTER 5
# Man

*"Treat a man as he is and he will remain as he is
Treat a man as he can and should be
And he will become as he can and should be."*

*-Goethe*

Let us take the gloves off right away. We are not all born beautiful and our parents, mainly our mothers, and all of their friends do us a horrible disservice right from the get go by, and I know you all have experienced it, saying "Isn't it a beautiful baby". "You are so cute and adorable" etc, etc. If you saw the one Seinfeld episode ("You have to come see the baby"), you will understand that we are not all attractive and sure things change over time. Some of us are late bloomers, but it is horrible to make someone believe they are something that they are not. Looks do not fall under the category of the American Dream unless of course you have enough money and time to endure the surgeries to change your appearance or want to be humiliated on national television on one of the new reality shows that use people as guinea pigs. Even then there are no guarantees of success, look at Michael Jackson for instance.

## *Seed's Sketchy Relationship Theories - A Guide to the Perils of Dating*

Come on parents, if your child is ugly face it, don't fill their heads with crap and get them thinking they are something that they are not. Sure, you can do things to enhance your appearance, like stay in shape, dress well, keep your hair trimmed and in style, but unfortunately you can't pick your parents. If they are at the bottom end of the gene pool, well this is one area of life that is determined for you and your parents should realize it and start preparing you for what lies ahead, instead of feeding you that *"beauty is in the eye of the beholder"* crap. Because that is exactly what it is: crap. Sure we all have different tastes and beauty, or more to the point attractiveness, is a subjective thing, but get real: all you have to do to see what most people find attractive is to go to the magazine section of any store, or for that matter, watch any entertainment show. This brings us to the *Theory: Beauty is a Consistent Thing.*

In the beginning, at birth, we are either born to be beautiful or we are born ugly - and everything else in between. We are born into families with means or we are born into a family in the poor house - and everything in between. We are born into loving and caring families or we have a single crack whore for a mother - and everything in between. I could write a whole other book on the perils of changing our social standing and moving out of one class and into another, but that is a little too deep for this book and I don't want to depress too many people. This is meant to be a guide on relationships, not a social commentary on how fucked up the world really is. Ok, maybe it is a bit of a social commentary, but just a bit. One other thing worth mentioning here is at times this book is very, very good and sometimes it is not so good - and everything else in between. Anyway, in order to map out the course of the male relationships I have decided to create a fictitious character by the name of Johnny Player and outline what happens to him throughout his life.

Let us say that Johnny is born into a suburban middle class family in Big City North America. Johnny is a reasonably attractive guy, on a scale of 10 he is about a 7. In the infant stage, his loving mother starts out right away by lying to him constantly, telling him how beautiful and handsome he is. Mommy, along with the supposed loving and caring Grandparents, Aunts & Uncles and

*Penned By: The Seed & German Seed*

friends, all perpetuate this lie by joining in on this great conspiracy. *Theory: Your Mother is Probably Lying To You.*

So right off, the person which in your formative years you have the closest relationship and in fact your first relationship, a person of the opposite sex is misleading you. Perhaps this is one of the reasons later on in life some of us are not sure whether or not we should trust women (more on this later as I have mentioned before, during the course of writing this I found out some earth shattering news about my mommy dearest). A short note to all of you mothers out there: if your kid is ugly or even if he is only average looking don't participate in the lie. You don't need to focus on his looks, instead you can start to focus on some other attributes. In Thailand it is actually considered bad luck to say a baby is beautiful. We are not telling you to tell him he is not attractive, because that could cause a lot of other serious scars, what we are saying here is just find some other positive attributes to focus on and or encourage him to strive for excellence in other aspects of life.

Now Johnny has spent 4 or 5 years of his life being lied to and now it is time to start interacting with other children: enter the Elementary School years. Right from day one in school, the hierarchy of life starts to be revealed, kids start to form little cliques, the athletes, the brains, the good looking kids, the rich kids and so on and one of the beautiful things about this age is that kids are brutally honest to the point of being cruel. So if you kept telling dear Johnny that he was attractive and he really isn't, his new classmates will quickly let him know if you were lying or not by where he is accepted in the school world. This is also the time when it is constantly re-affirmed that attractiveness, especially in the case of girls, is very important. The pretty girl has a ton of friends and is popular in spite of herself. This, though not entirely true for boys, boys have other ways of gaining popularity through sports, developing a sense of humor, etc., etc., even at this early age it starts to become evident that the attractive kids are going to have doors opening for them and the less attractive you are, you had better develop some other talents. *Theory: If You are Not Hot: Find Something To Excel At!* This is where our dear mothers come in and if they only were honest and let us know:

*"Hey Johnny, I love you dearly but sweetie, you know your friend Mike, though he is an ass, you know why everyone loves him honey. Just look in the mirror, he is a young 10. And honey, though you are not grotesque, you are only about a 7, so to save you a little grief later in life, let's get you heavily involved in sports and, by the way, honey, I have started to put aside some money so that I can enroll you in Medical School".*

*"But Mommy I am only 5".*

*"Sweetie I know you don't understand now, but Mommy is just looking out for your future".*

(The previous dialogue is just a hypothetical example. In no way do I encourage the use of the word grotesque when you are talking about the looks of your child. At least, not while they are in the same room).

If only most mothers could face the facts, this kind of honesty would greatly enhance the quality of life in the adult years. An important note here is - that though it is not the parents place to map out our futures, gentle persuasion can help us eliminate lonely nights and keep us out of the trailer parks and help to lead us into the Penthouses of the world. I am not trying to say that the father has no role in the raising of a child. Like I mentioned before, he plays a very vital role and that is to bring home the income that allows you to raise your children yourself in the best possible environment. And come on all you mothers out there, you should know that males, have not evolved enough to be able to handle the gentle subtleties of child care.

Back to Johnny, he is now entering some key years of his life: High School. It has already been decided for him where he fits in the school society, whether he is likely to be popular, whether he will get a lot of dates or if he will be spending weekends at home with his computer games and with the other outsiders trying to find the magic formula of how to meet and to impress girls. If only our parents were honest with us instead of trying to lead us down the path which will end up in the same misery that they are going through. That is, if by this time Johnny still has two parents kicking around in his life. Statistics indicate that it is only about a 50/50 chance, and even if they are both still around, that doesn't guarantee that they are not fucked up and "just sticking around for the kids sake". I have a good friend whose parents did just that – however, they never slept in the same room, screamed at each other and fought the whole evening, every evening. What fucking message does that send and what potential therapy are the kids going to need in the future to have a chance in this big mean scary world?

Anyway, I digress. We all know the formula and if we don't, then here it is: right from the beginning, our families, friends and society start to tell us that we eventually need to find a mate to share our lives with. This is re-enforced every day of our lives. We are bombarded with it on television in all types of advertisements and then again through weddings, family get-togethers, Christmas and family vacations. Now this need to pair up starts to put a lot of stress upon our children early on in their lives, our teachers make a big deal about such commercial days such as Valentine's Day. This starts basically in Kindergarten. Guys, we were all made to give valentines to girls at this young age, even though we maybe thought girls were "yucky" and we weren't yet aware of what pleasure we would receive from them in the future. This momentum keeps building through Elementary, High School, College and right into our working careers. We are all led to believe that we are a lower quality of person if we cannot find someone to date and bring to special functions throughout these early stages of our lives. Nice fucking going adults, just because you are miserable doesn't mean that your children wanted or should suffer through the same shit that you did. Now the problem with all of this is, the mixed messages that are being sent out, on one hand we are being forced to work towards these couplings, but on the other hand, why do Mommy and Daddy hate each other? If it is so good to be in a couple, why is Mommy always bitching about Daddy and the fact that he does not make enough? And why is Daddy banging that girl from where he works? And coming home 3 or 4 nights a week smelling of beer? And what does banging mean? Let us face it we are failing miserably at this relationship thing and I believe that it is because no one has the guts or balls to tell how it is *"Most of the Time"*.

What also happens, as guys, we learn very quickly that, regardless of what we have looks wise, we still desire the hot girls. At this stage, the hot girls really just want the hot guys. And the hot guys realize this. For most of them that is the only thing they have been able to figure out thus far and due to this they usually don't develop any other aspects of their personality. These guys can be pricks but the girls keep coming back to them (ahhh yes, the start of the girls desiring the bad boy). They don't have to worry about dates because if one girl decides enough is enough, it doesn't matter because another one is waiting for her chance. Now a little subculture develops here, the *"Nice Guy Syndrome"*. For every hot girl out there, there is at least one nice guy hanging around; the guy that is always there to pick up the pieces. The guy to do stuff with when the real boyfriend wants to fuck around with his buddies and brag about how cool he is. This guy is the equivalent to the *"Fag Hag"* that is present in the gay world. Who does the real boyfriend usually brag to, he usually brags to the nice guys and the poor nice guys sit there trying to figure out what they need to do to be just like him. The thing is he can't. There is no way because he doesn't have the looks to attract. Sure, at this stage he gets the middle of the road girls, but he doesn't want that: he wants the babe, even if the beauty is only fleeting, because through this period of life up till about 25 all it really is about, is popularity. So now you have this endless cycle of "Hot Guys" and "Hot Girls" treating each other badly. "Nice Guys" hanging around just hoping for their shot or some magical formula. It just doesn't happen. And this is part of the reason why relationships fuck up so much. We all want something else, something just a bit better. Especially at this stage of our lives. Now back to that pressure to hook up. Well it is all a load of crap. It is not that important at this stage of life and we don't need to keep following the same path that our parents did, and their parents and their parents' parents and so on.

    So early on, the biggest attribute a guy can have is his looks and secondary to that is to excel at something like sports, because that is how the world works, at least the Western World. Depending on where you stand on the attractiveness scale, if we were told the truth at an early age, this is an excellent time in a child's life to develop some skills that not only help him in the future to attract the girls he wants, regardless of whether it is to just get laid or if he wants more of a commitment. If our parents were honest, we could start honing other skills, these skills are

*Penned By: The Seed & German Seed*

the things that will eventually level the playing field with the "Hotties". It is very important for guys during these early stages to not sit at home and hide from girls, instead this period is an excellent time to learn to like yourself and learn to not to be afraid of being alone. Of course you could join a lot of clubs and play a lot of sports, however, it is important not to do this just to hook up, but solely as a way to learn how to interact with others. If you are to use this time wisely, by developing a sense of humor and excellent social skills, these traits will help you with every aspect of your life in the future. It is also vitally important to learn how to dress and to work on staying in shape, all very critical to what will happen later on in your life. You may think that some of this is shallow and superficial. Well it is not, it is just the way the world works. If you are so ugly that you don't keep mirrors at home, all of these points may be the most important things you learn during these years. They may be the only things that keep you out of the trailer park.

Johnny has now gone through High School. He had a lot of lonely nights when the popular kids were out partying. He did have some things going for him, he was quite adapt at sports, he had developed a keen sense of humor and stayed in good shape. His problem was that he was a nice guy. A lot of girls hung around him and really liked him, but they all wanted, remember, Mike. Fortunately for Johnny, even though he was naïve, he was developing other attributes of his character and personality, exactly the things that Mike wasn't. Johnny was stocking up for the future. He was at the point where he had accepted who he was and wasn't too worried about getting dates. He realized his mother had lied to him a lot. He even realized why his mother had lied and that was because she simply didn't want to face the fact that she too was only average *("Mommy why are you so self-absorbed?")*.

After High School Johnny took a little hiatus from the real world and he became involved in some Junior Athletics (Quarterback of a Football Team). For the first time, he started to have a little bit of his own money, so he was able to afford a nice car and some nice clothes. Though Johnny was only about a 7 he noticed some interesting things starting to occur. Girls at his work were starting to show some interest in him. Though in school he wasn't at the top of the class and there was a lot of competition, he now had a few things going for him. He was in good shape, he was a very good athlete, had a sense of humor and some ambition (a bit of an illusion because he had not moved on to college yet). *WELCOME TO THE REAL WORLD!!!* Suddenly, Johnny was becoming popular. A bit of a leader the skills and characteristics that he developed earlier on were starting to become more important attributes now. His lonely nights were of his choosing and when he was out with attractive girls other attractive girls were showing interest. *Theory: If You Want To Date Babes You Must Surround Yourself With Babes.* This is a very cold but true statement, all of you un-attractive girls out there be honest with yourselves, this is reality.

Still at this stage, Johnny had not quite figured it out. Over the next couple of years he stayed in the work world and as a reasonably decent-looking funny guy, with a nice car he really didn't have to make much of an effort to get dates. Usually very attractive dates. Albeit, sometimes he was still the nice guy and when the girl didn't get the call from the guy she really wanted, Johnny was not that bad of an alternative. He was smart though, he realized this and used this time to attract other girls and to acquire an understanding of what these girls really want. Oh yeah, not to forget, some mental images for when he was alone with his hand. But Johnny knew, to get the girl he really wanted, that unless he made it big at Football, working for others sucks, especially without the education to bump up your earning potential.

Now off to University. Johnny still had a shot at sports. He had done all he could do at the junior level, so he had to move on. He enrolled in University and continued his football endeavors. Johnny, with a little maturity, was actually becoming a little bit more attractive. He at this stage, moved up to about an 8 on the looks scale, somewhat because he remained in shape, had a sense of humor, always dressed fairly well and due to this, something started to happen. Johnny all of a sudden became very desirable. Not only to girls that were 5's, 6's and 7's but even to 8's, 9's and even the odd 10. At this stage Johnny was becoming quite a bit of a stud. There was rarely a weekend where Johnny wasn't sampling the co-eds, and the beautiful thing is he never had to try. It just came naturally. Being average in earlier years had become a bit of a blessing. He had honed other skills, developed his own personality instead of copying the personalities of the popular kids. He had become quite a hottie himself, yet far from the most attractive. *Theory: To have a chance you must learn to like yourself (YOU must learn to be alone)*. Hell, at this stage, even the good looking guys were trying to figure out how Johnny was ending up with the girls that they used to have no problem with.

Unfortunately for Johnny, this all came unraveled. He was unmotivated in school, he did not have the focus or desire to pursue the program he was in - sure football was good - and he was having no problem with the ladies, but some things in life were starting to happen. His father became ill and after a lengthy illness passed away. Shortly after that, his mother became ill and passed away as well. This all greatly affected his schooling and everything else in his life. He had become a bit insecure, fortunately what he learned earlier would help him deal with these traumatic events.

Johnny at this time he went down that life-altering path that so many take: he got into a serious relationship. His first one, probably as something to hold onto during these difficult times. For the most part, it was good. However, like any relationship it did have its problems. First of all, the whole course of the relationship took place while his father and his mother were ill and dying. Johnny however kept a brave face during these trying times and he had become quite popular. He was a leader amongst his friends. Their sisters and girlfriends wished that their brothers and boyfriends dressed like Johnny, were funny like Johnny and even were as attractive as Johnny, the whole package. One of the challenges ahead for Johnny was that though ambitious, by leaving school he had created some limitations for himself. He fell into a world of Hospitality and Sales & Marketing and though reasonably adept at both, it was becoming apparent that even with all of his pluses in these positions it was unlikely that he would ever be making a 6 figure income: life was going to be a struggle. To make matters worse, after leaving school, breaking up with his serious girlfriend and the death of both of his parents, he started having a series of athletic injuries that led to several surgeries over the next several years of his life. Not only did this cause a lot of mental and physical stress, the prolonged periods of inactivity left him financially strapped. So Johnny fought through and as tough as it was, kept for the most part a positive attitude as he still had a lot of friends as well as a few exceptional friends to give him support through the tough times. Oh and did I mention, he had a relatively good sense of humor.

The next period for Johnny was a bit of a roller coaster, he still stayed in shape through it all and for some reason he still had no problem attracting good-looking girls. However, he seemed to be noticing that these encounters never really were much more than short-lived flings. This activity continued and continued and continued for Johnny with the odd serious relationship thrown in. One of these serious relationships occurred at the end of the series of surgeries he had, where, when it ended, he was devastated. He had forgotten the important theory about learning to be alone. He went into a self-help frenzy trying to figure out what went wrong, trying to hold on to someone who had dumped him. Eventually he became pathetic. But at the end of all of this, he learned a lot about relationships and he figured out what is really important. He was developing a tremendous understanding of women. To this day, several years after all of the life-changing experiences and challenges, he still has no problem meeting women, even if it is just for sex, while at the same time knowing his limitations. As for Johnny's future. Who knows.........it looks bright.

What Did Johnny Learn? Let us take a step back, back to the formula, the one that is not working, in its short form. We are all pressured to hook up, it starts early in life, this leads to a lot of people not developing all areas of their lives, such as, social skills, like learning how to talk to others. By high school we all start looking for our future mates, this quest continues into University and our working years and usually women by the age of 24 and guys by 27 have hooked up and gotten married. Fuuuuuccccccck! What do we know at this time? Guys, you are probably trapped in some job you hate and are pressured into buying a home, which most of you do. Then a picket fence and next some offspring. Well, congratulations you have now likely realized you're in your early 30's, you hate your job, probably don't like your wife and have a couple of hungry mouths to feed for at least the next 18 years or so. **NICE LIFE: WHEN DID OUR PARENTS TEACH US THAT WE WANT TO LEAD THE SAME LIVES AS THEY DID?** Along the way, you likely forgot to have fun. If you hooked up in your early 20's, you

*Penned By: The Seed & German Seed*

know, the years during which you think you have got it all figured out, you have now spent the good part of a decade with someone, in a serious relationship you don't really know. Remember life reveals character it doesn't build it. And now your wife is likely overweight going to the local coffee joint with your 2.2 children, in sweats I might add, and is bitching about how much money you don't make. Did I mention she cut off all of her hair to simplify her life. Or even worse yet, if your wife decided that a career was what she wanted, then why the fuck did you and the selfish bitch have kids to begin with? *So someone else can raise them?*

The nice thing for the guy, as his wife gets baggage and a fatter ass, his earning potential grows as time goes on and all of a sudden that 24 year old assistant starts looking pretty good. If he is making a good income – say 6 figures – maybe he even has a chance at trading up. Remember the divorce rate. One of the problems he faces, is that he missed his 20's. He was hooked up the whole time, so instead of learning how to talk and interact with people normally, quite often guys will unfortunately revert back to what they remember it to be like. Fuck - that was 1988 and things have changed. Yet, a key thing here is since you have $$$ those shortcomings can be overlooked. If you are a lawyer, doctor, athlete or celebrity, what you *"do"* becomes part of your introduction. If you are not any of the above, your introduction will consist of just your name. *"Theory: Hot girls may fuck the bartender but it is not long term"*. Did I mention that women fall for now, but are really looking for the future and what may be. On the other hand, guys are simple creatures – we fall for now and stay in the present. If our wives and girlfriends are hot, that is really all that matters. We will overlook a lot of the shortcomings. If we are with a 9 or a 10, what most of us don't realize is the following: other 9s and 10s want us as well, as they know that *"Most of the Time"* a 9 or a 10 is not going to be with a dead-beat trailer park boy. Mom teaches their girls this early in the game.

Important Note – Johnny is a fictional character and any resemblance he may have to anyone living or dead is purely co-incidental. His life story was completely invented by the authors. It was made to seem somewhat difficult in order to illustrate what could happen and that *"life is fucking difficult"*.

*Seed's Sketchy Relationship Theories - A Guide to the Perils of Dating*

One last thing. All of you guys out there who, once you have a bit of money, trade up because your wife has developed some baggage. You selfish pricks a lot of what has happened, you are directly responsible for. Perhaps look at yourself first before you screw up a bunch of lives.

# CHAPTER 6
# Woman

*"When You Were Born
They Looked at You and Said
What a Good Girl What a Smart Girl
What a Pretty Girl"*

*-Barenaked Ladies (What a Good Boy)*

Now for the same experiment in the same town, this time with a sweet little angel. A little girl is born. Her name is Chastity. It is evident that she is a pretty little girl, she truly is a beautiful baby. Therefore, Mommy is a little more honest with her beautiful baby and starts her off with *ready, set, manipulate...* She starts to teach her little angel that if she smiles, pouts and does certain things, she will be able to wrap men around her finger and anything she wants, she will be able to get. The better looking this little girl is, the easier it will be. This doesn't mean these little angels won't have other emotional problems along the way. However, the game of love, sex and dating will come a little easier for her. Yet just like with the boys, sweet Mommy, the relatives and friends lie to these little girls by giving them the illusion that they are attractive when they are not. Just like with the boys, these parents need to take a look in the mirror and realize if they are average, that is likely all that is in store for their children as well, unless of course the kid gets the genes of the mailman.

So now little princess Chastity enters school and immediately she becomes one of the popular kids. Other little girls, though jealous, want to be her friend. They learn early that if they are around a popular girl maybe there is a chance of some people discovering their inner beauty (remember, guys, if you want to date hot girls, you must surround yourself with hot girls). Other girls understand this very early on in life. Right away, Chastity has lots of friends. Quite often she is the teacher's pet (perves). Let's face it, people like to be around beautiful things. By this time, Mommy has taught her little angel how to wrap Daddy right around her little finger. Mommy has taught Chastity what looks to use, what to say, and so on and so on, to have Daddy open up his wallet. The funny thing is quite often Mommy is even manipulating her girl, because Daddy started noticing Mommy getting bigger and Mommys only way to Daddy's wallet is to use Chastity's charms. The big difference between a little boy and a little girl to gain popularity, is this, for a boy looks are important, but being good at sports and other activities are equally important. Whereas for a girl, it might help to be well rounded, but it is in fact simple: the main way for a girl to be popular in school is to be attractive. Sure you can dress well and stay in shape, but if you are truly a looker none of that matters. Your course has already been set for you.

So Chastity goes through Elementary School being popular with lots of friends, she gets lots of attention and she learns that she really likes it. The big problem for society is that most of society is average. Only a small portion of it is in the upper echelons of attractiveness and by promoting this, thank-you fashion magazines and the numerous glamorous entertainment shows, we are not doing society a favor. Indeed, we are fucking up society.

All of a sudden when Chastity hits about grade 5 (it might even be grade 3) and starts to show interest in boys, an interesting thing starts to happen. Chastity starts to realize that the boys in grade 6, 7, 8, 9 and even older have already noticed her and though she has guys who are friends in her own grade, the fascination with the older kids is a bit more intriguing. Mommy may deny this and claim that she doesn't want her little angel hanging with the older kids, but Chastity is not stupid: she realizes that there is a reason why Daddy is 4, 5, and even more than 10 years older than Mommy. The main reason the older kids are frustrated with the girls their own age, is because they are doing the same thing as Chastity, they have moved onto the older guys as well, even guys in university if they are hot enough (fuck supermodels – some of them are 12 or 13 years old. When I say fuck supermodels, I do not mean that term literally, that is of course unless you have a chance, in that case go for it. If you are dating someone and you have a chance with a supermodel, keep it in your pants. What the hell are you? A Stock Broker, Lawyer or Car Salesman? And another point you sick bastard: if you are hanging out with 12 or 13 year old supermodels you belong in prison).

Chastity now starts to get it, she knows the gifts, the parties and the guys are all a little better if she hangs with the older crowd, however, she also realizes that the competition is fierce for the attention of the popular older guys. One of the big differences now is to get this attention a price has to be paid. These new guys are expecting a little something, something or their interest will wane. Girls realize that to even get in the running, they need to do several things: like dress seductively or be aggressive, but fortunately in this highly competitive world, Chastity and all of the girls who are pursuing the older, richer, more sophisticated guys realize one thing is very important, to get noticed you must be a bit of an *Attention Whore.* By the way I am a guy, I have played a lot of sports, hung out with the rich, the poor, the intellectuals, the funny, the not so funny and so on, and I have never once met older richer – ok, I have met older and richer but I have never met, not once, these more *sophisticated guys.* They just simply don't exist. Come on, I don't even really know what sophisticated is supposed to mean. Does it mean he actually eats all of his fruits and vegetables that he bought, before they go bad. Maybe that is how we should judge sophistication. A guy should get a badge, just like the scouts, a merit badge of sorts, let's say if he eats all of his bananas before they go bad. I really think that is how sophistication should be determined. Come on do you have a better idea. Let's hear it!!! Anyways this brings us to the next *Theory: Most Attractive Women Are Attention Whores.*

Chastity has now attracted a guy 4, 5 and even 10 years older than her, a guy who thoroughly enjoys his bananas by the

## Seed's Sketchy Relationship Theories - A Guide to the Perils of Dating

way, and though it is a stretch to find things in common, he likes Springsteen, she Likes J. Lo, the two of them pretend that all is well and for the most part, it is, he has his trophy girl on his arm, so he can be cool with all of his buddies, and she is the recipient of better gifts and gets to eat at better restaurants instead of at the mega mall food court. Unless, of course, the mega mall food court has one of those fresh turkey franchises. Who doesn't like fresh roast turkey? It fills you up and makes you sleepy, could anything be better than that? Chastity, just like the good looking and athletic guys, is coasting through life. It is easy, attention, gifts never a lonely night, hell, when her star guy goes out with the buddies, she even has some Poindexter to shower her with attention. How could life be better? Well, there is one way, Chastity: could you please go out and develop some character? Quite frankly, society is teaching you how to be a bitch and we already have enough of those in the adult world (of course if you are an *exception* please disregard the last comment).

Chastity is now in university and has two options: free agency, where she cuts her man loose for an updated model who is higher in the social standing pecking order, or stay with him for the next 10 years, have his kids and end up divorced with short hair and you know what's coming next. How many kids does she have? Come on take a guess. Come on. *Bang on!!!!* You got it on the first guess: *2.2 kids.* I would like to take a moment at this time to say I really thank you for paying attention while reading this book. It touches me and the fact that you guessed that right on the first guess, well it has brought a tear to my eye. That is right, my eye. Yes, I have two but I am blind in one of them, so they both may very well have tears in them, but I can't see it. So I can only tell you what I can see, and that is the tear in the one eye. You may have known that I have only one functioning eye if you already read the *"Who is the Seed Section"* at the back of the book and if I had mentioned in that section that *Seed* is blind in one eye. However, at this point I am not sure what relevance my eyesight would have on writing this book. Well, it would have some relevance, as I would have a difficult time deciding what beauty is if I was blind. And proofreading would be a bitch. The fact is I am not. I am half blind and that is it. Chastity is beautiful. A little socially inept, shallow, superficial, an *attention whore* and destined to be a cougar unless she develops some depth of character. Or, unless

*Penned By: The Seed & German Seed*

she latches onto some rich blind guy when the love of her life trades up for a newer younger model. So Mommy, you have a big responsibility to your sweet little girls. Can you teach them to be sweet, beautiful and well-rounded adults as well? Money, though great, is not everything. And while you're at it, can you also work on teaching your boys not to be such self-serving pricks? If you can do these things, I tell you, the world will be a much better place. Don't you think?

# CHAPTER 7
# Theory: Your Mother Is Probably Lying To You

*"Is there any way you could phone your parents and ask them who your real parents are"*

-A Civil Servant
(informing Seed the people he listed as his parents are not his real parents)

*Penned By: The Seed & German Seed*

This chapter took on an interesting twist during the creation of the book. A series of events occurred which gave me tremendous insight into the subject matter. These highly volatile and traumatic events made me consider changing the title of this chapter to: *"Your Mother is Probably Lying to You, along with your Brothers and Sisters, Aunts and Uncles and any other Family Member Who You Have Come In Contact With. And, quite possibly, the Family Pets Have Been Lying as Well"*. No, really. But at the last moment, I decided that title was a bit too long and confusing and would warrant another book in itself. Even though I am sure the pets were in on the conspiracy, if I was to spend too much time trying to convince you, you may actually think I am a bit more off my rocker than you already do. So, having said that, I am going to stick with the original title. By the way, as I reveal some things, you may find it eerie like I do that I wrote this chapter before I received some earth shattering news, which will be revealed to you later. I have you curious, don't I?

Mom, God bless her, she means well. Or does she? Is it that she does not actually want to admit her own average existence? Mom, from day one, starts with the "aren't you cute" and "isn't the baby beautiful" routine. A mother may find her wrinkled little child to be cute or beautiful and maybe in an ET sort of way they are, but I tell you what, no guy finds babies beautiful and I mean no guy. A mother has an excuse: she had to get knocked up by her spouse or some other loser, then carry the child for 9 months, going through God only knows how many hormonal changes and when it is finally over, she does not likely want to admit that her hairless, wrinkled creation is anything less than beautiful (the father, if he is still present has to go along with this as well, by proxy, for his own good). So Mommy, if you want to do your child a tremendous favor and aid them in their future development: once some time passes and the child's looks start to develop, start being honest with both yourself and your child before society starts to let them know what reality is. If your child starts developing into some sort of troll you can encourage them to work on other strengths. Sure, they can do the things to enhance how they look, like developing a sense of style, good grooming habits, stay in shape, etc. By the way, you have a heads up on this whole troll thing, it is called the mirror and the family tree, look in one and go back a couple of generations and you should have the troll thing answered for you.

That is, of course, if you are honest with yourself to begin with. That is, also of course, if you did not get busy with the young, hot pool boy. Who are we kidding? If you come from a family of trolls, like you are going to have a pool.

Some things our genetics dictate for us and the sooner you stop telling your children that they are beautiful or handsome, the sooner they will be able to understand how the big cruel, beautiful, scary world works. The sooner you face reality, the sooner your child can start developing into a success later in life, both in relationships and business. You can give little Johnny and Chastity a head start on all of the other 5's, 6's and 7's of this world by being honest. That is, all you have to do, is be honest. That does not mean being cruel, blunt or anything of the sort. It just means encouraging and letting them know that there are other things that are just as important as looks. Most importantly, let your kids know how much you love and support them and ultimately that you want the best for them. A little side note, we live in this big fucked up world where athletes are the new ruling class. Remember back in the 14$^{th}$ century when the statues were of Machiavelli, David and famous philosophers. Well, now we have statues of Gretzky and Mike Tyson. Ok, probably not Mike Tyson – I hope. At this particular moment I would like to say that I am thankful that I do not have any children, because if I did, there would be a chance that if Mike were to read this, my children would soon be on his dinner menu in the near future. Fuck, what is going on in the world?

Now back to the kids. If Johnny turns out to be a non-looker and a bit of an athlete, you may gently encourage him to go down that path (don't neglect education to do it, since only a small percentage of great athletes make it) and who knows maybe Johnny some day will be your gravy train. Hmmm ... Gravy!!

Speaking of gravy, another way Mommy starts lying to us at a very early age is that cooking is such a big tremendous fucking chore that wipes them out every day. So much planning, time and effort to make nutritious meals for the family. This is a bunch of crap as well. I have been (on and off) on my own for some 20 or so odd years and I used to believe that. Until, of course, my first Christmas that I spent alone. Now not to wallow in despair, I decided fuck it, I am going to have a great time and cook a turkey

*Penned By: The Seed & German Seed*

with all the trimmings and fixings and dessert all from scratch. Sure, I was going to have some wine and beers and watch the game while I did all this, but damn it, I was going to do it. And if it did not turn out, that was fine: it was going to be a blast. What I discovered was that it was simple: including the clean up. No stress whatsoever, no getting up at 5 am to start the process. It is all a big scam. It takes little effort and it is actually quite a fun experience as well (insert booze). And the kicker, I have done this for about 12 years now, sometimes for myself, sometimes for a dozen or so people and every year it has turned out great and tasty as well. This also goes for nightly meals. Guys you can come home from work, walk to the store and cook a great dinner for your family all in a matter of about an hour and have it all cleaned up. Don't believe the propaganda! The only thing that is difficult is trying to decide what to eat each night. That is it. So Mommy, please quit lying. You are stunting our development. I know I am not a 10 – my classmates have told me so.

So, there you have it. Section 1 is complete. I hope you found it entertaining and informative. As a little bonus I am digging deep into my mental resources and giving you a little extra material. So grab another gin & tonic. Maybe a sandwich and enjoy. You may thank me later.

**Now for a Little Rant On the Responsibilities of Parenthood**

*"The more people I meet, the more I like my dog."*

*-Author unknown*

If you stop to ponder the problems in your life and the problems of many others in the world today, it will occur to you that the vast majority of these are created by people. People chasing "Gravy", the "good life", "success" or what people consider to be success, namely $$$. What's the rapper slogan I last heard: "Get rich or die trying". A sign of the times. Perhaps, though, other people aren't the cause of your problems, you're right: maybe you're the cause of your own problems. But that's OK, because you're people too, and Gravy is your goal.

I would like to take some time now to add a little bonus material for you. Once again this is likely to bring me a bit closer

Sainthood. However, that is not the reason for the bonus material, the reason is I thought now would be an appropriate time to share this with you. By now I have given you an understanding of what it is like for the Johnny's and Chastity's of the world growing up. The intense pressures that they face each and every day on this planet. It is not easy being a kid. Or have you forgotten what it is like. I have illustrated some of the misinformation that parents feed their kids and how sometimes they actually increase the heights of the hurdles their little angels are going to face. Having said this, I had spoken to some kids about the topics of parents, school and stress just to get a perspective on how hard life is and what some of the obstacles are for them. One older kid in particular submitted this letter to me as an example of his take on growing up in this day and age. So at this point I decided to include his letter, just to illustrate this issue.

**Dear Seed,**

I was born into and brought up in a fucked-up dysfunctional family. Nonetheless (at least) my mother instilled in me, respect for others and politeness. I have always held these attributes in high esteem, well at least until fairly recently, when I began to think: why the hell should I constantly be polite and nice to other people? No one, or very few people, appreciate it and even fewer practice "respect for others" and "politeness" anyway. Have you ever driven to work on the freeway? I have with my parents and it can be very scary. Your fellow motorist will drive like a fucking maniac and cut you off so that he or she can get ahead of you by two and a half feet. You may get pissed off, but hey, it does not matter whether you are polite or not, because the maniac might be armed.

Have you ever been shopping in a crowded mall? Think about Christmas shopping for example, the spirit of love and friendship is in the air, peace on Earth, blah, blah, blah. People jostle, push, shove and behave like animals just to get the newest doll or coolest video game for their kids, because, after all, that's what Christmas is all about. It's all about having the trendiest and most expensive toys and bragging to your family, "friends" and neighbors about how cool you are and how much Gravy you have (keeping up with the Jones).

*Penned By: The Seed & German Seed*

Have you ever rode in a crowded subway car or bus? Do you think people will make room for you, when you're carrying bags, or give up their seat for an old lady? People in our society are raised to be selfish. The feelings, wishes, needs or ideas of others are meaningless: "Just see to it, Son, that you become successful." That you get ahead. At what price? Parents hammer that into young peoples minds from the get go. "You gotta win that spelling bee, Johnny." "You gotta pass that Biology test, otherwise you'll never make it later, or you'll never get to college." You don't want to end up being a loser, do you Johnny?" Because then you will have no money, no one will like you and no woman will want to marry you. (...).

And if you can't be a winner, then there's only one other option, right? Fuck that, I will live my own life on my own terms and I am happy that I have finally moved out on my own.

### *-Johnny (exerts of a letter from a typical teenager)*

Let's read between the lines of these statements. Remember kids, you have to be on the honor roll, so that your "proud" parents can tell the whole world "My kid is on the honor roll". Yeah, kudos, kid, you made the honor roll – too bad your parents are fucking idiots. All of the stress and pressures exerted by parents, teachers and other "well-meaning" adults through the course of life does not really help, they just add to the pressure and stress that already makes growing up in our society so challenging. Maybe you can't remember what it was like in school, so let me remind you. Kids aren't nice to each other. They neither respect others, nor are they often polite to one another: for example, the quiet, non-athletic kid is of course branded as a loser, unpopular or a fag. Hmmm....Have we already forgotten Columbine? So many people wonder why there are so many suicides in this day and age. Or why kids flip out, take Dad's gun or hell, buy their own these days and simply start shooting. Sure, maybe gun laws also have something to do with this, but that's a topic for a different book – or at least a different section. At least it has little to do with video games, heavy metal or violent films, as most self-appointed experts and religious nuts contend. A kid doesn't listen to a song and start shooting. If only it would be so easy to solve this problem. There must be a reason why these kids have become so desperate and depressed that they take such measures. Finding the reason

*Seed's Sketchy Relationship Theories - A Guide to the Perils of Dating*

and solving the problem requires honesty about the way kids in this world are being treated, which the majority of people do not want to face. No, they will most likely just continue to point their fingers and blame others for ultimately their own failure.

The point is, your kids already have enough shit to deal with as it is. Maybe instead of piling more on them, screaming at them or giving them hell for failing the Spanish test, perhaps you should just listen to them for a change. They probably have a lot to tell you, that is unless they don't really like or respect you because you're too busy on the quest for Gravy to ever notice, really that hey, that guy or girl you see for eight minutes at the breakfast table every day is your kid.

(Now a few words of encouragement from Seed for any stressed-out kids reading this book: first of all, don't say fuck as much we do. It's not polite. Secondly and far more important, pay no attention to the crap or stress various adults are giving you, because in real life, your marks from the Grade 9 biology test won't interest anyone. And the kid on the honor roll, whose parents are so proud, will likely be living in the small town you've moved away from, managing at Burger Joint long after you've become successful at the job you've chosen that truly interests you and that you're good at.)

One other thing to make perfectly clear: kids should apply themselves. Life will be easier if they do well. Kids shouldn't become doctors, lawyers or engineers just because Mom or Dad did. It is best if they are encouraged to cultivate new interests, to learn and to want to go to college on their own accord. Not because they've been forced to go, or even worse to take some career path that was pre-determined for them. The results may ok, although they are well educated and perhaps even rich, they are likely not happy. At least not as happy as they could be. Sure, they got married and have a husband or wife with looks that correspond with their salary. They may even have a family, because that's what you're supposed to do, live shallow lives and continue the gravy-indoctrination with your own children. More likely than not their spouse is simply riding the gravy train, as today true love, character and happiness do not seem to matter. I can just hear the self-righteous justifications: "No, I'm not spoiled, I'm just well taken care of." No, you're just fucking conniving and calculating. Good thing you found a partner that's just like you though - you can now show off the ring. A match made in Gravyland.

Nowadays, one must own fancy cars, houses, go on trips to Australia and be able to present the highest possible standard of living to the world. That is the goal in life for most people. So you think I'm a cynical bastard - well you're right. That didn't just happen by chance. Take a moment and think about your family, your "friends" and acquaintances for a second. Be honest about the individuals you know (or are related to) who will lie, cheat, stab others in the back just to get a ride on the gravy train. Maybe you'll see that I'm not so cynical after all.

There you have it the take on the way things are from a typical well adjusted teen. The name has been changed, he was ok with me using this in the book, however he did not want his real name to be used. Johnny is a good kid, funny smart, and full of life. You would not get the impression that he felt this way from talking to him. However, when I asked him his opinion on what it is like growing up that is what he wrote for me. For all you parents out there I hope when you read this it opens your eyes. And for those of you planning a family, please pay close attention to what Johnny had to say as well. If you don't think your kids think this way. Ask them. Actually let them read what Johnny has to say and see whether of not they agree with it.

So your kid flunked the math test. Lighten the fuck up. Then encourage him or her to study more, get some help or take some time off yourself and help them yourself - your golf game might suffer for it, but your kid won't. The math test isn't the end of the world - I know you'll say: "In this dog-eat-dog world, marks and results are important. "Results, results, results." What are your results as a parent? Your kids are probably keeping the stats. They won't tell you anything though, because they hardly know you and after a certain point in time probably don't want to know you any better anyway. And by the way, dogs don't eat dogs - the world is such a fucked up place because of the people in it, not the dogs. Dogs are faithful companions that just bark and wag their tails. Dogs can't talk and it's probably better that way, because if you neglect your kids then you're probably not treating your dog much better and he'd most likely have a lot of shit to discuss with you. And maybe he'd buy a bumper sticker that says: "My owner's an asshole." Chances are he is probably a better driver though.

I would like to thank little Johnny at this point for submitting his letter and also for his use of the word Gravy. This crazy kid has inspired me and I think you will see the results of the inspiration later on in the book in a Chapter called Gravy. Also little Johnny's rant on growing up has also inspired me to include the following pointers on being a parent. I am sure you will find them helpful.

**The Parents Responsibilities'**

- ✓ Plan your pregnancy make a choice to actually be there to raise your own children both financially and emotionally. Do not pass the responsibility on to someone else like daycare or grandma. Or at least, be there for them in the important formative years, preferably until school starts.

- ✓ On that same note, it is important to have one of the parents take on the full time job of raising the children (preferably, if possible, the mother). Who is in better in touch with the emotional well being of the child, after all she carried the little one for 40 weeks? If she wants to get out of the house and neglect the child, fine, that's your decision. Simply wait approximately 15 years and you may very well have other much more serious problems on your hands.

- ✓ **LISTEN, LISTEN, LISTEN.** Your children have a lot to tell you. It is tough growing up and they are looking for answers. No matter how trivial their questions seem to you, they are important to them. Make sure you listen and treat them like their thoughts matter.

- ✓ Be honest with your children right from the start and this means: be fucking honest with yourself.

- ✓ *Encourage, Encourage, Encourage.*

*Penned By: The Seed & German Seed*

- ✓ Did I say **"Encourage"**, when I say Encourage I don't mean "live your child's life for them". As your kids age it is important to allow them to be their own person. That means just because they didn't like broccoli when they were 3 that they still don't like it when they are 18. Let your children speak for themselves, make their own mistakes and most importantly dream. Just because you worked at the same place for 20 years does not mean that will be the best lives for them. If they want to shoot for the stars, let them. Don't hold them back. With your encouragement, nurturing and gentle persuasion, who knows, they may have grander lives than you. Don't be jealous of that, be happy for them. Remember you helped them along the way and that should be enough of a reward.

- ✓ Oh yeah, one more thing for you parents out there: stop using crack. It is apparently very bad. Your kids will try it when their dysfunctional friends lead them down the wrong path. They don't need to get it from their parents.

*You're Welcome.*

# SECTION 2
# Getting In The Game

*"If you don't fail enough
You will never succeed"*

-the seed.

*Penned By: The Seed & German Seed*

The groundwork has been laid. You now have an understanding about what Love is or at least should be. What a Relationship should be. As well, you probably had a few good laughs and realized this Seed fellow may have his finger on the pulse of what it is like growing up. You may actually even go a step further and think this Seed fellow has a pretty good grasp on how the whole friggen world works (That last sentence felt quite invigorating. I had every urge to use the f word but some greater power came over me and made my fingers type "friggen"). Hell, Seed has even thrown in a few helpful hints for the parents of the world to help them in the child-raising process. Once again, he is either nuts or a bloody Saint. I know, the jury is out still. I personally am leaning a bit towards a bloody saint who is slightly nuts and bordering on some sort of manic genius. Just a note, when I just typed genius I spelled it wrong.

So section 2: Getting in the game. First off, a quick question: why are you single in the first place? Have you not given into the societal pressures to hook up? Are you deformed in some way? I know at any given time a certain percentage of society has to be single. That is just the way it works. With the exception of the un-dateable, who closely resemble the unemployable members of society. The only difference is that the unemployable still have the ability to impregnate, hence, the ghettoes of society and welfare. It is a fact: the stupider you are, the more likely it is that you will have larger litters. Ouch, that was harsh. Did I just say that? Please - if you fall into this category and I repeat, please - get some form of education. I am begging you.

Back to the subject at hand. In this section I am going to assist you in the process of getting dates. As well, I will explain some of the signs and things to look for and tell you a bit of how things are operating now. Not to mention what women look for and basically how just to have a blast without being malicious in any way. If you are already in the game, good for you, the wisdom you are about to receive may help you stay in it longer and also help you to see some of the warning signs before it is too late. If you listen, the sections that follow about picking up the pieces really won't pertain to you: you will be a champion.

For those of you in the parental role, whether it be single mothers, dysfunctional family units or hopefully strong loving and nurturing families, I hope your little Johnny's and Chastity's are enjoying the wonderful toys that you have picked up for them at **Seeds Magnificent Boutique** at <u>www.seedenterprises.com</u>. I hope the wisdom and perhaps the copy of this book or one of the others that you gave as a gift to some of your un-evolved friends has been helpful. If you haven't purchased anything as of yet may I ask you something: why are you depriving your kids and loved ones of reaching their happiness potential? Now come on, don't be selfish. I didn't write this book for just you. Well, at least I hope not, because if that is the case you will be able to find me at the drive through window at a local burger joint and unfortunately I will not be in a car. So buy something. You will not be disappointed. I really don't want to have to sell burgers.

# CHAPTER 8
# Theory: How to Get Dates Or Pickup Lines Don't Work

"Okay, so I came over here to ask you to dance, but I'm kind of concerned. I mean, we could hit it off really well, end up having a few drinks, next thing you know you're giving me your number because I'm too shy to ask for it, I finally get up the nerve to call and we take in a movie, have some dinner, I relax, you relax, we go out a few more times, get to know each other's friends, spend a lot of time together, then finally have gotten past this sexual tension and really develop this intense sex life that is truly incredible, decide our relationship is solid and stable, so we move in together for a while, then a few months later get married, I get a promotion, you get a promotion, we buy a bigger house. You really want kids, but I really want freedom, but we have a kid anyway, only to find that I am resentful, the sparks start to fade and to rekindle them we have two more lovely kids, but now I work too much to keep up with the bills, have no time for you, you're stressed and stop taking really good care of yourself, so to get past our slow sex life and my declining self-confidence I turn to an outside affair for sexual gratification. You find out because I'm careless and a lousy liar, you throw me out (justifiably so) and we have to explain to the kids why mommy and daddy are splitting up. That's just too sad. Think about the children. For God's sake,

# Seed's Sketchy Relationship Theories - A Guide to the Perils of Dating

if you dance with me and we hit it off, let's just keep it sexual, because we both know where it's going."

-Author Unknown.

## "Hey Baby"

I would like to start this chapter out by saying, the title of this section sucks. "Getting in the game." Come on, what the hell does that mean? Relationships are a game? My god, no. This is probably, not probably, it is the most important part of your life and to refer to it as a game is bluntly an insult. A lot of people (ok, ladies, you're right: a lot of males) approach the intimate part of their lives much like a salesmen. They figure it is a numbers game. The more contacts that you make, the more trips to the plate, the more "no's" you hear, the more likely that one day you will get a big "yes". What a fucking crock of shit that is. Come on now, imagine on your wedding day when you toast your bride saying: "Honey you were 74th on my list and I cannot tell you how much I truly love you. With you it was definitely love at first sight. Maybe not the first, but 74th sight." How romantic is that? Sure, sometimes you have to date a few people to truly find out what you want and even if you must go out, and I shall venture to say - bang a few, just for the sake of it. Unless your girl is from the bible belt, she likely doesn't want her man to be wearing white on the wedding day. Experience is not necessarily a bad thing.

*Penned By: The Seed & German Seed*

Which brings us to the whole concept of lines, pick up lines. If when I said lines, you were thinking along the lines of South American, well my friend, you have other problems and I can't help you. But when it comes to the use of using pick up lines to win over your love............ Is that really the way you want to *"meat"* the most important person in your life. Pick up lines, though they may be cute, offer few things. They lack any originality. Quit lying you didn't invent yours. And they are also quite insulting. Sure they can be fun or cute, but you must have the ability to be non offensive in your delivery. They also reek of desperation. If they work, ask yourself, how many has your new dream girl fallen for before. Anyway, here are a few for your enjoyment.

- "Let's do breakfast tomorrow. Should I call you or nudge you?"
- "If I could rewrite the alphabet, I would put you between f and ck."
- "Nice dress/pants, can I talk you out of it?"
- "Your eyes are as blue as window cleaner."
- "Your eyes are as blue as my toilet water at home."
- "Help, I'm lost. Which way is it to your house?"
- "I'm new in town. Could you give me directions to your apartment."
- "Hey...somebody farted. Let's get out of here."
- "If I followed you home, would you keep me?"
- "Wouldn't we look cute on a wedding cake."
- "You must be a thief 'cause you stole my heart from across the room."
- "Bond. James Bond."
- "My lenses turn dark in the sunshine of your love."
- "My name isn't Elmo, but you can tickle me anytime you want to."
- "If you were a booger, I'd pick you first."

I think you get the general concept. There are thousands of these little gems floating around and some of them are even funny. However, if you want to meet the girl of your dreams, I highly recommend not using any of these or any of the others that you come across. Instead show some depth, show that you have a brain, anyone could memorize lines out of a book and spit them out. It is no different than telling jokes that have already been told hundreds of times before, they are insulting and condescending. Believe me, they have all been heard before. And if you actually think you are lucky enough to go home with a girl because of some cheesy line, may I suggest two things here. First, when the liquor wears off in the morning take another look at her. Secondly, you are a moron clean out your locker, high school is over.

Wow! Seed sure has bashed pickup lines. You know what, if you are out with the buddies and just having a good old time, go ahead, use as many cheesy lines as you want. That macho bravado pack-like mentality, where you each try to impress one another, girls really love that. At least the *"Attention Whores"* do, which we will be exploring a little later on in the book. Let the locker rooms lies begin. Anyway, the point of this is to help you have a chance at finding and more importantly, keeping love. Like said before, experience is a good thing, but be careful of how much experience you boast about. Telling a girl you would like to have a long relationship with, that you have been with several hundred before her.... Well, use your brain. There is a time and place for everything and my friend if you boast about this, you are a fool. Remember, women want commitment. A future. Not a macho idiot.

So you ask. How do you attract? How do you approach, someone you are interested in? What separates you from all of the other guys out there? To start off, if you see that one woman that makes your heart start beating just a bit faster, or makes it miss a beat, you are a lucky guy. So how do you not blow it? First, go home, take a shower, take of the Budweiser shirt and put on something you bought this decade. And very important here, make sure you have some shoes and belts that actually don't have sports logos on them and perhaps even match. Now that you have gotten this far, the mullet has to go as well.

You have now gotten all spruced up. Maybe for the first time in years, but you still think your efforts won't be noticed.

*Penned By: The Seed & German Seed*

After the initial physical attraction, our fine female friends have been taught by their lovely mothers and their peers to check out shoes and belts. You think I am lying? Well you are wrong, this is a fact. I may have made it up, but it still is a fact. Its my fact, so pay attention to the following. They can tell a lot from these two things, for instance, your sense of style and an indication of potential income. I know you are thinking this sounds like a game. Unfortunately, it is a bit. But just remember you are not actually playing: you are "sincere" in your quest and these are just a few of the guidelines. If you don't want to dress well for yourself anyway, what type of Neanderthal are you? It is no wonder you are still driving a Pacer or a Gremlin. If you have not figured out by this point that looking good just for yourself is a sign of self-respect, you have a painfully long way to go. Oh yeah! You are one of those people who just want to be themselves? I wish you luck. Remember trailer parks are often the only places hit by tornados. Ok, so now you look good. It is very simple, what comes after not looking like a slob in the rank of importance is: having a little confidence. If you don't, women can and will smell that out. No confidence means no future and though some people like taking on projects, like you will learn later, few will stay if the project takes too long.

**"NICE WHEELS...SUPERSTAR!"**

What do you do now you ask? What lines do I use? Were you even listening, maybe you are a moron after all. No Lines. Not on someone you are generally interested in. First off, I suggest, having

## Seed's Sketchy Relationship Theories - A Guide to the Perils of Dating

and using your brain. If you don't have one, *"oafodasgodashg."* That is probably the only thing you have understood so far in the book. By using your brain, I mean have some interests in your life. Maybe read some books and develop a personality. It is not that hard to do. Just stay away from the macho packs (the wolf packs) and their lines. Develop some sort of style that makes you an individual. Have confidence and find things to talk about. It is as simple as an observation and a "Hello", now the challenge is to do this, with no expectations of anything in return. If you learn how to do this, your lonely times will diminish greatly. And while I am at it two more things: don't travel in a fucking pack. Even if you go out with a group, try to separate yourself from the group somewhat. And when out with friends, do not set a goal of meeting anyone, just have fun and talk to people, without pretense, without agenda. It is that simple. Oh yeah try not to be a troll! Unless of course you live under a bridge and are interested in meeting other trolls.

That is it, the secret of getting into this supposed game. I know you think it can't possibly be that simple. Well it is. How do I know. I am a living example. But I will not boast. At least not too much. Let's just say I have a little experience.

# CHAPTER 9
# Theory: Don't Listen to The Pressure to Hook Up. Stay Single. Have Fun. Sleep Around If You Must At Least Till You're 25.

**Scenario:**

You are 23 you have been with your high school sweetheart since you were 16. What the fuck were your parents doing letting this happen. You now have just finished your marketing degree and the insurance recruiters and office companies are at your school, they are there trying to offer you a bright future full of glamour and riches. You have the world by its proverbial balls. There is nothing but smooth sailing ahead. Hell, your parents are only in their early to late 40's and they fit in at the local pub with you and your friends.

Now that you know it all, you decide to ask your sweetie to marry you. **WRONG!!!!!** What is the rush? You have already spent seven years with her and you have only had sort of sex with one other girl and it was only sort of. You don't know shit my friend and unfortunately you likely won't realize it until you are in your 30's or 40's. So wait, break-up, sample the other merchandise let life happen. Maybe you will be confronted with some trauma, like death, illness or job loss. Believe me it is going to happen and how you respond will reveal your true character. So I suggest not putting any other burdens upon yourself until such time that you discover who you are or are truly becoming. Gone are the days where you have one or two careers in a lifetime, the average now is between 6 and 10. If you examine that and say your working life is composed of 40 years. That means something new approximately every 4 years. Handle that a few times before you commit to marriage. And as morbid as this may sound, see how you handle the loss of someone very close to you. These are character revealing events. In fact the five most traumatic events one can experience in a life time are as follows and in no particular order.

1) Loss of a Loved One through death.

2) Job Loss.

3) Moving to a new location.

4) Loss of physical well being.

5) Loss of a loved one through divorce, separation or breakup.

If you want to stay married or give your relationship the best chance of success, the key is, no matter how much you think that you are in love, no matter how mature and well adjusted you think you are, no matter how much you think you have found the person you want to share the rest of your life with, here is a very important thing to remember. You don't know shit. For Gods sake you are less than a quarter century old, how can you possibly know anything and how can you possibly be sure that this is your lifelong soul-mate. Fuck - you probably don't even know what you want to do career wise yet, you probably haven't lost some loved ones, so you don't even know what type of man you are going to become. How can you possibly know what type of girl your sweetie is going to become. I cannot stress this point enough, until at least 25, have fun who wants to be tied down to just one girl, don't waste your 20's, because you will likely regret it later. I even recommend not committing to any one particular person,

*Penned By: The Seed & German Seed*

that is if you want the relationship to have a chance of lasting. Who really stays with there high school sweetheart for life? It is important when you are discovering what life has to offer you, to kick the tires, try on a few different types, that way when you decide it is time to settle down you will not have any questions to answer and that means if the high school sweetheart is the one for you, you will never have to question your decision.

# CHAPTER 10
# Theory: We Attract What We Can Afford Beginnings (Finding and Keeping Dates) How not to get Fucked

*"If you can make a complete stranger laugh or smile everyday*
*Regardless of your own personal circumstances*
*Without motive*
*Then you are living a successful life"*

-the seed.

*Penned By: The Seed & German Seed*

# PERSONALITY -- OPTIONAL

    This Chapter is meant to help you attract the woman of your dreams, maybe have a little bit of fun, but definitely it is to help you get on the playing field. So let the controversy begin. The absolute best and most sure fire way to attract the girl of your dreams is as follows:

## $$$$$$"BE RICH"$$$$$$

    Now before you get all defensive and try to say that is not the way the world works, let us examine this a bit further. This may require some brutal honesty, which I am sure it is something that some of you have avoided for years. You may think that I am trying to portray women as gold diggers, only interested in money and possessions and that love is really a secondary consideration. I want you to understand that unfortunately love is a secondary consideration. Remember as it was explained at the beginning of the book there are exceptions to every rule, so if you are truly one of those well adjusted exceptions just sit back and smile.

    The evidence is overwhelming, ugly people still wish they were with beautiful people, there are several theories that try to tell you that we all end up with someone of an equal level of attractiveness. Those theories though somewhat relative, are really full of shit. People have several qualities that make them attractive to someone else, such as, a sense of humor, skill at a sport or a nice car. However, the number one thing that attracts

## Seed's Sketchy Relationship Theories - A Guide to the Perils of Dating

the other sex is $$$$. If you are fat and ugly and have a lot of great qualities you have no chance of attracting someone out of your league, however if you are fat with cash, the more cash the better the chances of catching someone hot increases tremendously. That is just a cold reality of the world.

To examine this in further detail and to understand why this is such an important point, we must look at a few examples and believe me we all have them. To begin with, we just need to go back as far as the start of high school (believe me it all starts a lot sooner than this). If you can remember going back that far, what was the most important things at that point of your life and what did it take to be popular. For guys to fit in you basically had to be in one of the following groups, the athletes or be from the right side of the tracks, it was that simple and to be the most popular, if you were from the right side of the tracks (the rich kids) and you were an athlete as well, your days in school were easy, you kind of had it made, you were on the top of the food chain everyone wanted to be with you, be like you but, unfortunately most of you did not develop any of the other skills needed to excel in life.

As for you girls, the rules were a bit different. To fit in, the criteria changed: the most important thing was to be good looking. Sure you could fool some people with make-up and a good fashion sense. The next criterion was being from the right side of the tracks (once again, the rich kids). For girls, if you were both hot and from the right side of the tracks, you had it made. But not without a price. For most hot girls and hot guys, being hot actually limited social skills. For the most part, they could get by with their level of attractiveness. Unfortunately, this limited them in so many other ways: like, education, interaction with other people and ambition. It was wonderful in high school but for most of the hotties, I am sure they wished they had done things a bit differently. We all know the High School Quarterback (you may even be him), who had it all but after his school days were over everyone passed him by and he keeps, as Al Bundy and Bruce Springsteen say, looking back at those "Glory Days".

In light of this *"Seed's Sketchy Guide"* is really a brutally honest educator, something that most of our parents and the school system fails miserably at. To have a chance in the world it is important to be honest, and I mean brutally honest to your kids

*Penned By: The Seed & German Seed*

and students so they can prepare themselves for what lies ahead in life.

In life, if you want to succeed with the opposite sex there are several things which you may do. Like mentioned before, being rich would be the number one thing you can do to increase your potential audience. But that, though it may be enough to attract and perhaps even have the woman of your dreams marry you, is not the end of it. If that is all you have to offer, welcome to an unsatisfying and boring life wondering if things could ever be better. Here is where Seed becomes a bit of a sap. I had the girl of my dreams and lost her. Am I rich? No, but I am comfortable. I have a lot to offer, ambition, looks, some people think I have a great sense of humor (I will let you guys and the book sales be the judge of that), and I have a lot of character. You will be able to read about that in one of my future books *"Inside Seed's Head"* which will give you tremendous insight into who I really am based upon the events that have taken place in my life (in bookstores sometime in 2004 or 2005). Or visit our Website and check out the book there. You won't be disappointed. I gave everything to my girl, I left it on the table and was madly in love. Did that matter? Sure it did to me, but to her, well maybe, she still managed to find someone with a little more $$$ and he was able to provide fancier trips. Sweetie, I would just like to say I wish you had told me your definition of Love was *Bling, Bling*. You could have saved me a lot of time. And Patrick thank you for being just as shallow and superficial as her. Just hope your money never runs out or she doesn't meet someone with a bit more along the way. Fuck that, I hope she does.

Do you get the point here? You could be the greatest guy on the planet, but it is out of our control. There are so many societal pressures and that constant desire for more that leaves us all vulnerable. All you can do is be the best you can be, don't strive just for riches in order to try to attract and find your perfect mate. As much as it is ok for your girl to want more, there must be some sort of limit. People don't always deserve more. So if you find yourself making a good living, you have ambition and character and your girl still wants more, then there is only one answer: send her packing. As hard as that may be and I know love fucks you up sometimes, you will be better off in the long run. You will save yourself a lot of mental anguish and who knows, maybe you will actually meet someone worthy of your love and devotion, instead of spending your time with a pretentious unappreciative bitch that makes you feel like you are not good enough. Let guys named Patrick date those types, after all that is what they deserve. I feel it is now necessary to say that I really don't have anything against guys named Patrick other than they should quit being so fucking pretentious and start calling themselves Pat, definitely don't try to be cute and call yourself Paddy – that is just sick and lacks all originality in itself. It is kind of like calling a person from France, "Frenchy". Please come up with something better than that. It is just simply a coincidence that I have chosen the name Patrick to illustrate a point, it has nothing to do with my ex dating someone named Patrick. It could have just as easily been Stephen or some other name that sounds stuffy when you say it in its proper form. I bet you all of the Patrick's and Stephen's of this world never have any problem finishing their bananas. Anyway, I digress.

Continuing on with this theory, at the risk of being redundant. I have decided to include the following scenario to illustrate the point even further. I believe it is important to get this point across, please remember there are some exceptions. But, just some. If you are still resisting this as being reality a recent Newspaper Clipping (actually front page, from Vancouver, BC. Canada) where a 34 year old man who was I believe a maintenance man or something like that had just won 10 million dollars in a lottery, read as follows:

"The Most Popular Bachelor in Town"

Guess what? The reporter was a woman.

**Next Scenario:**

This is an observation more than a scenario. Go to McDonald's or Burger King. Then go to a Denny's or somewhere similar. Next go to a middle of a road dining establishment in your city. Finally, go to a finer or upper end establishment. What do you notice? I don't mean the age differences, if you look carefully with the exception of the youth, the level of attractiveness will become quite clear to you. Do you see it. The better the establishment the more attractive the customers and the staff are for that matter.

*Penned By: The Seed & German Seed*

My friends, that should need no explanation. We are all trying to impress and if we can only afford fast food, don't expect much in return, maybe some instant satisfaction and then that sick feeling in your stomach. If we want more from this life, we must want more for ourselves. Mothers teach their daughters this at an early age, they teach them to go for the best and there is absolutely nothing wrong with that, like everything else, within reason. The poor guy I feel sorry for is the bartender. He likely has to work all of these nights if he wants to earn an income that makes him in the top of his field.

Here is the great equalizer between men and women. In the beginning it is looks that are most important. As we get into the real world it is the $$$, the cabbage, the bling bling or whatever the current term for money is, which will attract women. Most women and more importantly most attractive women may notice the bulge in the back of the pants far before they notice the bulge in the front. This is a hard thing for both sexes to accept, they may think that it means true love does not exist, women may think if they admit this, they are shallow. Well I am here to tell you, that in the world today, this is the basis of true love and not a sign of shallowness. It is what gives the Poindexter's of the world a chance, sure during high school and parts of college the hot girls were dating the hot guys. Whereas, Poindexter assumed the role of the nice guy. He still craved the hot girls but he usually was the guy who had to listen to how much the babes want someone else. The huge advantage Poindexter has, if he is smart he is busy becoming a well - rounded person and he is also busy working towards things that will help him make $$$ in the future. If he does these things all of a sudden in the real world what happens is that sure, the bartender who used to be the Quarterback may have a hot girl on his arm, but when she realizes that if she wants to go on that exotic vacation with cocktail boy, she will have to pay her own way, whereas Poindexter is making six figures and it is first class all the way, all expenses paid. This is the way the world works 999 out of 1000 times: Poindexter gets the girl, at least for awhile and probably in the long run as well.

Before you get too upset and start getting defensive, there is nothing wrong with wanting better things and an easier life. If these opportunities are not presenting themselves to you, you

## Seed's Sketchy Relationship Theories - A Guide to the Perils of Dating

are more than likely not that hot. I know this is probably going to piss off a lot of people, but I will also tell you that if my girl is happy with me and my food court, warehouse, or whatever my menial job is *"I DON'T WANT HER"*. Fuck guys if you have a girl that is happy with you in any of these roles and you don't already have kids, get the fuck out before you do. If you don't here is what likely is in store for you *"We're pregnant"*, we have 3 kids, we are fat, we need more channels on the TV because we need every possible way to numb this existence that we have gotten into. Congratulations if your girl doesn't want you to achieve, you will be spending the rest of your life trying to raise your 2.2 kids paying the mortgage on the house you are not sure you really wanted and all of a sudden your 40 or 50 and you go down to the local watering hole trying to escape what you have become. My friend you are living a life full of regrets.

Here is how the great equalizer works. Ultimately we end up with the most attractive girl we can afford (of course if we are not hideously ugly, then there is no hope period. Wait a minute, maybe surgery. But then you need money. See above.). The more attractive your girl is, the more temptation there will be for her to jump classes. If you are dating a Halle Barry, you'd better be earning seven figures and if you are dating a Miss Piggy $10,000 may be sufficient, but even she will have some shipper/receiver she met drunk at the meat draw at the local pub who may offer her a way out of the trailer park. At the end of the day, you can correlate it to where you live. If you live in Any town, North Dakota or Hollywood, the richest Prick will get the hottest babe. Without exception. Now stop crying and claiming you are not this way and start living. In no way do we condone anyone becoming a prick, it is not a nice way to be. If, unfortunately, you are already one, could you please stop it, it is quite frankly annoying, your shit is no more important than anyone else's and as we're past the age of 22, ok 25, we really don't care who you banged last night, ok – well maybe a little bit – but really just stop being such an ass. Treat others with respect and the same way in which you wish they would treat you. Have you ever heard of the Ten Commandments? Ten very simple rules for life, as the vast majority of people back then couldn't read, and the rules had to be simple. Can you read? Ok, then you get it. Fuck, to tell you the truth, the bartenders of

*Penned By: The Seed & German Seed*

this world are tired of listening to your bravado. Evolve already. Quite frankly you have become boring.

That may have seemed to be a lot of discussion on this topic, maybe Seed is bitter and hurt from past experiences. In reality, yes I am a bit. It is just very important to have an understanding of how things really are. And, more important, not just to understand but to accept the way the world is. We all must strive to be the best we can, at whatever it is that we choose to do. Whatever career choice we make has some severe ramifications and limitations on every aspect of our lives. It affects where we live, what we drive, what we eat, where we go on vacations and ultimately who we end up with. It is time for us all to face reality.

# CHAPTER 11
# Theory: If You Are Not Hot! Find Something to Excel At

*"The key is to be a light, not a judge,
a model, not a critic;
a programmer, not a program;
to feed opportunities, starve problems;
to keep promises, not make excuses;
and to focus upon our immediate circle
of influence, not upon the larger circle of concern."
-Unknown*

*Penned By: The Seed & German Seed*

# Be A Rising Star!!!

This ties in with the previous theory nicely. The sooner you realize you are not George Clooney or Brad Pitt, the sooner you can start working on the things that will impress the ladies and hopefully help you to earn the kind of income that will in turn help you to attract and to keep the girl of your dreams. This works as well for the 9's and 10's of the world, unfortunately a lot of those individuals spend too much time looking in the mirror or being told that they are beautiful that they forget to develop any of the other attributes which make life a happy, smooth ride. Aren't looks fleeting after all? Actually, for a lot of guys, looks develop with age. Life can go something like this: homely kid, cute adolescent, sort of attractive young adult and then - wow - hot man. For women, life can go the other way. Beautiful kid, cute adolescent, hot sultry young adult and then: "Is that you"? "Where did all your beautiful hair go"?

My suggestions here are that no matter who you are, male or female, no matter how hot you are: stop listening to what others think of you. If you are hot, accept it. It is going to open doors for you, but you have a responsibility to yourself to develop other aspects of your life as well. Though reading fashion magazines may be fun, may I suggest also learning some other skills as well, because if you are both beautiful and intelligent, funny, compassionate and caring, you can pretty much have anything in this world. Your looks may be able to provide you with money and even fame, however, if you can take that and expand your abilities, the fame and fortune will be tenfold. I suggest watching the movie "Zoolander" if you want a full understanding of what I am saying. It may actually be better to be beautiful and stupid, that way everything in the world would be fascinating. You may not know why, but it just is.

For example, imagine if your IQ was, I don't know, say 12. If that was the case, you could be told that your whole family just died in a car crash, as devastating as that would be for normal humans, an individual with a 12 IQ, though likely to be upset, that feeling of upset would likely subside as soon as a butterfly flew by. Sort of something like this: "My family is dead". "Oh, look, a butterfly". There is only one thing wrong with my analogy here and that is, a person with an IQ of 12 probably would have trouble speaking and maybe even standing, so lets say that the IQ would have to be around 17.

While we are on the topic of butterflies, can someone please explain to me why the Germans are so angry. Just think about the word "butterfly" in English. Butterfly is of course butterfly, in Italian – "Farfalle", in French – "Papillion", in Spanish – "Mariposa" – but for the Germans it is "SCHMETTERLING". Why do they need to yell so much? Is it because of all the pork that they eat? Come on Germans, pork does not constitute all of the food groups. Eat something else.

Back to the topic at hand. For the rest of us, the less fortunate ones, we must work hard and do all of the things we can, to look the best we can. If you don't agree, I am sure your self-esteem is probably in the toilet. We don't go through this life looking good for others. We do it for ourselves. If you don't believe me, try to remember what your sweetie wore to the last 10 social gatherings. You probably can't, but I bet you can remember what you wore, at least most of the time. We are too self absorbed – our own struggles distract us and dominate our thoughts, which sometimes makes it difficult to notice others. The thing that you likely can remember is that she looked hot and that is all that matters. And if she looked too hot, hey, who is she

*Penned By: The Seed & German Seed*

trying to impress? She has already got you, or is she still shopping? (Just a little food for thought).

So guys, and girls out there, I issue you the following challenge: no matter what your pecking order on the genetic looks scale, forget about it (please do not read the last 3 words of that sentence like an Italian, it is old and it has been done and hopefully you are not stupid). (OK, I am in no way implying that the Italians are stupid, well the stupid ones are, but the rest of them are actually very lovely intelligent people just like people in every country. What I am implying is that the saying "forget about it", though it was cute in its time, has lived it's time, which was about, I don't know 15 minutes, unfortunately it has lived on for years. And while I am on the topic of Italians and Italy, I have to say I loved your beautiful country and its culture after spending 5 days in Germany and eating all of that pork and drinking a little too much of the Maß Beer, it was a pleasure to eat a vegetable again. So, thank you Italy, for restoring my health after Germany took it away). (Relax Germany I had a great time there as well but frankly for the most of it I think I was drunk, my little Schmetterlings).

So as I was saying, do what you can to look your best and don't fret it, there is only so much you can do. More important, start to develop other aspects of your life, whether it is through taking classes, with the guidance of mentors or just picking something and becoming an expert on it. There is nothing more attractive than intelligence and beauty combined. Be a leader, not a follower. And whatever you do, don't listen to anyone else's opinion of what you can or can't do. Fuck, I wrote this book and if I would have asked a lot of people whether they thought it was a good idea, you know what replies I would have received? You know, the ones like: "It is a cute idea, are you going to write in your spare time?" Or, even better: "Oh, you're writing a book. That is great, are you still looking for work?" That's the sort of thing I mean and though not always meant to be negative and mean, sometimes it is just the product of mediocre people trying to keep you down in their comfort zone. Most people in your life may want you to succeed but not too much, because if you do too well it will just illustrate how much of a failure they actually are. Don't listen and quite frankly, they are being mean. If you have an idea or a passion, don't let the nay-sayers take that away from

### Seed's Sketchy Relationship Theories - A Guide to the Perils of Dating

you. If your sweetie or your friends can't encourage and give you some support, get rid of them. You don't need them in your life to begin with.

However, in some instances you have to use your common sense. If you want to be a boxer, and your nickname is "Armless Joe Brown", maybe your friends are just trying to look out for you. After all, they don't allow head butting in boxing. But if you have done some research and have an idea. GO FOR IT!!!!!!!! The worse you can do is fail. And frankly if you don't fail enough, you will never succeed!

# CHAPTER 12
# Theory: Though Early on in Life For Guys Looks May Attract Women.
# As We Age It is Power, Money and Fame That Attracts

*"To Really Succeed In Life
You Must
Bite of More Than You Can Chew"*

-the seed.

*Seed's Sketchy Relationship Theories - A Guide to the Perils of Dating*

**POWER, FAME & MONEY**

**Scenario:**

You are now 28 years old, you are a few years out of University but you still are lacking any direction and you have gone through a few career changes. Fuck, you just don't really know what you want from your life. You are lucky – you are a 9 on the looks scale, so you have no problem attracting good-looking girls, well at least initially. But now something is starting to happen. Your uncanny ability to name every player in pro sports and the number that they wore for the last 20 years may have been cute at the keggers, however, now you may just as well tattoo a big "L" on your forehead, because unless you are dating girls in there teens, my friend, you are starting to become the epitome of the "one-night stand".

Inevitably, the big question is going to be asked and that is: "What do you do?" Trust me when I tell you this, if you want to be in the game, your answer is imperative. Although the question itself may be shallow, it is probably the number one way of qualifying potential. If you say you are a dishwasher at Denny's, you may still be taken you home for a quick romp, but that is about all there is going to be. Face it guys, looks may get you a long way in this life, but eventually the "bling, bling" does the talking. Don't get upset with this, there is nothing wrong with this attitude. Well, at least to a point. Women and society place a lot of importance on career and titles. We forget that some bartenders, managers and members of other professions, who perhaps don't get the glamour of the doctors and the lawyers of the world, earn enough with the added bonus of a better quality of life due to better working hours and above all less stress. Those who only date the doctors and lawyers have a title of their own: namely, "Gold Digger". Yet, they are most likely to end up as a statistic when their loving mate trades up for the candy striper.

    Back to the point at hand, it is OK for a woman to want her mate to be a success in life and to make a decent living. If she is content with you living in a trailer park without an ounce of ambition, then do you really want her? Wait, of course you do, you have zero ambition. You are just a lazy bastard to begin with. Fuck, if you are content with that, then the question I'd like to ask you is: when did you give up? So the big point here is even in the adult world your looks can still get you things for the short term and they have likely helped you get places in your career. Let's face it, society rewards beauty. However, if you have not developed any other skills and are just sort of coasting through life, you have a big problem. You may have found the love of your life and know that you want to be with her, but unless you have some potential (that is, <u>earning</u> Potential) - even if you are lucky enough to marry the girl of your dreams - you are going to end up as a divorce statistic unless you develop some ambition. Life's pressure will eat away at your love bond and more and more, the lack of cash, ability to go on a vacation, the ability to spoil and clothe your offspring will grow to be a major problem. So get some ambition and some drive or enjoy being a man toy. The choice is yours.

    I know this section seems to focus primarily on looks and currency. This topic is a very important thing for guys to understand and the earlier in life you learn this, the better off you may be. Johnny is a prime example of how this theory and many others play out. Now fortunately for Johnny he was not born hot. He was only about a 7 on a scale of 10, so very early in his life he learned through interactions with others that his looks were not going to be enough. And though on the basis of his looks he was able to attract girls at a comparable level of attractiveness and, on the basis of his personality, to be friends with the 9's and 10's of the world, he realized that he would have to excel at something if he wanted have any chance at being with these girls (or get a penis enlargement). Regardless of whether that was sports, academics or business. He also realized that he would have to remain reasonably fit and dress and groom himself as well as he could within his means. So the lesson one learns here is that early on in life, the attractive girls are very drawn to the equally attractive guys or to the more attractive guys, but as we age and develop our personality and character this changes. As we get into the adult world, the attractive girls realize that if the attractive guys have not developed any other aspects of themselves, those looks will not be enough to provide them the material things and security that they are desired.

So as man ages here is what happens: though looks may be an important attribute, the things that really attract women are Money, Fame and Power. Those are all things that will provide us with the capacity to earn the income we need to be able to have the beautiful things that we desire, either clothes, cars, homes or the women we settle down with. Guys, this doesn't mean you can be a fat fucking slob. Let's face it, there are very few John Belushi's, Chris Farley's or John Candy's etc. in this world. By the way all 3 quoted examples are DEAD. Do you get my drift?

Not to dwell on the topic of looks, but you can't be horrifically ugly or a troll (there is a correlation between looks and earning potential). You don't need to be a 10, but for that matter you shouldn't be a 5. And be honest with yourself: should you be a 5, then you have little choice. Work on your personality, fitness and grooming and you will at least be able to salvage 1 or 2 points (maybe even 3) to bring yourself into a different league, my friend. You must still strive to do the best you can with what you have been given to succeed in both the business world and the "World of Romance".

Basically, most men are juvenile idiots until they've reached a certain age. Let's say for argument's sake: 25. The "magic age" of maturity depends naturally on the individual and of course, life experience, education, travel and to be honest, relationships. If you stop and think about the guys you knew in high school, who married their "sweethearts" and started a family (or knocked their sweetheart up and were forced or "convinced" at the point of a shotgun to get married and start a family), you probably can't recall any that are still married, or at least happily married. Those that front and pretend to be happily married are probably stalking chicks in their spare time or are quite conspicuous when they go out with the guys for a beer, the only thing that really interests them is the possibility of picking up a bit of skank on their "night off" from the wife. Or bragging or boasting to the boys about all of the girls they had in the good old days. If you are doing this, stop it. You made your bed. If you love the person you are with, refuse to participate in this type of "glory days banter". It is quite bluntly, disgusting.

Wow, that's a fucking ad for getting married at age eighteen, isn't it? Why should it be otherwise? In high school, we had our own little world. Jocks, Geeks, Popular People, Losers, Punks, Surfers, Drama Freaks, Goths and People in the Band. Everyone had their place. After high school, we entered the real world, where everyone has to find or fight for their place. Looks might carry you a little bit further, still, if you are not prepared to study anything or start working, your looks won't carry you too far. After all, looks, as opposed to diamonds, are not forever, and if a woman is going to stay with you for more than a few days, weeks or months, then you'd better be able to offer more than good looks and wild sex. (In no way does Seed want to discourage wild sexual activity. In fact the opposite is true he encourages it. Whip!!!!) If you can't offer it right away, then hopefully you can at least give her some hope that you will be able to make something of yourself someday (soon). Good looks can never hurt, yet the vast majority of us are not 10's and have to make up for this fact, sad but true, with other attributes. What is the SECRET to success? We don't know either, but for starters, making something of yourself has a little bit to do with the word "secret".

Let's just look at a small example. Johnny is working as a consultant in a large firm. One day he hears that the company is planning to expand and open branch offices in European major cities. The first offices are planned for London and Paris. In two

## Seed's Sketchy Relationship Theories - A Guide to the Perils of Dating

years time, the firm will open an office in Madrid. Johnny had gone to Europe after his first year in college and had a blast in Spain. How can you not have a blast in Spain: beautiful people, great booze and good music. He had even learned some of the basics in Spanish. The company was looking for qualified and interested employees for the various start-ups. However, an average "Johnny" isn't exactly what the bosses are looking for. Let's face it, there's no free lunch and they're always going to ask the question: How bad do you want it? Doing an MBA and improving his Spanish would naturally improve Johnny's chances of coming on board. He sees the chance and wants to take it, so he enrolls in a MBA night course for professionals accompanied by a Spanish course at the local university. That means four nights a week of class for two years, regular tests and bad-ass exams at the end of it all. Still, Johnny is psyched, his friends haven't seen him so motivated and excited in quite some time. He dives into the courses and tells everyone who will listen how great it is. But what happens now?

Of course, his girlfriend is not thrilled with the idea. First of all, he's no longer available four nights a week, as he's got to go to class. Then there's the homework. He never has time to cook, to go to the movies or to hang out like before. There is the issue that if he gets the job he will be going to Europe. She has no desire to leave home but does not know how to tell him. Resulting in: "Honey you know your full-time job plus MBA is way too stressful. It can't be healthy - you will work yourself to death."

After a while, his buddies at work ask him how he can manage to handle the courses on the side next to the enormous workload and pressure at the office. Others ridicule him around the coffee machine because "he has no chance to get the job anyway, as he's only been with the company for a couple of years." Some of his other "friends" start to complain because he no longer comes to watch hockey or football at the bar on Wednesday nights, because of course he's busy - he's got to go to class. One of his friends from high school asks him how serious he really is about learning a new language, because, as we all know, "none of us was any good at French in school." His mother worries about the stress he's under. Once again, that "can't be good". Then there's the thing about his plans to leave home, and of course, he wouldn't want to lose that nice girl. Plus Mom's friends start to take sides. "Look at my son,

*Penned By: The Seed & German Seed*

he's an accountant and is making good money." Well, look at your son. He has an ugly wife, he's fat and has no life. As well, his kids are fat. Of course his Mom's going to sing his praises, after all, if Mom was lying to him as a kid, why should she stop now?

Enough about Mom, his girlfriend and his "friends". What are the consequences of all these comments? After a short while, Johnny starts doubting himself. He starts thinking about whether he will be able to pass the exams. The constant stress and stupid fights with his girlfriend start to make him think: "am I really working too much?" Fear creeps into his head: "maybe the course is too much for me." Perhaps Girlfriend is right: "maybe I have bitten off more than I can chew." Then of course, every time Johnny comes home to visit his family, the questions start flying. "Why is that course taking so long?" "Why aren't you done yet, Johnny?" "My degree didn't take so long." Dad chimes in with a commentary: "When I went to university, we didn't have to learn Spanish. I started working in Canada, why does Johnny have to go to Europe? Why doesn't Johnny just stay in Canada?"

The constant questions about how far he is start to get on Johnny's nerves. When will he finally be finished? He can't possibly be serious about this course. Johnny thinks: "Why don't you all just fuck off?!?" Weren't we taught as kids, if you don't have something nice to say then don't say anything at all? Unfortunately, most adults or so-called loving family members simply don't have anything nice to say. They're just pissed off because they had to get married at the age of eighteen. Or twenty-one. Or twenty-eight. So much for friends and family. A lot of people don't want the best for you. Quite the opposite: if you fail, then it will only serve as a confirmation that their sad lives aren't so bad.

Back to Johnny. After a few months, he starts to hate the courses. He begins to skip class on a regular basis before he finally quits. Maybe you are asking: what's the point of this story? Have you ever tried to learn Spanish? Probably not. I feel that the point is that on the one hand, there are those among us, who might be pleased when we strive to achieve something new. Unfortunately, they're the extreme minority. If you haven't yet realized it, people aren't nice. They don't want the best for you. Quite the opposite, when you achieve, or God forbid overachieve, then they see that as a personal insult. Most people, and especially most of the "caring and loving" family members are simply jealous. They're pissed off and purposely want to stop Johnny from achieving more than they've achieved in their sorry lives. Of course in all fairness, there are others who honestly are worried about Johnny and only want the best for him. Yet, without harboring any evil intention, their constant nagging, doubt and above all irritating questions start to distract Johnny from his plans. Furthermore, Johnny can never simply talk about his courses and his plans; rather, he constantly has to defend his decision to better himself. This robs him of the energy and, more important, the enjoyment he had when he started taking the courses. Then there are the people, the "friends", who, although they can barely speak their mother tongue, somehow managed to get a B.A. or B.Sc. explain to Johnny: "Oh yeah, I know how that is. It's just like when I did my degree in basket weaving. I know what you're going through, man." Well, no you don't. Yeah, you studied, but the focus of your energy was spent on picking up ugly chicks and committing stupid pranks. It might have been different if it wasn't for all of those hits from your bong.

Sadly, the point in time comes, when Johnny decides "fuck it". He stops taking the courses. At first, Johnny experiences a huge relief. An enormous weight falls from his shoulders. Yeah, good, but wait. Those people who always questioned his decision to make something of himself, who always questioned his goals, revel in his failure. They start to talk about him behind his back: "I knew he wouldn't see it through." Furthermore, whenever Johnny mentions that he'd like to do this or learn that, people simply smile smugly and remind him that the last time he tried something, he failed. One quote comes to mind: "The more people I meet, the more I like my dog." At least you can count on your dog not to fuck you over, as opposed to your so-called "family" or "friends". Unless of course your dog is one of those evil lying dogs that I had mentioned earlier on in the book. Like I said, most people aren't nice, they're only looking out for No. 1. Your success is their failure.

Naturally, there are exceptions. There are some individuals who honestly want the best for you and are happy for you when you succeed, or even way more important, are there to support you when times are tough. Most people, either consciously or

*Penned By: The Seed & German Seed*

subconsciously, don't want you to succeed. The fact that you want to make something of your life, that you want to improve your situation, travel or make more money only sheds light upon their inability to do the same.

You may think this is all superficial and shallow. There is nothing wrong with wanting more as long as it is within reason and is in check. If you are driving a Mercedes and you want a Bentley or Rolls you are just one greedy bastard or bitch and eventually karma is going to dish you a large dose of reality. And by the way who taught you to be that way?

# CHAPTER 13
# Theory: To Have a Chance You Must Learn How to Be Alone

*"The sooner you learn to do things for yourself
The sooner you learn to enjoy your own company and time alone, The far more desirable you will become to the rest of the world"*

-the seed.

**Scenario:**

You are a good looking guy. You have been dating someone ever since you were 15. You always had an attractive girl on your arm. You were a star athlete and the prom king. Sure you had periods when you were single but they usually were only about 3 or 4 days long. It always seemed that as soon as your heart was broken, someone else was there to ease your pain. Fast forward and you are now 27 and the girl of your dreams who had been dating you for the past 6 years dumped you about a year ago because she did not see a future with you. Fuck - you wonder, how could she be so shallow? After all, you are a manager at a Foot Locker. She must hate stripes. So over your year of despair, you think: "I will show her. I will get in better shape because how could she not want to be with the guy with the hottest body in town?" So you work out diligently, get in great shape and sure, you even get laid a bunch because the 22 year olds have not figured things out yet. But your nights are still lonely, you pine for your ex and meaningless sex. Drunken debauchery does not seem to be filling the void. May I ask one thing of you, could you please quit writing her all of those fucking poems, you are not a poet. Poets are poets. Leave the poetry to the poets, it is hard enough eking out a living as a poet to begin with, so they don't need the competition from you. Now back to you Mr. Lonely-Pants. You don't know what to do. How will things ever get better?

Well, my friend, there is no easy answer for your dilemma. Actually there is: "You are Fucked". Before you go and slit your wrists thinking that was as good as it gets and because I just told you that you're fucked (you probably couldn't slit your wrists anyway, because when your girl left she took her cutlery with her, so ever since you have been eating with a spatula and a soup ladle, since you don't know how or where to buy cutlery). I am just kidding, what I am trying to say is that you have your work cut out for you. You have been a serial monogamist since you were 15, which means you probably forgot to learn to like yourself. You spent so much time with others, you never learned how to be alone and treat yourself well. This is one of the curses of being attractive, someone always will want you, especially when you are younger. But as you get into adulthood, keggers no longer cut it. Your girl left you because she no longer saw a future. The staff price on Nikes were not going to provide enough for a comfortable life together.

My friend, you now need to do a few things. First, as scary as this is, go out by yourself occasionally. You will be surprised what you learn. Pursue some of your interests, read and find that ambition that you never needed because you were always with someone. Learn to cook. Don't just eat TV dinners and crappy canned food because you are single and that is what single guys do. That is not what single guys do, by the way. It is what losers and under achievers do. People who have accepted their place in the pecking order of life and would rather mope around and whine about what they don't have instead of going out becoming the best that they can. So when the next dream or love of your life comes around you actually will have a chance at keeping her, because your pad looks great, you can cook, you can dress yourself, you read more than Sports Illustrated and you have not given up on ambition. If you can do some of these things, you are learning how to be alone and like yourself. If you do this a beautiful thing will happen: you will become more desirable. That is of course if you haven't slit your wrists already.

    This is an area of just about everyone's life that is usually underdeveloped. I feel this topic is very important, so at the risk of being a bit redundant I am going to ramble on a bit here and give another scenario illustrating my point. I am also doing this because I wrote the scenario that follows a long time ago and when I returned to finish this chapter I neglected to read it first. After I read it I realized that at least to me it is funny and I think in the process of giving this insight it would be amiss if I did not let you, the reader, form your own opinion on it.

    Society is constantly putting pressure on us to hook up. It is cheaper to do everything as a couple. I am sure you have seen all of the 2 for 1 coupons out there. Unfortunately, we don't develop this area of our lives, namely personality and people skills, until something tragic happens and we are forced to do so, whether we like it or not: death, separation, and divorce, we have all been through these or know someone who has. The scenario plays out sort of like this: the High School Sweethearts have been together for 7 years, they are now 24. However, the hot cheerleader girlfriend realizes that there is a big $$$ world out there and though she loves her boyfriend dearly, his memorization of all of the words of the new Eminem CD, though cute, coupled with the job down at the factory is not going to put her in the latest fashions or provide her with the dream life she so desires. And by the way, the 35 year old Lawyer who is pursuing her, may be a bit of an ass and not capable of making her laugh like her boy does, but he does drive a BMW, owns his own loft and is offering a trip to the tropics instead of a trip to the Beer Garden at the state fair. So she tells the love her life one of the standard lies: "Its not you, it's me" and drops him like a 2 foot putt. So now welcome to "Dumpsville", population "you". If you have never in the past learned to be alone and like yourself, this can be one of the most traumatic experiences in life. If you are hot, don't worry, you won't be single long and can jump into an equally fucked up relationship with a younger model, because she doesn't realize that you are likely going nowhere, and who knows, maybe you can hold on to this relationship for a few years before she sees the light. Then once again, the story repeats itself until suddenly you are 50 (it will happen long before 50 my friend), out of shape and can't attract the babes you so desire anymore. Or the day will come that you settle for the not so attractive slightly overweight girl with great depth who doesn't mind you going down to the local watering hole every night for 2 or 3 or even 8 pints of medication so you can drown the fact that you have failed miserably in your life.

There is good news, however, it does not have to be this way. Now though this experience may be traumatic, it can be a great time for self discovery. Hey, you can learn to jerk off with your other hand. This is the time to redefine yourself. If you have been in a long term relationship you need to take some time off, not just a week or two, but instead however long it takes you to change course (unless of course you are so pathetic and don't care if you keep repeating this cycle). Fuck - if you are working in a warehouse, come on pal, use your brain: the Halle Berrys of the World are not going to end up with some schmo in a warehouse, so do some serious soul searching. Sure, the hot chicks in Fargo may not take a Hollywood superstar to win them over, but even they are not going to end up with the shipper/receiver, at least not long term. There is a Pig Farmer down the street who will attract them (Don't take offence, Fargo, I really know nothing about your city, I don't even know if you have pig farmers in the area. It was just the first city that popped into my head while I was typing this and frankly this is a book about relationships and to do the research on Fargo will be saved for my second book: "How to score a 10 in Fargo").

So if you want to succeed later in life, you might initially think you should do the things you need to do in order to try to win the love of your life back. But don't waste too much time with this as you will quickly realize that your ex-girl will get over the guilt (remember women are taught early on in life how to manipulate

*Seed's Sketchy Relationship Theories - A Guide to the Perils of Dating*

and the power of guilt) of dumping a loser like you (maybe a day, maybe a week). So don't go out and buy a bunch of self-help books on how to win your love back – for God's sake, didn't I already tell you to STOP writing the damn poems!! – because at this present moment if you try too hard, no matter how pure your intentions may be, it will quickly turn pathetic and can, and will be misinterpreted. Also, there are stalker laws and you don't want to sacrifice your remaining shreds of dignity and make your own personal life worse. Come on guys, you have been dumped. As hard as this may be to face, your sweetie does not want you anymore. There was a better offer out there and like anything in life, who wants to be with someone who doesn't want you. Have some self-respect. Develop new skills and get out of the trailer park. This is a new beginning and if you use this time wisely, you will find a new way and understanding of how things work. You don't have to become bitter – this information can help you stay in the game just for the sex you need, but also help to develop the skills that will enable you to attract the girl of your dreams for the long term. Wouldn't it be sweet if, in a few years, your now fat ex is down at the local coffee shop with her short hair, 2.2 kids, wearing sweats and her lawyer pal has traded her in for a newer fresher model and you drive up in not a BMW but a Mercedes? So fellows, it is up to you to find a way out of the warehouse.

The big message here is quite simple. At some stage of every person's life we need to learn to like ourselves. It is imperative if you ever want anyone else to ever like you. The sooner you come to this conclusion and learn to do things for yourself and to enjoy your own company and time alone, the far more desirable you will become to the rest of the world. The real kicker here is, if you learn to do this, the likelihood of you ever being alone will diminish significantly, people will want to be around you, you will exude confidence, character and charisma. Not to mention you will learn how to please yourself.

# CHAPTER 14
# Theory: If You Want To Keep Her Interested Don't Be A Nice Guy (The Girls Want The Bad Boy Theory)

**Scenario:**

"Honey can you pick up my dry cleaning?" "Yes, dear". "Honey can you drive me to the store and wait for me and then drive me home?" "Yes, dear." "Honey can you go to the store and pick me up some feminine hygiene products?" "Yes, dear." "Honey can you paint my nails, rub my feet, ...?" And the list goes on and on. It is quite simple: the more you say "yes", the less desirable you become. Unfortunately, relationships are constantly being tested and you need to get a spine. Sure, it is ok to do a lot of things for your significant other as long as it does not take away from the things you want and need to do. I am a big fan of true love and putting another human being first, but my friends, there has to be limits. If you constantly are there to do every insignificant task for your mate, you really aren't their intimate partner. You have actually become their servant. I know some of you guys out there know what I am talking about. You gave up something important to serve your mate and eventually they dumped you for some ass. Don't let this happen, only do things if it does not detract from your quality of life. By this I mean it is OK to say "no" once in a while. Your girl actually wants to know that you have a backbone and if they were ever in trouble you would be able to stand up for them. If you are just a yes man, guess what? You are letting them know in a time of danger you are likely to back down. It is, after all, a survival of the fittest world.

"Nice Guy's are Fucking Boring." Just about every girl claims that they just want a nice guy. I am telling you that is a big, big fucking lie. There is no more boring type of individual than the nice guy. Girls walk all over them, families walk all over them, bosses walk all over them for Christ's sake the whole damn world will walk all over them if they are too nice. The term nice guy should actually be changed to "Disposable Guy". I am not saying be a prick or an asshole, what I am saying is this: if you want to keep the girl of your dreams, then have a backbone. Believe me you are being tested every day and sure for a while she may like that you will drop everything you are doing and drive 20 miles out of your way to pick up her kitty some special food. And yes, it is ok to do it once and awhile but not every fucking time you are asked to drop what you are doing or going to do. If you do, I guarantee that "Most of The Time" she will end up fucking someone else while you are running her errands and when she finds someone more intriguing in a higher income bracket, you will be gone. Guys, it is very important that you believe this. If you want to have a happy relationship full of sex and surprise, no matter how much you love her, don't tell her all the time. Don't even tell her she is beautiful all of the time, even though you may want to. Believe me, it is much better to have her feel a little unsure, maybe even a tiny bit insecure about herself. I am not saying play head games, just don't be a little wuss and constantly wag your tail and tell her every 15 seconds how much you love her, how beautiful, wonderful, lovely – gag – she is. Telling someone 20 times a day "I love you" doesn't make the feeling or the bond stronger, it only waters it down. Think about it, if you behave this way she will never respect you and even if you have kids together you will be the one staying home and raising them. So do you want to be that

*Penned By: The Seed & German Seed*

much of a pussy .... Only you can answer that and you don't want the answer to be meow, meow, meow...

Note: When you are sure that your relationship has evolved and is full of Love, Trust and Respect it may be ok just to be a nice guy. Once you are very confident that you have found your true love, the person who will stand at your side through thick and thin, in sickness and in health, then the rules change. You can tell them you love them and that they are beautiful every day. But then and only then, when you are to that stage of your relationship. The kicker here is that very few relationships ever get to this point, so be careful. A little attitude can go a long way to keeping things fresh.

This is one of the biggest clichés in the dating world. For centuries, we have been constantly told that nice guys finish last and that the bad boy gets the girl. For years, testosterone-filled guys (you're right ladies, "idiots" is maybe more applicable) everywhere have constantly tried to prove that they have a bad streak so that they can win over the girls. The point that is sadly being missed here is that the girls they are attracting are bar girls. The girls who like to have drama in their lives. We all know the ones. They are the ones playing the game, pitting guys against each other to see who will go the farthest in the pursuit and defense of their honor. To illustrate this all you have to do is go down to any bar or night club any night of the week, or primarily on weekends, to see the game in full knock down, drag out action. The problem here is that the people in this game are not in committed relationships anyway. Most people who are spending their nights in the clubs of our cities are still shopping. That is not to say that you can't go out to clubs with your mate once in awhile to have a night out on the town. However, mark my words, if it is a regular part of your social package you are being set up for a fall and eventually will likely find your nights lonely again, as your true love moves on to "next". The really sad thing about this is that it is likely that your true love was shallow to begin with and hurting you was only going to be a matter of time. "Oh well", you will be told, somehow you deserve it. They will constantly try to prove to you that the next sad sap is better, that there was something lacking in your relationship. The fact is, what was lacking is that your sweetie is a shallow bitch or bastard.

What does all of this have to do with this theory? Basically it is simple: stop playing the fucking bar games. High School should be over for you now, so graduate already, you are in the adult world now and the bar stars are not worth the effort. Sure, they may be a fine shag now and then if you are single, but eventually that will grow old and tiresome as well. As for the theory, what we are trying to say to you is, that girls, although they constantly long for the "nice guy", don't really want you to be too nice. You are always going to be tested in your relationships, right or wrong, that is just the way the world has been conditioned. If you give into every whim of your girl, she will eventually think of you as more of a servant, personal assistant or lap dog, instead of a partner or lover. A lot of us have heard this line while being dumped: "You are the sweetest guy I have ever met, I don't know what I will do without you". The translation is, you were too nice and they are not sure who is going to do their errands for them now. The funny thing is you probably still will or would gladly and depending on how heartless they are, they will probably let you.

Women do want their mates to have a bit of a mysterious side to them, a bit of an edge, so don't reveal everything, at least not right off the bat. You can tell your best friend everything but don't tell your sweetie. That is right, my friends, tell your best friend everything. I know you may be thinking the following: "but my girl is my best friend". Well, you are wrong. Think about it: here are things that you can only tell your best friend, for instance, stupid pranks, stupid mistakes or behavior, sexual adventures from the past and your mate has the same stories as well. Don't get me wrong: we all have a past. After all, this made us who and what we are today and that is a good thing (unless of course your mate is a psychotic murderer fleeing the long arm of the law or, as George now and then says, an "evil doer" – didn't you ever ask yourself why he was constantly going on business trips to Kabul?) Plain and simple, people, it is not fucking healthy to reveal everything about your life to your partner. Frankly, we cannot handle some of the things and this will affect either consciously or subconsciously how we treat each other. Remember this: you are now living in the present. The past is just that, the past and that is where it needs to be left. Don't put that pressure upon anyone, you will not like the response. Unless of course you want the relationship to end, then you may want to reveal some of your deviant past to your

*Penned By: The Seed & German Seed*

mate, as a way to cut free. But other than that, keep things to yourself. Without a sense of mystery, life can be stale. Remember you have your whole life to learn about each other, you don't have to do it in the first week and a half. The reason that women are fascinated by the bad boy is the insecurity that it arouses in them. We have all at one time desired things that we could not obtain and the bigger the challenge, the greater the desire. So with the bad boy and mystery comes a yearning: you want more and more and more. You sort of want to unravel this great big mystery, but you probably never will. We are not encouraging you to play games here, on the contrary we are just letting you know that very few are really bad boys and at the end of the day, women want a good guy with a bit of a mysterious streak in them. That way life can remain fresh. In the end the true bad boy likely leaves, goes to prison or something along those lines.

In our lives I am sure you have heard the saying: "Never judge a book by its cover". Well, that is often the case in the world of the bad boy. A lot of women are attracted to guys who wear leather and ride motorcycles. It has a romantic feel to it, an image of danger. Whereas, in reality a large majority of motorcycle riders are actually great guys constantly putting safety first. They have wives and kids to come home to, so they take every precaution to ensure their safety. They would not think of getting on their bikes under the influence of alcohol or anything else. And when you break it down they are not big risk takers, they just simply like to ride motorbikes.

While at the other end of the spectrum there are stock brokers and stock promoters. A lot of these characters drink at lunch, drink after work, will put anything they find up their noses and would screw anything capable of getting up on two legs that is not capable of outrunning them. They give the illusion of success, of having money and power and a lot of the bar stars that go to the pretentious trendy establishments that we talked about earlier want them. Well, they think they want them, they really just want some of what is in the bulge in the back of their pants. Now you may think that a large portion of these individuals are the real care free mysterious, fast living, fast loving, bad boys. Well, actually, they are just PRICKS. (Not all stock brokers and promoters are this way, there are just a few more in these careers

## Seed's Sketchy Relationship Theories - A Guide to the Perils of Dating

than some others. Ok, throw in lawyers as well. And to clarify things, 98% of stock promoters are pricks, hell they can't even get licensed, so that should tell you something. Oh, did I mention Car Salesmen. Ok, I will stop now.) By the way, those of you in any of the above mentioned fields that do not fall into the PRICK category, hey congratulations, you are the exceptions and should be very proud of yourselves. Fuck – it must be annoying working with the others though. Come on tell us the truth. We won't tell anyone!!!! By the way, how does that quote go again? Oh yeah, "all generalizations are false." Discuss.

# CHAPTER 15
# Theory: Beauty is a Consistent Thing

*"It is wonderful to surround yourself with beauty.
But it is far greater on the scale of importance
To find someone whom you truly love and cherish
And feel that sharing your life with them will only greatly enhance yours."*

-the seed.

*Seed's Sketchy Relationship Theories - A Guide to the Perils of Dating*

**Scenario:**

This theory pertains to the cliché: "Beauty is in the Eye of the Beholder". What a load of crap. Sure there is some room for different tastes and there is such a thing as inner beauty, but in most cases what we find beautiful is very consistent. It is easy as a trip down to the local book store or magazine shop and a look at the different fashion magazines and though as time goes by there may be some changing tastes of what is hot at the moment, it remains pretty standard. Why do you think that the Sports Illustrated "Swimsuit Edition" is always so greatly anticipated and such a tremendous success each and every year? Now the only reason big chunky guys end up with whom they do is because their income dictates the kind of girl they can attract. Now you are probably thinking: "That can't be true!" There must be more to it than just financial standing. To a point you are right, for the most part there are not that many big, fat, super-rich people (when compared to the number of non-fat ones) and the ones that achieve this status, where they can afford whatever they want,

*Penned By: The Seed & German Seed*

usually have this horrible habit of dying too young due to health problems.

One must go no farther than looking at some of the comic greats of the past 40 years to see this point clearly illustrated. By the way, these individuals all likely had there own demons and issues haunting them – that is, indeed, part of the reason for their comic genius. It is amazing how much great comedy comes from some sort of almost debilitating pain. As for beauty, it is decided for us by someone else, more so than ever in this pop-culture society that we live in. We have television, movies, music, magazines, beauty pageants and the fitness industry telling us how we should look, feel and dress. From the beginning of our lives it is drilled into us what we should like and above all buy, starting with the "in" toys and dolls to the "cool" clothing, cars and other possessions. We have all become some sort of sheep for the media. Their success is based solely on us buying into it. And my friends, we have bought in to the tune of hundreds of billions of dollars per year. And it is not going to change anytime soon. It can't change. It would take a major catastrophe for us to change our perspective and that is not likely to happen in our lifetimes. Or is it?

Everyone is beautiful in some way. Ok, not everyone, let us eliminate the real "evil doers" of society; the rapists, murderers, child molesters and the religious zealots just to name a few. If I missed you and you are an evil doer, you know who you are, could you do us all a favor and go jump off a bridge or something, you are fucking up a lot of lives and frankly, you can just go piss off. Now back to the beauty thing. Sure, there is beauty in just about everyone. Remember, it is not always physical beauty that attracts, but at least initially that is the case. And as much as there is beauty in everyone there is also likely someone out there for everyone as well. Don't fret if you don't find that person early in life – you have your whole life ahead of you to do so. Don't over analyze. Just live. Refer back to the previous parts of this section, there are some excellent pointers on living and having a good time.

As life goes on, things do change dramatically. We have childbirth, aging, injuries and sickness along with the toxins which we ingest ourselves and the ones which we breathe in. Our cities are over-populated and polluted. We even have masses of water which are so polluted that satellites no longer recognize them as water. You can just imagine the effects of these pollutants on our beauty, at least our outward beauty. You are probably thinking: "Where is Seed taking us now?" He is talking about beauty one moment and now he is listing a whole bunch of things that affects this beauty. Why is he doing this? I am doing this just to illustrate, that beauty is a fleeting thing. Very few people can hang on to it for a life time. Some of the truly vain in our society try desperately to do so through cosmetic surgery. The message I am trying to get across here is, sure, it is wonderful to surround yourself with beauty. But it is far greater on the scale of importance, to find someone whom you truly love and cherish and feel that sharing your life with them will only greatly enhance yours. Despite of all of the challenges which we all face every single day of our lives, they will never leave. They are in it for the long run.

Maybe your true love has dropped from the 10 they used to be down to a 6 or even a 5. Maybe life won't be kind to them. But as long as they are content and doing as much as they can to maintain who they are both outwardly and inwardly, now that is true beauty. Consider yourself lucky. If you want and crave more and as a result you disrespect this person, cheat on them, treat them badly, etc., well perhaps you are one of the evil doers and we will eventually find you, uncover your ways and then.... you ain't gonna be beautiful much longer!

# CHAPTER 16
# Theory: If You Want To Date Babes You Must Surround Yourself With Babes

**Scenario:**

You wonder why some bars get labeled as pretentious and full of "Gold Diggers". You always go to your local pub or hangout on the weekend because you can go as you are. But you notice that the most attractive girl in the pub is carrying around a rump roast and is missing a couple teeth. Sorry, let me clarify that, her butt may resemble a rump roast, however I am referring to the pub's weekly meat draw, in which she won a rump roast. As well, rumps and roasts come in all different sizes. So if I was referring to her rump in the first place, I may have not been calling her ass large. Because of the simple fact that she is missing some teeth, I am going to guess that she has a lot of junk in the trunk. Anyway, you likely crave going to one of the pretentious places, but you are probably intimidated by beautiful people and in all probability would not know how to dress in order to go in the first place. It is a lot easier to wear your 5 year old Budweiser T-shirt on your big night out, than to ever attempt to climb the social ladder. The point here is this: the beautiful people hang with the

## Seed's Sketchy Relationship Theories - A Guide to the Perils of Dating

other beautiful people. They don't try to win meat, they don't stumble into places where people are trying to win meat. They expect more out of life and if you want to be in their league, you have to try to fit in. That means staying fashionable, learning how to speak properly and if you are a single guy and you want to date someone attractive, find a way to hang out with attractive people. I know this all sounds pretty shallow and yes, like I said before, inner beauty is a wonderful thing. But don't you really want to find someone with both inner and outer beauty?

This theory is very simple and is based upon one of the ways women are very competitive, especially beautiful women. If you want to attract a 9 or 10, of course the first way to do so, as long as you are not hideously ugly or obese, is to be rich. Women can overlook a lot and discover inner beauty if they believe you can provide them with "security". However, one other way to attract beauty is to surround yourself with beauty. Girls are fiercely competitive and want what others want. They will always turn their heads and see who other hot women are with. There is a belief that if someone is with a hot woman they must have the means to attract them. It costs money to surround yourself with beauty. Clothes and hair cuts do not come cheap. Above all, it takes discipline and time to train regularly and eat sensibly in order to stay in physical shape. I am not suggesting shallowness here. I am just stressing a point that has been made before. Look the best you can within the means that you have. Don't spend your days in your old stinky sweat pants and expect good things to come your way. Don't expect a supermodel to stay with you if you wear brown belts with black shoes, a fanny pack or socks with sandals. They won't and you will just look fucking stupid. Yes, even if the fanny pack is a name brand one. So use some thought and pay attention to how you dress and present yourself, surround yourself with people who also have some self esteem and try to do the best with what they have as well. See, you thought I was just being an ass, trying to tell you to dump all your friends and become shallow and pretentious. In reality, I was just telling you to dump your loser friends, you know the ones I'm talking about. The ones, who on your big night on the town wear old ratty sneakers and a T-shirt. The ones that have changed the course of your night to: "I don't think we can go there because they won't let Carl in because of his sneakers" (who the fuck wears sneakers

*Penned By: The Seed & German Seed*

on a Friday night, and who the hell says sneakers anymore? Just stop it, it is embarrassing!). Don't let your friends keep you down, of course unless you want to spend your nights winning meat and unless you have a great dental plan where you work, because your wife is going to need it.

# CHAPTER 17
# Theory: Most Attractive Women are Attention Whores

**Attention Whore, a definition:**

Someone who goes to great length to assure that everyone else in a room or at a social gathering notices their presence. They will do this with clothes, or props or by any means which are available to make sure they receive the most "exposure" possible in the shortest amount of time. They are not necessarily extroverted, but they do know that if they can attract higher numbers of potential partners, they will increase their possibilities of success. Quite often they are insecure, shallow and superficial, with little more to offer than looks. Also quite often as they age and their looks become fleeting, they drop the word "Attention". Second cousin of the "Crack Whore".

*Penned By: The Seed & German Seed*

LOOK AT ME!

### Scenario:

It is Saturday night and for the tenth Saturday in a row your girl wants to head to the hottest club in town. You are not too keen on the idea, even though you will probably have a good time. You would much rather stay in, maybe have some dinner and watch a video or two before retiring for some "Sweet Loving". However, you do not want to be a prude, so you give in to her desires and it is off to "Club Available" for a night of dancing and frivolity. Now, your sweet gal is hot but she dresses a little too revealing for you. You are always wondering why her skirt has to be that short or her top that low, but she is yours and in a way it is flattering to you to know that you have the hottest girl in town. The problem, though, is that you go out to be with her and she goes out to show off and attract attention to herself. You can't understand this. You know she is going home with you at the end of the night, so you do not make a big deal about it. Should you? As the night progresses for you it is kind of boring, all you want to do is be alone with your girl. She on the other hand is lapping up every ounce of attention she is getting. Is it innocent? Well, it appears to be that way, but as they say, appearances can be deceptive. These nights are starting to eat away at you. You know she has it good, fuck you are a great guy. You're ambitious, funny and attractive with a killer body and killer personality to boot. Basically, the whole package. But for some reason your girl needs to receive attention from the everyone. It is like she knows she has it good, but she wants more.

My friend, you are dating an *"Attention Whore"*. And as much as you think you may be able to handle it, it will eventually end in ruins. You are probably staying for a whole series of reasons beginning with the obvious, she is hot, up to the fact that you may actually love and trust her, as you have seen her true beauty and the potential is unlimited. This wonderful girl may even be your soul mate, your true love. The problem is that she unfortunately most likely does not feel the same way about you. She may know that she has it good. But the *attention whore* is very much like a drug addict. Their drug is having the masses worship them. They usually have charm and personality. Their personality is usually very infectious and they make a killer first impression. However, when you scratch deeper and go beneath the surface, there is not much else there. In truth, they are disrespectful and cruel. The world is solely about them and what they can get from it. If you find yourself in a situation like this, you may stick it out because you are in love. You may even believe that they love you, you know, they might. The sad thing is you are going to inevitably get hurt. *Attention Whores* likely will cheat and when you eventually challenge them, they are going to leave since they likely have someone waiting in the wings. This is a sad reality. Now let us scratch just a little bit deeper into the world of the Attention Whore.

Let the gloves come off and let the controversy begin. Ok, the gloves have been off for quite a while, I am sure I have somewhere prior to this point offended at least one person. After all we are now 17 chapters into the book and it doesn't resemble a nursery rhyme. At least I don't think that it does. I am sorry

*Penned By: The Seed & German Seed*

about offending some people. Ok, I am not sorry about that at all. This chapter, I believe, if it has not gotten you to take the gloves off yet, for sure it will get you to do so now. And if you do, place them somewhere easy to find because who knows when you will need them again.

We are now getting into the meat of the whole dating world. If you can be honest and not get too defensive or hot headed when you read this chapter you will start to make great strides. By understanding this one fundamental rule you will be well on the way to success. This chapter is as simple as the title, but let us add one quick bit: *"Most attractive women are Attention Whores!!!"* Relax now, remember *"Most."* This is one area where women and gay men are fiercely competitive. They are taught early that if they use their looks properly, they can use them to attract, capture and eventually control their dream man's life and bank account. But they also realize that this is a time sensitive proposition and that in their late teens and early 20s they are most capable of attracting potential equally attractive or financially potent partners. During their 20s they are still in the game and if they can hold on to their looks and their bodies into the early 30s there is still a hope. But after that sweetie, if you have not succeeded in this game, it is likely over and you better have your own career and your own bank account, because honey no one is likely to be paying your bills.

Now, I would like to address you, the reader, should you happen to be one of the *attention whores* who is playing the game. First off, I hate you, you despicable human being. Did you forget that love is an important element in life and designer clothes don't look that good on you anymore anyway, so I hope you live an unsatisfying life. Secondly, while you had your looks, you probably scouted out the bank accounts of the suckers you were after and the divorce settlement probably has you covered for the future. It just is no way to live, and those of you who live that way are really cancers of society. You should have your own islands where you can just go around constantly fucking each other up, because ultimately that is all you deserve. [German Seed is sensing a bit of anger here in Seed. Hmmm.... Time to call Seed for a bit of anger management.]

## Seed's Sketchy Relationship Theories - A Guide to the Perils of Dating

To understand this theory further, you just have to look once again at the fashion and cosmetic industries. Women, regardless of how hot they are, constantly spend big dollars on trying to look the best that they can. For what? Do you honestly believe the garbage that they just want to feel good about themselves? Here is the simple answer to that question. Sure they did when they were trying to attract you, but come on, how many of you girls or guys are dolled up all of the time at home or dressed to the nines? The answer? Fuck, you know the answer. How many of your girls spend a lot of time getting dolled up when they go out once they already have you? You also know the answer here: all of them. Now don't be naïve, you may have a fantastic relationship and I am sure you want your babe to look hot, but I guarantee you that they are all not doing this for you. Some of them are still seeing what type of interest they can attract on the open market and they are letting you fucking know that if you slip up, there are interested suckers in the on deck circle. If you don't believe that this is the way the world works, your sweet girl probably does have your balls in a jar.

There are some simple tests to illustrate that *"Most Attractive Women are Attention Whores."* Women will spend a long time getting ready for a night on the town and even single women, if they meet a guy that they are very interested in and for illustration's sake let us say that they would definitely like to spend some time between the sheets with, if they meet him too early in the evening, he is likely out of luck. It is just that, to early. They have not been hit on by enough guys or received enough compliments about how good they look. Most women go out to be noticed. They of course are competing with all of the other women out there, whether they are single or not and it is like a game to secure your position in the pecking order of life. Remember, before you get too upset with me and say that Seed is just a chauvinist pig, I know this because I was a high end call girl in a previous life. So I have first hand knowledge of how it really is.

Now guys let's reverse it a bit here. Say you have spent a couple of hours getting ready, got the right hair cut, had someone pick out a smoking outfit for you and now you are off to the bar for the night. Here is the question: a hot girl you are interested

*Penned By: The Seed & German Seed*

in asks you to go for a romp in the first 15 minutes of getting out? What do you do? I thought so.

Girls, before you get too upset and try to prove that you are not one of those girls, come on be honest. The level of the Attention Whore changes based upon the level of attractiveness; the more attractive you are, the more time you will likely spend on beauty and looking good in order to get noticed. And as you go down through the beauty chain less and less time is spent and if you are homely enough perhaps you can become a CEO of a fortune 500 company, because let's face it, no one is likely going to be paying your way honey. OUCH!!!!!!!

I think it would be prudent at this time to give some dating pointers according to Seed. The pointers that I am giving you now have already been touched on before in the chapter about pick up lines. I feel it is very important to repeat one point again. The last little bit of this book was a bit harsh, perhaps even a bit too edgy. The Seed is a big supporter of looking great when you go out. Your clothes and style say a lot about who you are and what your first impression on others will be. Select them wisely, figure out what message you wish to convey. The difference here compared to the Attention Whore is that you want to look good for yourself. Take pride in the person you are. You do not desperately try to attract attention for the sake of hooking up with some rich "keeper" or to stroke your fragile ego. Remember, you should look good for YOU! Not for the Sugar Daddy or Mama! Like often in life, it's all about how you use it?

So now fellows you are out in the dating world. What do you do? How do you attract attention to yourself? Do you want to know the big secret here? It really is not that big of a secret and it is NOT about playing any kind of game. It works well regardless of where you are in the world and it works with just about everybody, even if you do not speak the same language. How do I know this? It is the way I live and if you were to ask any of my close friends they would verify the gold I am about to give you. I am not going to brag about the numbers or anything like that. This is NOT even about numbers and in fact the actual numbers compared to the amount of occasions that I declined are only a small percentage. Why am I keeping you waiting so long. I don't know, I think maybe I am just trying to fill a page or something. Anyway all of the stuff

### Seed's Sketchy Relationship Theories - A Guide to the Perils of Dating

that I have been telling you up to now is important. Before you use this info, please (and I urge you) have your house in order. The number one way to meet and date successfully is this: "STOP CARING", "STOP TRYING" and above all don't use (or stop using) any fucking lines. What I mean by this is simple. When you go out, don't have an agenda. If you are out with friends, be just that: out with friends. Have fun with them, don't go looking for anything. And when you are in these social situations and you find someone that you want to talk to, simply smile and say hello. It is ok if you make a simple observation about something and you bring it to their attention. But that is it. Don't impose. Don't desperately try to be "cool". If they want to talk to you, they will talk to you. Maybe not at that precise moment, but perhaps sometime later. If you follow this advice you will be thanking me. You will spend fewer nights lonely. Your life will be much more fulfilling, this is not just simply dating strategy, it is also life strategy.

I believe that regardless of career, marital status and your own personal family situation, if you can go through your life and on each and every day find a way to make another human being smile, most importantly without expecting anything in return, you are a successful human being. I know it sounds so simple. It is. Treat people like they are gold and you will get gold in return. Treat them like you are playing a game and you to will be played my friends. You are an adult, now act accordingly.

# CHAPTER 18
# Theory: Hot Girls May Fuck The Bartender But They Are Not Staying For The Long Term

*"Do you really want to spend your life
Pouring beer and making Bloody Mary's
For some dickhead who thinks he is better than you"*

-the seed.

Seed's Sketchy Relationship Theories - A Guide to the Perils of Dating

**Scenario:**

You have spent 5 maybe even 10 years working behind some of the hottest bars in town. You make outrageous coin and usually have a great time. You have honed your skills to an art form and have the ability to communicate with all types of individuals, from condescending assholes, to the powerbrokers of your town. You are able to give insight into which girls may be fun and which to stay away from. You are like the pusher to the stars, you have wit, charm and charisma. After all, everyone knows that the bartender can solve their problems. If not with advice and a good ear, at least with the libations that make them forget their worries. As for the girls, you have what they want – the personality enhancer: a martini here, a special cocktail there, an appropriately-timed complement. The world is yours. You have hundreds even thousands of friends and quite often, pardon my language, a good romp or two (I got you there – you probably thought I was going to say "fuck". Well my friends I am several chapters into the book now and I would like to say that I have matured as an author, I have become much more reserved). My friends, please use this time wisely, learn, develop some mad skills at interacting with people and please, please realize that very few, if any of these people are your friends. Sure you might have made some excellent connections for yourself, but ask yourself this: How often is that excellent connection in your bar? The answer will give you the insight into how excellent the connection is.

As for the hot girls that go home with you: they probably find you attractive, they may even sincerely like you, but the fact here is that they are likely looking for that same excellent connection that you are. And unless you want to get into a deviant sexual adventure with them and the connection at the same time, you must make your own way in this world. Use your connections but don't count on them. They are likely full of shit and impressing you is part of the game. If they impress you, then you will do work for them. After all, you have your finger on the pulse. Don't you?

Now if you want to have a chance at success with the 9s and 10s of the world you must understand this theory. It is also important to be above a normal level of intelligence or you are going to be spending a lot of lonely nights at home with your hand. Sure you can switch hands now and then for variety, or of course dress them up in cute little teddies (a bit fucking weird don't you think?), but at the end of the day if you bartend and you want to take home the babes you must understand your place in the pecking order of life. Bartenders have couple of advantages over the general population. They have the ability to intoxicate. They usually have exceptional people skills. They usually can talk a bit of bullshit and they are usually dreamers who can convince people that they have some big plans for the future. However, in the world of *"Most of the Time"*, most of the time bartenders are just bartenders and they, can have a tendency of becoming the worst type of regular in their own world. The regular that truly does not have a choice. They have to be there. It is their way to pay the bills and to do so they have to listen and put up with the shit of all of these regulars that they cannot stand. In the world of $40,000 to $60,000 a year, they can become kings. They are the entertainment. What the construction guy and the marginal sales guy wish they could be. The problem is that the bartender craves more, at least the intelligent ones. He craves to own his own place. He always looks at what is out there until the day that he is broken

## Seed's Sketchy Relationship Theories - A Guide to the Perils of Dating

The important part of this theory is that the bartender, of course, depending on where he works, can have the 9s or 10s. Actually the bartender can have the best looking girls regardless of where he works. It doesn't matter if it is your city's hottest club or the bar out by the truck stop. The difference is in the club, the hot girl might be a true 10 where as at the trucker bar the hottest chick may be wearing stirrup pants, be missing a couple of teeth and be trying to win some meat. It is all relative. Ahhh, the meat draw. You can usually tell the attractiveness of the clientele by the type of promotions a bar has and frankly, if it is people trying to win meat, one word: argghhh!!!

My friend, if you want to have these "non meat-winning girls", you have a tremendous advantage. You are the dealer, the focus of entertainment. If you are good at what you do, you can convince these girls that you have *"POTENTIAL"*. What this will do for you, if you can talk a good game, is to get them into your bed. Maybe even get them to stay for a while. But fuck fellows, unless you are actually showing some strides to accomplish something with your life, even if it is trying to become the owner of the bar, *"THEY WILL NOT STAY FOR THE LONG HAUL"*. As much as we like to think we are more intelligent than the fairer sex, they will quickly realize that you are just a bartender and the big game that your talk, is just that: talk. They will quickly calculate that though you may be a funny, attractive and the life-of-the-party-type of guy, the food court is not where they want to eat and "the maybe there is a chance if the tips get better, we will be able to go away" is crap. They are gone. There are a lot of broken bartenders all over the world talking about their glory days. So unless you are stupid and that it doesn't bug you to have your girlfriend's friends introduce their men as Doctor Ken or Lawyer Stan while you are just being introduced as Johnny, your choice is a simple one: get off your ass. Instead of just talking about what you are going to be, become something or the babes will be a thing of the past and you will end up settling for the cocktail girl who had the looks, lost them and had a kid (nice going single mom). And due to the fact that you work together you will come to realize you already are fucking married because you see each other every day. Don't do it, it is sad and pathetic.

*Penned By: The Seed & German Seed*

This is not all about just getting the hot girls. It is much more than that. It is about sanity and trying to make the best for yourself and your life. Come on do you really want to spend your life pouring beer and making Bloody Mary's for some dickhead who thinks he is better than you? I know the answer. You don't have to tell me. If it is yes, all the power to you. I do ask one small thing of you. Do it with passion and at least strive to be the owner of your own place. Life is too short to spend it working for that same dickhead. So take the bull by the horns and you my friend, that is right you, strive to be that dickhead. Ok, you don't have to be the dickhead at least not in public, maybe during your intimate moments. Just be something!!!!!!!!!!!

---

There you have it Section 2, hopefully it was both funny and informative at the same time. Personally I find Section 2 a bit depressing. Like I have said on several occasions, this is how the world is currently operating. I myself do not like some of it. I will not participate in the game. You may use the information to your advantage, if you are playing the game. However, if that is the case, you are likely just following the norm and becoming another sheep. Another faceless clone without personality or passion.

If, on the other hand, you strive to be different, one of the *"exceptions"*, I am sure you will use this information to help you figure out what is important to you in life and to help you to strive to achieve those things. This information will give you some insight into how the majority of people are thinking and if you are actually attracted to someone who is treating this part of their life as a game, at least you will know what to expect. Just think of how valuable this information will be if you would like to hold on to your true love - perhaps you will recognize whether this person is the one you have been hoping for. You have the advantage. Now use your head and seize it!

After reading this section you may want to remain oblivious to reality. Perhaps that may be an easier course. If you choose to do so then you will likely become a statistic. Do you truly want that? There is no excuse for ignorance or apathy.

## Seed's Sketchy Relationship Theories - A Guide to the Perils of Dating

In summation, Section 2 is as follows, at least for me: love and meeting your potential soul mate is really not a game. Instead it is probably the most important aspect of one's life and to treat it like a game is insulting. Be yourself, develop some interests, some skills and strive to be the best you can with whatever you have been given to operate with. In your youth, develop some character and have some fun. Don't tie yourself down until you have some clue as to what life may have in store for you. If you are motivated by beauty, understand it comes with a price and to attain it you likely need a level of success in you life. Don't become jaded and bitter by the way it is now. Understanding and accepting it gives you power. If you are an *"exception"*, or if you want to become one, this understanding is crucial. It will give you the ability to stay clear of things and especially the people that do not help you achieve your goals. If you spend your time having fun developing a personality and some skills you are well on your way. If during this process you learned honestly to like yourself, your own company by pampering and nurturing yourself, you are making great strides. Well my friends, you are developing a great gift that you will be able to share with others. If you can do all of this, while at the same time gaining an understanding of how the world is working, then the world is yours. You are unstoppable.

*Penned By: The Seed & German Seed*

# SECTION 3
# You Have Someone You Think You Want To Keep Now What?

*"Whenever I'm Alone With You
You Make Me Feel Like I Am Whole Again"*

-The Cure (Love Song)

*Penned By: The Seed & German Seed*

## Drift Away----- Time For Some Romance

    You have just met your dream girl. At least you think you have. Your heart is racing a little faster. You think about her all day long. She is on your mind when you go to sleep at night and when you get up in the morning. Fuck this is special! You are on your best behavior. You don't know what is going on. You have never felt like this before. You feel your ambition coming back. You want to be someone. You start blowing the guys off on Friday nights. My friend what do you do next? You only know one thing you don't want to blow this one.

    The only problem is that you have blown every relationship before and never took the time to examine what has always gone wrong. Hell, there was even that one drunken night in the frat house when you blew.... Never mind that was a whole different story. My friends you have now entered uncharted territory. If you would have only had a copy of the book before, you would be so much more evolved. Well, I am sorry. I was too busy evolving myself and going through the pain and hardship necessary to learn the valuable lessons in order to be able to share them with you.

## Seed's Sketchy Relationship Theories - A Guide to the Perils of Dating

I hope you appreciate the hell I went through for you. At this point of time, due to my pain and suffering I would like you to take some time to stop at *Seed's Amazing Boutique* at <u>www.seedenterprises.com</u> and purchase one of the fine products in appreciation of my efforts. While you are there maybe buy a book for a needy friend as well.

As for your dilemma.... You think this might be the real thing: true love. How do you make sure that you stay in the game? Well that is what I am going to share with you. In this section I am going to encourage you to make sure that you are genuinely interested and not just dating because you feel lonely. You are going to gain some valuable insight on how life's traumatic events change you and how better to handle these events when they arrive. As well, I will explain to you the *"Myth of Security"* "Security" just does not exist. I will give you some additional insight on what may be necessary to keep the girl of your dreams for the long haul. You will learn about the ways women use their looks as a type of currency. In addition, I will touch on what happens to men as we age and how best to prepare and cope with it. Finally, I will share with you some of the warning signs, the "red flags", which might help you to decide when to run or when to stay. So pay attention. Very close attention. I may quiz you on it later.

# CHAPTER 19
# Theory: Never, Never, Never, Never, Never, Never Absolutely for No Reason Did I say Never Settle No Matter What

*"Couples love to have everyone safely attached and will try to see that you get that way as soon as possible."*

-Unknown

*Seed's Sketchy Relationship Theories - A Guide to the Perils of Dating*

Seed Lives Do You????

### Scenario:

You are in love with Chastity and she is the only one who will make you happy. But you know what? Linda is ok, maybe she will do. Quite frankly, this is the most important chapter in this book. If you for whatever reason do not follow this chapter and its advice, no matter how harsh it may seem, then there is nothing else to say to you and I wish you luck on your dismal journey through life. This advice is so imperative and yet it is difficult to truly believe and above all practice, as it requires not just honesty but also courage as well. This is also the chapter that if you want to say "Seed what the fuck are you telling us? Where did the edge go?" Go ahead. As I have mentioned throughout the book and will continue to do so, I am a big fan of relationships. I believe that relationships make the world a better place. I believe it is vitally important to find an individual that you value and put before yourself. Period. Also I seem to be a big fan of using the word period as a sentence on its own to get a point across. It is the greatest gift you can give (not using period as a sentence, rather putting another person first) and is a sign of true love. I know I have felt and given it and unfortunately lost it. I don't know if it exists more than once in a lifetime and frankly, it is my greatest fear that I might never experience it again. However, having said that I am open to the possibility, but one thing I guarantee is that

I will never ever settle. If the magic is not there or if the magic is not sustainable, I can't be unfair to whomever it is I am seeing. It is not fair to them and primarily it is not fair to me. Love should be magic, if not everyday at least most of the time. If you are only holding on because it is comfortable, or for companionship, you may even be in love, I just ask you to do some soul searching and as long as you have no children set your mate free. The initial pain may be great, but the pain of a life unfulfilled will be much greater. Wow, who have I become, a chapter or so ago when I said I had matured I was just kidding. Maybe I am deeper than I think.

So my friends, if you want to date or marry someone like Halle Berry and that is the only person you can ever envision being truly happy with, then please don't all of a sudden decide to settle for the copy girl just because she is nice and you don't want to be alone. Ladies before you get upset: the message is the same for women as well. If you can only see yourself with Brad Pitt, first of all, you may be crazy. Secondly, don't settle for the video store clerk. We all have our vision of what we need or want to be truly happy, we all have characteristics, looks, personality, social standing etc., that we look for in our dates and eventually spouses. This is a very important theory to follow and it is the key to future happiness. It is Ok to be alone and we all don't have to marry. There is no time limit on finding what you want and just because your family, society or your already trapped friends look down upon you if you don't follow their paths (it is funny as I age and by age I mean that some of my married and hooked-up friends are envious of me – they at times live vicariously through my actions). People who are miserable want company. The guys want to hang around other guys, who get shit and flak from their wives about anything and everything and the girls want other unsatisfied, fat chicks to bitch about their lazy fat husbands with. It is a fucking cult, you do not have to go down this path. Oral sex does not have to stop with "I Do". You don't have to spend your Weekends at the Home Depot, Wal-Mart or at the kids' soccer games.

This is not to say that the family unit is not important, you don't have to have a family just because others (your family, relatives, friends, co-workers and acquaintances) pressure you to do so. Get married, have kids: but for God's sake (no, actually for your own damn sake) do it for the right reasons! It doesn't have to be a life-long ordeal, where your only "way out" is to flee to your stool at the local dive bar. "Normal" is a highly subjective term and what is normal for the sheep of this world does not (I hope) have to be normal for you. Furthermore, "normal" is not necessarily "right", a look at the divorce rate will only confirm this. What is "normal" is to keep looking for what you want and never, never, never settle for something just because people tell you that you are too picky. Be picky: most of these people are miserable and heading down a marginal life path or worse yet, heading for an eventual and probable divorce. I encourage you not to join them. Try not to become one of the husbands who gets together with the other husbands and always talks about the hot girls that they used to date or bang before the inevitable "time to settle down" was upon them. What does settling down actually mean? Is it resting up for death? I know for myself personally, when it comes to death I do not want to be rested up for it. I want to be spent. I want to have danced more and lived more than anyone else on the planet. I don't even think I want the inevitable death to be a pleasant experience. I am pretty sure I want it to occur while I am leaving it on the proverbial table as opposed to having a group of my loved ones and those who feel obligated, gathering around me to watch me take my last gasping breath. I want mine to be remembered. Hey, maybe that is the moment when I will become an "Attention Whore" at my death, or let's call it simply my "death party". Can you think of a better time? I know, I know – how selfish opposite the mourning guests to disturb their misery and suffering. Yeah, but whose party is it anyway? Oh, and another thing, the only hot chick that I want to talk about when I am having beers with the guys, is my "True Love".

In conclusion if you want certain things don't be a big gigantic pussy and settle for less. We only get one go around as this particular life form, so don't settle, don't let the other cult members drag you into their misery and just like we are *"Not All Meant To Procreate"* we are *"Not All Meant To Marry"*. Please don't marry because your man has money. Please don't be that shallow. You do know when the bling, bling fades, there will be nothing left. Most important, don't ever, ever give up on what you want or it will be your misery; fuck, you will be more alone settling than you will ever be getting to know yourself and learning to like yourself. If that means trying to fuck hot chicks till your

*Penned By: The Seed & German Seed*

70 and trying to make your first million, so be it. Or would you rather have a fat bitching wife, 2.2 kids and a house with a 3-hour commute every day because that is all you could afford. The choice is yours.... Really, it is.

The only real reason to get married is if you have been lucky enough to find your "True Love" and your partner has found theirs as well. Period.

# CHAPTER 20
# Theory: Life's Troubles Don't Build Character They Reveal it

*"Our true character,
Whether we are a follower or a leader
A fighter or a quitter,
Are all revealed by how we react
When life altering events take place"*

-the seed.

*Penned By: The Seed & German Seed*

### Scenario:

You watched your parents die 17 years ago one year apart. You actually watched them each take their last breaths. You then faced a series of 10 operations over a 4 year time period. Your girlfriend and you broke up and shortly after the breakup she had a brain aneurysm.

Fast forward 17 years from the death of your parents and this time the true love of your life dumps you. A week later a young friend commits suicide. One week after that another close young friend informs you that he is dying of cancer and a few days after that, in an attempt to cheer you up, he informs you that your ex and him cheated on you. Is that enough drama?

Let us make it a bit more intense. You get a call from your closest relative an Aunt. You have 3 older brothers and 3 older sisters, but this Aunt and you have some strange bond. She informs you she is going to be changing her will and cutting some people out and oh by the way, she might be dying. Now your sisters and brothers start to load the guilt on you to drop your life and go and watch your Aunt die, but you can't and your Aunt is ok with that. She understands how much you love her. But the family still alienates you. At the same time all of the mutual friends from your relationship, instead of seeing if you are ok and giving you an occasional hug, decide that your lying and cheating ex is fun to party with, so they all alienate you as well. And get this, some of them tell you the reason is "because you have changed". No shit you've changed, your whole fucking life is changing in front of your eyes, and there is nothing you could have done to alter the outcome.

Within a month, you get a call from your sisters, you sense a guilt trip coming, instead they inform you your last uncle passed away in his sleep the night before, unexpectedly. So there you go: a break up with a true love, 4 deaths, family and friend alienation and a whack of infidelity. Could anyone handle that? Well, let us spice it up just a bit more. You decide, because that was too intense for a 3-month period of time, that you need to get away to clear your head. So you go to renew your passport. In the process, you need a new birth certificate. However, the vital statistics department of your state won't issue you one because some of the information you gave them does not match the records they have. Next - you find out that the people you listed as your parents, the ones you watched die 17 years ago, get this, they weren't your parents. Which means everyone in your family sisters, brothers, aunts, uncles and everyone else have been lying to you for your whole life. To top it off, your actual parents are still alive. Oh yeah, the family members are not what they seem. They are not actually brothers, sisters, aunts or uncles. Strangely things are starting to come clear to you. Why you were treated poorly throughout your life? Why you don't have many fond memories of growing up, other than the ones with your friends. Can you handle it? Is it believable? Probably not, no one could go through that much in a short time frame and be fucking OK at the end of it.

The point here is, this is an unlikely scenario but life can be difficult and extreme, "unlikely" and unexpected things can, and likely will, happen. We all experience death and separation, job loss and other traumatic events in our lifetimes. It is unlikely that so much can happen to one person in a lifetime or in the short period of time mentioned above. It is even far more unlikely that these events would not have a significant impact on that individual and significantly influence who that individual becomes. I just hope if something like this ever happens to any of you, you have some solid friends to help you pick up the pieces. Events like these are extremely traumatic and I believe that you either have character or you don't and when events like this occur, whether it is one or all of them, when the dust finally settles, if you are meant to survive, you will. You are a person of character. If not, you will end up in the gutter, destroyed and broken. Yet in consideration of events as extreme as described above, I am not sure if anyone on the planet would not end up destroyed and broken.

*"Life's Troubles Don't Build Character They Reveal It"* is another important theory. There is a lot of what I feel is misinformation out there about how one develops character. I believe that the way you are brought up, the values, morals and standards that are instilled in you by your family, relatives and your early social groups help greatly in the shaping of who you eventually become. But our true character, whether we are a follower or a leader a fighter or a quitter, are all revealed by how we react when life altering events take place such as the loss of a loved one by death or separation, the loss of parents, the loss of a job, health problems such as operations and so on. These are all very traumatic events that everyone and I mean everyone has to go through at some point of time in their lives and until these events begin to occur we will never really know the true individual that lies beneath.

Another point which falls under the category "misinformation" or just plain bullshit can be summed up in a simple phrase: "Get over it." With this simple, short phrase people possessing absolutely no compassion and often with no comparable life experience attempt to put you down and minimize your trauma. "What, your true love just left you for Dr. Ken. Get over it – it's just a break-up." Another potential gem: "So, your family was killed in a car accident? Get over it. Be positive, things can only get better." If only life would be that simple. If it were, we could create a table or a list of appropriate periods of time required to "get over" traumatic events, for example: job-loss – 7

## Seed's Sketchy Relationship Theories - A Guide to the Perils of Dating

and half days; break-up with true love – 15 days; death of a loved one: 32 days, etc.

As we are human beings and not robots, traumatic events have an effect on us. Whether this effect is earth shattering, long lasting or of shorter duration depends of course on the event itself. This effect also depends on the character of the individual who has experienced it. If you cut your finger, and even though it really hurt, you probably won't require sixteen sessions of therapy and a home nurse in order to help you deal with the trauma (unless you are, as mentioned earlier, a gigantic pussy). The point is simple: grave situations or life-altering events have a severe impact on people. Life-altering events, as the adjective suggests, ALTER your life. Therefore, they shape and change you, how you feel about or view certain things and perhaps even how you think and act. You CAN'T get over these events as they become an irreversible part of your life. They don't go away or undo themselves; they stay with you for the rest of your life. You can't get over or digest the death of a loved one, but you can eventually come to terms with it.

A lot of people believe the crap from Nietzsche: "What doesn't kill you will only make you stronger". Well I am here to tell you, that is not the way it is and if you would like further proof you could ask the Johnny's of the World. Once again bare with me here for a moment as I switch gears and go off on another tangent. I am not sure why, but throughout the book I have on several occasions started a sentence with "I am here to tell you." As if me telling you things may be my sole purpose on this planet. There are some severe limitations to that thought. Such as, who are you? I am going to assume the book buying public. As for that being my purpose. I hope it is only a small portion of my purpose. I like to think I have a wide variety of talents and as much as I would like to share most of them with you, I simply do not think it would be feasible. And to be blunt you really need to earn it. That is if you would like me to share one specific tongue talent that I have with you. And frankly I don't think I have enough tongue for all of you.

Back to the cliche', that cliché may be true in some cases but most of these life-changing events usually just break individuals down and if you are not a person of great character it causes people to eventually quit and become bitter individuals. Maybe even regulars in bars wasting away their days complaining about what could have been. If you don't believe me go to any bar or local hang out and you will be able to find hundreds even thousands of people whose life's challenges got the best of them and they have given up on anything new and exciting ever fucking happening to them again. Sure they all have a sad story to tell and what I am going to say next is not really going to be that popular, all of these stories for the most part are *"Fucking Boring"*. Most of these people, when life gave them challenges revealed that they were weak of character, were not well rounded and had decided to give up. Cowards in a way. They have taken the easy way out and are now just killing time until they die. I am not trying to diminish the significance of your life, by saying your stories are boring, they are not to those that love you. What I am trying to illustrate is that we all have had challenges to work through and unless they are unique these challenges are nothing new. It is just the way life is, **you live, you die, you change along the way**. I just want the change to be positive, don't quit. Look for the positive in everything and though it may be tough to find it, it is there, even in trauma.

Why is this important in the World of Love, Sex and Dating and finding that attractive girl you want in your life? It ties in directly to some of the other theories. Guys, there is no rush to get hooked up. Society and its pressures are wrong. We don't have to hook up and get married and have kids, a home (ok, we do need some sort of home) and the whole fucking kit and caboodle figured out by the time we are 30 or 40 or even 50. Life is too important to follow this stinking, goddamn formula. Fuck, the world is overpopulated, people are way too over stressed. We all need to slow the fuck down and this also means slowing down in the world of relationships and settling down as well.

How many of you know couples who wasted their 20s thinking they had life all figured out. Then they started experiencing life's challenges and found out that their respective partner was not the person they had originally fallen for. Some of us don't handle trauma and challenges well and quit, and you don't find that out till shit starts to happen. This is why I recommend not even bothering to get into a committed relationship until you are past

25. "Have Fun". This doesn't mean you can't date or be with one guy or girl. Believe me, if you really love and want to be or spend the rest of your life with the person you are with, the only way you will have a chance is if you listen. If you wait and you must wait as it will take some time before you find out if your mate is a winner and full of character, if they will stand by you in times of adversity and treat you how you deserve to be treated. On the other hand, perhaps your partner is a wimpy little cry baby waiting for the chance to tell anyone who will listen about all of the shitty cards life has dealt them and why they need to cry their beer every single day because it was not meant to be. Would you want to be with that wimpy assed cry baby anyway?

Now I know once again, all of you bleeding hearts out there are going to say this Seed fellow is fucking harsh. What gives him the right to be so blunt in his opinions. Well before you get too uptight remember the *"exceptions rule"*. If you are one then you have beat the odds. Feel fortunate because it is rare. The reason Seed can be so blunt is because he believes in telling the truth from his *"point of view"* and believe it or not it is a positive point of view. Life has dealt Seed more crappy cards than just about anyone and yet he is always looking for the silver lining in things. It would be easy to quit and think that all the good in life is done, however, that is not in his nature (character) and regardless of what is next, he knows it will always get better. *Life that is*. He even whines and cries sometimes in his beer, ultimately he knows that what is paramount here is that he limit's those periods of time and tries to move forward. Not get over it, but move on if you will. Unfortunately a lot of people believe that moving on, means to forget what has happened, getting a new lover or whatever to help them to forget the past events. That may be a necessary step, but it is far more important to look in the mirror. If you lose the love of your life, that fucking sucks. Don't just climb onto the next one until you have done some soul searching or you are destined to end up in the same traumatic situation somewhere down the line. It is very important that when the challenges of life come knocking or in some cases kicking down your door, you don't just diminish there importance. Take as much time as you need to get through them. Lean on your friends for support and if your friends put some sort of conditions or time frame on your recovery, well unfortunately they are not really friends. Your life is to important to surround yourself with shallow uncaring people. Purge yourself of them. As long as you believe that you have a fighting chance in this big world.

(The above scenario loosely represents Seed's life of course not exactly, no one could handle that much trauma. Could They?) Ok, in an attempt to show great honesty and integrity here I am going to tell you something. That is Seed's Life. None of it has been embellished and in fact a lot of events have been left out or just barely mentioned, because if Seed put the whole story down at once he may explode, and we would not want that because who would finish the book first of all, and secondly, Seed really doesn't want someone to have to clean up his exploded body, it just wouldn't be a pleasant thing.

# CHAPTER 21
# Theory: There Is No Such Thing as Security

*"The supposed security of relationships
often makes people comfortably self-neglecting
and keeps them from becoming more than they already are."*

*-Unknown*

**Scenario:**

You are a beautiful 29 year old woman and you have dated the man of your dreams for 4 years. But due to the fact that he is a Vice Principal at a local High School and has pretty much maxed out his career and earning potential, you don't see the finer things in life coming down your lane anytime soon. Sure, the middle class life is ok. He for the most part makes you happy and he knows how to send chills down your spine. But the fact is that you are a babe, a real 10 and you have had many offers for a finer lifestyle. Offers, which of course you turned down because of your happiness. But for some reason a year ago you decided to split up with your love, to test the market and you have found yourself dating the CEO of a major company who is making well into the six figures. Life is good. Or is it? Sure this guy is giving you

*Penned By: The Seed & German Seed*

the good life, clothes, trips, fine dining basically the works. He is not even an ass, but something is missing, that spark that you had. Despite of this, you wrestle with this decision and you have decided to marry him. It won't be the happiest existence, but it will be comfortable and it will be able to provide you with that one vital thing: Security.

People get hooked up and married for several reasons but one of the main reasons is they believe it provides them with Security. Well, in life as well as relationships there is no such thing. Security does not exist. Before you start saying this is a bunch of crap, give it some thought. Is money security? No. At any time you could have an accident, develop a terminal illness, be a victim of crime or the stock markets could crash and though money while one is healthy and all is going well it can appear to provide security. Remember just as there are rags to riches stories, there are just as many riches to rags stories. So don't be fooled.

Is Love and Marriage security? No. Once again it can create the illusion of security, however marriage is really just a business contract where the parties that enter into it believe that they will be able to operate better as a single unit instead of two separate entities. I know that does not sound in any way romantic. However, that is what marriage is in its simplest form. Sure, marriage can be a great provider of support and nurturing, it may help you get through the day to day grind, however, just by signing a piece of paper does not mean your spouse will not go out and cheat with your neighbor or the milkman tomorrow. Or get struck down by a debilitating injury or illness or at worst, even death.

As time goes on, it is important to get this point, it contradicts a lot of the things that have been said before. It is ok to want more and sure, in the society of today the male's earning potential is unfortunately still greater than that of the female. That is a simple fact. We do not have to get into an equality debate here. The fact is men and women are not equal, I have said it before in the book and I will say it over and over again. It is a simple fact. All people must be treated equally before the law, yet all people are not equal physically, emotionally, intellectually or in the area of child birth period. And if you argue we are, you are an idiot. Listen, I am not saying that one is greater than the other, we are just not equal.

*Seed's Sketchy Relationship Theories - A Guide to the Perils of Dating*

      Now for those of you ladies out there who have experienced the scenario above and left your man for the bling bling. You may even be a great person, but can you please stop being such a bitch. If you have found a relationship that fulfils you in virtually every way, stop looking for the greener pastures. They don't exist. There is only one thing out there and that is money and if that is what you are after, to the point of giving up something good and pure, then take your Prada and Gucci with you and go get hit by a train. Because that is what you deserve and believe me your Vice Principal boyfriend will be better off without you in his life. No matter how devastating that may be to him initially. However, if you are sweet, stay, support, encourage and love – that will be the closest thing to security that you will ever find. I guarantee that your CEO boyfriend will not, no matter how good of a guy he is, be able to put you first. He can't. Otherwise he would have become the Vice Principal.

# Chapter 22
# Theory: Women May Fall for the Present
# But They Stay For The Future

*"You will never leave where you are until you decide where you want to be."*

-the seed.

**Scenario:**

This is another reason that people need to "wait" to settle down. In general, when attractive women meet you, especially in University, they are not just looking at your level of attractiveness, physical beauty or sense of humor. What they are looking at is what you may become. I know what some of you may be saying: there is no way that women would be that manipulative or conniving. However, that is the way the world works. Believe it: if you are a good looking guy with a great body you are not going to have a lot of lonely nights in your school years, but, and this is a big "but": where you are heading in life is what they are looking at for the long term. Ultimately, there is nothing wrong with that. If you want to be with a 9 or a 10 at the end of the day your chances are

## Seed's Sketchy Relationship Theories - A Guide to the Perils of Dating

better if you are in Business, Law or Medicine. Whereas, Physical Education, History and Arts may give you the time to pursue and have a good time with girls, yet they know that if they want the materialistic things they crave in their lives the first 3 faculties are where they need eventually to end up.

The problem with this is that they are falling and going for something that is not based on reality. They are basing their future on the projections of who they want you to become and not of who you are. If you fall for this and they fall for you and you end up married with kids, should the life they want for you not be the life you decided you wanted for yourself, guess what: the next exit is "Divorce City". So once again, take the time in your life to find out who you are before you jump. You know what – if you never find out who you are meant to be, it doesn't mean that it is the end of the world. It doesn't mean you can't have love, sex and relationships but don't be so selfish that you want to drag someone into your mess to help you figure out who you are supposed to be. I am not saying don't commit, what I am saying is don't make the ultimate commitment until you are pretty sure of what you want from life, your career and business ventures. And for Heaven's sake, whatever you do, until you do have some sort of clue: "Don't Have Offspring". Remember this, you can always change course several times in your lifetime, so it does not mean that you have to commit to one thing for the rest of your life, just do it with prudence. If you decide to follow the book, there is however one thing that one should commit to during this lifetime and that is their true love. Nothing is better than having someone who really loves you and who thinks you are so damn wonderful and beautiful that they will be beside you to help encourage you, as you do them, through this wonderful challenge of life.

Guys, do not and I repeat do not fall for the trap of letting someone else project on you what they want you to become in life whether it is family, friends or your love. If you do, it is only a question of time before you will be a broken pussy drinking pints with your new loser peer group daily at the local pub, wondering why you did an engineering degree, which sure has left you with a decent job full of stress and a lack of satisfaction, when your true passion and gift was being a DJ. Society has a habit of repeating itself – that is why generation after generation of families ends up

*Penned By: The Seed & German Seed*

in the same business or vocation and seldom does anyone change social status. As a matter of fact because what is happening in the world presently the middle class is slowly being eroded and the poor are becoming poorer and more numerous and more dismal, while the rich become über-rich. Who else can afford to go to sporting events or concerts? The whole point here is the following: it is your life. All anyone else should be doing for you is encouraging and supporting you in whatever choices you make. That is showing love. Fuck this trying to keep the ones we love in our own pathetic comfort zones. Most of the great successes of our time stepped outside of the norm and went after their dreams whatever they may have been.

The message here is that if you want to have the best chance for you and your true love to make it, both in the relationship world and the world of marriage. I simply ask that you wait until you have decided on some direction for your life. Without at least doing that you are just delaying the inevitable. You may as well just divide up half of what you have and give it to your girl now or vice versa. Another suggestion: start labeling your CDs and writing your name in your books. The positive point here is fortunately you likely don't have anything at this point. Let us just hope you have not gone down this road and decided that you needed some children, because if you have, my friend, you have just guaranteed yourself at least 18 years of having nothing. And have I mentioned how attractive single parenthood is to your next true love? People just love the holidays now, but throw in some children that don't belong to them, along with their insecurities and dysfunctional behavior and the special events become, shall we say, festive nightmares. The good point is, these events will likely never be boring!!!!!

*"If one does not know to which port one is sailing, no wind is favorable."*
*-Seneca*

# CHAPTER 23
## Looks & Currency

*"Fire is the test of gold; adversity, of strong men."*

-Seneca

*Penned By: The Seed & German Seed*

More controversy here, this chapter explores the different currencies in the relationship world. Looks for women, power, money and success for men.

A Simple Scale

| Name | Annual Income Required |
|---|---|
| Halle Berry | Seven Figures ++++++ |
| Jennifer Aniston | Seven Figures ++++++ |
| Drew Barrymore | High Six Figures |
| Jennifer Love Hewitt | High Six Figures |
| Miss Piggy | Maybe $20,000 |

Do you get the drift here? Of course, for the bottom end of the scale we used Miss Piggy as an example because we believe and hope that she is the only one of the group that cannot sue. At least that is what we hope. As for the others, in no way would we illustrate any of the above celebrities as shallow, quite the contrary all of these celebrities have had successful careers and they do not need the assistance of any man. They have all made it on the basis of their own merits and beauty, sure the beauty thing may have helped them along the way. As far as looks being a currency I am sure that anyone of them would acknowledge that despite their tremendous talents, that if it was not for their extreme beauty a lot of doors may not have opened for them. At least not as quickly. Sure, early on in their careers, their beauty may have actually been a hindrance, due to no one taking them seriously. However along the way, it has likely opened some doors, giving them an opportunity to display their talent and eventually being able to share it with the rest of the world. So I would like to thank you all for being beautiful. These celebrities are also an example of a previous theory: "Beauty is a Consistent Thing". Oh, by the way, if you do not think any of the above are beautiful, I

## Seed's Sketchy Relationship Theories - A Guide to the Perils of Dating

must ask you one simple question: "What are you? Blind in both eyes?"

Since the beginning of time the sexes have been divided into two different categories with their own roles: Men and Women. The quest for equality has in a way fucked up everything in the world. Face it, as stated before, men and women are not equal in any sense of the word. I notice I stress this point a lot, I promise I will try to talk about it less. I think we all get it by now. That is not to say that one is greater than the other or that we cannot compete in certain arenas against each other. But, let us face it, there are some distinct differences and all I have to do is name one, in order to illustrate this point. Women can give birth. So in no way can we be equal. Women are in charge of the most important aspect of life, namely, the creation of life. I know that man has to be involved in the process, however, as science moves forward that is becoming less and less necessary.

So what is happening over time is that women have this internal clock ticking. They must reproduce at a reasonable age in order to give their children the best chance for a normal healthy existence and above all to avoid complications at birth. Not to mention who wants to be raising their children later on in life? Is that fair to the child? What this dictates is that at least during this period of fertility, the primary bread winner in the family unit is going to have to be the man. Unless you are of course like so many selfish families which decide to have a family before they can afford to, where both parents have to work to make ends meet. This creates a situation where in the key years of development the children end up being raised by strangers, the grandparents or some others who don't have the same vested interest in the child's well being as the parents do.

At this point in the book I am going to venture of tangent for a while. I feel it is a good time to share a little story about Seed's life. Seed was born in July of 1960 as the youngest of 7 children. Due to events in his life he does not have a lot of childhood memories, actually he has none until about the age of 5 and the majority of his family memories are not of the pleasant variety.

*Penned By: The Seed & German Seed*

In fact, his first memory was at the age of 5. His family lived on the edge of a small city and as his parents went out for the night, his older brothers, whose ages at the time were 9, 13 and 17 locked him out of the house until it was dark outside. Needless to say, little Seed had become quite scared being out in the dark alone. Shortly after it was dark, his wonderful siblings let him into the house. I know that older brothers can be cruel, but what they did at this point was shut off all the lights in the house and pretend they were ghosts going around the house chanting his name. This would continue up until the time the parents got home at 3 or 4 in the morning. At which time they would find their dear young boy hiding under a bed or couch shaking in fear. Pretty fucking traumatic for a 5 year old. Anyway there are several other stories like this that came out of Seed's upbringing. I think it is important to mention that Seed basically was a miracle baby to begin with as at the time of his birth his mother was 46 and his father was 56 and they had had 6 children before him, so it was very unlikely that they wanted another. Surely, no one would plan to have a 7$^{th}$ child at those ages. How could they have the energy to possibly raise one?

The point I am getting to here is, that they didn't. Both of them worked full time and were seldom home to help nurture care and encourage. A large portion of the upbringing was done by committee. By the older brothers and sisters who really wanted no part in it. Actions like the above story give you some insight as to their involvement. So little Seed actually became a product of society and the school system. He struggled to belong and always felt like a bit of an outsider. He had already developed a keen sense of wit. Hey, comedy comes from pain and I think he was feeling some. Fortunately Seed hung with the right crowds in school and from an early age his friends became his family. It is not to say that his parents didn't love him, they did. In their own way, his father however, made it quite clear he was not like the others in the family. As for his mother she was too busy working trying to eke out a living to survive.

Now for the kicker, I don't know if you remember way back in the book when I told you about the individual whose life had been turned upside down by a series of events only to find out at the end of these events, that his family had been lying to him his whole life. Well, Seed is that individual and the fact is that the people he thought were his parents, with whom he had spent 5 consecutive years of his life in his early twenties going to the hospital every day watching them slowly waste away and eventually die, were not actually his parents. They were his grandparents who took him out of obligation. It gets better: all of his sisters, brothers, aunts, uncles, nieces and nephews were not what they seem. The brothers and sisters became aunts and uncles except for one of them. The oldest sister and this makes me ill to type: she is Seed's Mother. "Bitch!" Was that subliminal? Oh well. She was 23 when I was born and working full time, but she just didn't want me. She was probably going on a vacation in a few months and did not want the burden of a child. Can I add something to the "bitch" comment above: "selfish bitch". To make matters worse she stayed in my life for my whole life up till now and has treated me badly. I can slightly understand my uncles treating me a certain way. I was taking away some of their time from their parents and I was not really one of them. The sad point is, she did not want me and passed me on to relatives for the first 3 to 5 years of my life, until those relatives didn't want me and they passed me onto my grandparents, who then took me out of obligation.

So, I would like to thank all of you for the wonderful upbringing and all of the pain it has caused. The way that I was informed of this gem of information was equally devastating, at 43 years of age I went to renew my passport and needed a new copy of my birth certificate. During this process, a civil servant over the phone matter of factly asked if I could call one of my parents to find out who my real parents were, because the ones I listed on the application are not the ones on their records.

So: "Shame on all of you". I cannot describe the amount of pain you caused keeping this lie from me my whole life and how much it hurt discovering it from someone else. On a little vindictive note, this is where they are all finding out for the first time that I know the truth about my upbringing. It is at the same time as you, the readers, because I wanted them to find out in a way similar to the way I found out.

The whole point of sharing this little piece of Seed is that it illustrates what families can do to an individual. I am lucky I had surrounded myself with some good people outside of my family and developed my own sense of what was right or wrong, not without some major mistakes. I have managed to become quite a well-rounded and charming individual. Hey, I know it may be somewhat debatable. Perhaps I should have known that people of that age could not likely be my parents, but why would I, I was a kid after all. They actually took me at 50 and 60 years of age. How unfair to them, but most importantly to me, due to my mother's selfishness I got to watch her parents die when I was way too young, only to find out that mine are alive some 18 years later. Can you imagine? I tell you I won't be there to watch my real parents die when their time comes. So you see, Seed not only has been a prime example in the world of relationships, but he has first-hand knowledge about what happens to a child when he is not wanted early on in life. The effect on my relationships must be intense.

A society of absentee parents. That is not an accomplishment. It is extremely unfair to the children of the world, to have it when their parents get home from their work to be with their little darlings, that they are too wiped out and stressed from their days, to be able to give the quality time that is so necessary in the child's development. I, unfortunately, as mentioned above speak from experience on this matter since both of my parents (grandparents) worked full time my whole life. Fuck, they were never there. I had no curfew, no direction in fact I think this has probably caused some significant psychological damage.

Anyway, this chapter is supposed to be on the different currencies, not my past or the whole equality issue. So here it goes, in the dating world: there are basically two currencies, money and looks. They are both equally very valuable. In general, the male of the species provides the money and women provide the beauty. How do you dictate what value is to put on beauty? Well, as we have discussed, society does that for us. By whatever is in. Sure, we have some input in the final decision. This input is decided by the magazines, clothes, movies and television that we buy and watch. It is all calculated for us. We are constantly being put to the test to help the ad agencies decide what we consume and virtually who we want to become. You know it is true. So don't even bother arguing. Who do you find hot? Sure as we move from the penthouses to the trailer parks of the world the standards may be lowered, but it is not due to not wanting more, it is just that people tend to quit and settle for less than they can become. We are a society of quitters and clones.

However in the world of the attractive women, the simple formula or the way that it works is that in their youth to their early to mid 30s the most valuable asset a woman possesses is her looks, her level of attractiveness. The more attractive, the more doors and opportunities that will be opening for them. If you are less than desirable, your education and hard work becomes more and more valuable. Whereas, if you are hot, well try arguing with that. All guys want hot girls and I am telling you, you do not see that many hot woman in the trailer parks of the world. Just think about it. The mullet died years ago and it is not coming back.

If you think it is some other way, quit kidding yourself. Love, honesty, integrity and ambition are all remarkable characteristics and if you possess most of these you are bound to be successful. That is, if you persevere and do not, no matter what, quit. But to attract and keep beauty, unfortunately, you need to have your financial house in order, and if not in order, at least on the way. If you do not do this, it does not matter what your intentions are and how strong your love is. Problems will arise. Period. People crave comfort and luxury and all the promises of having it one day will wear thin. Trust me my friends, you don't want love to become about money, and it will. So unless you want a girl who is happy with a trailer park existence, work towards something. That is if you want to keep the girl.

Of course this is how it is. Hopefully you have found someone to share your life with who understands the team concept of the relationship and is there to help, encourage and support you and not someone who is just waiting to reap the benefits of your hard work. If that is who you are with, you are likely better off losing her. Love and relationships are a team venture. If they are not, you are with the wrong person.

# CHAPTER 24
# The Role of Friends
# (Who Can and Who Can't Be in Your Relationship if You Want it to Succeed)

*"A True Friend Will Never
Put You In A Position
Where You Have To Choose".*

-the seed.

*Seed's Sketchy Relationship Theories - A Guide to the Perils of Dating*

# "True Friends"

This is a very important part of the world of relationships. Some would say the most critical part. Friends: who can stay and those who must go. Who are they? Well, there are some obvious ones that need to go right away. These people are not actually friends at all. They are relationship cancers. They are horrible puss-filled tumors and if you keep them in your lives they will eventually eat away at you and destroy every major relationship you have in your life. You all know them. They are charming, usually attractive, almost always funny, but they can not be trusted. If you bring your new girl to a function their competitive ways will not allow them to leave her alone. By this I mean, they are so fucking insecure and wrapped up in their own looks or whatever other complexes they might have, that they must see if they can out-compete you for the attention of your lady. They do this effortlessly and with no regard to the effect that their behavior is having on you. Your supposed good friend. That is not to say that you cannot have some charming, attractive friends who enhance your relationship. The line here is extremely fine and if you ever find a friend vying for the attention of your girl, without promoting you in the process, there is one solution and only one solution here and that is to punt

*Penned By: The Seed & German Seed*

your friend out of your life, because he is quite simply not your friend.

Another cancerous, leper "friend" who has no room in your relationship is the new friend of your partner who does not acknowledge your existence. At this time, I hope you are enjoying the visualizations that I am providing in this chapter. I am testing the waters to see if I have any ability as a horror writer. What do you think? Do I have some potential? Back to the subject matter. This is primarily if the friend is of the opposite sex. Believe me, this is very important and ties into the theory about the girl with a lot of male friends. I know a lot of people may say that this is not the case. It is ok to have lots of friends of both sexes. It is even healthy. I am not denying that we all have a lot of friends, both male and female, in our lives. Actually, you haven't been listening if you believe that. The fact is we have few friends and a lot of acquaintances. If you believe the rubbish about having a lot of friends then you are likely to feel a lot of pain throughout your life. I know you may be thinking, if I don't allow her to have her own friends I am controlling her. In no way are we suggesting you control your girl or restrict her activities and break the trust barrier. We are just telling you how it is. If your girl is hot and she encourages a lot of new guys to be friends with her, she is still shopping and she is not taking you seriously, or for that matter, she just may be the worst kind of "attention whore" and your days with her are numbered. If this is the case then try not to get attached because you are going to end up picking up the pieces when she finds your replacement (the same is true for the girl who is dating a guy with a lot of female friends, primarily new female friends).

The scene plays out sort of like this. The two of you meet some interesting people at a party and at the end of the night one of the guys gives your girl his number or e-mail addy. Next thing you know, they are keeping in touch with each other. You don't understand, but your sweetie assures you that he is "just" a good guy and they are just friends. Because you are spineless and in love, you let it go. Maybe they are "just" friends and after all you don't want to be "controlling". The next thing you know, he is starting to stay in touch more and more. Your girl gets a cut on her hand and she tells you "Patrick says if I rub vitamin E on it, it will heal faster". Fuck - Patrick must be a brain surgeon to come up with such tremendous advice (and your girl is a bitch by the way). But even though you think that is the case, you let it slide. Anyway to cut this story short. Patrick, or whoever, does not care that you exist. They have one thing in mind and that is the prize. Isn't it sweet that your sweetie is already in another relationship, while allowing you to pick up the emotional tab. This is the point here, should your sweetie believe that it is ok to have a bunch of new male friends who are solely hers, not both of yours. You have two choices, leave or eventually get dumped. That is just the way it is. I am sorry, but it is. There can be no other answer. Don't worry, some day Patrick will get his just reward as well. Let's hope it is something festering and puss filled that she brings home.

Now, as for the long term friends that your girl has from her past. These friends have a responsibility to her to express their opinions, to make sure she knows what she is doing and that you are not some doped-up fucker. As much as being judgmental is not a good quality, we all do it and we all need to continue to do it. That is the only way we can weed the crap out in our lives and decide who can and who can't fit into our lives. If we didn't quickly judge or weed out some people, life would just be too confusing. The point here is, that there is also a line that these friends cannot cross and that line will come into play if their intentions are not pure, but instead based upon jealousy. Remember to be sensitive here. Her old friends may feel you are taking their time away from them and resent you for that. But if you are not some psycho loser, you should be able to defuse the situation by just being the saint that you are. On the other hand, if her friends resent you and have no reason to do so, meaning you have been a saint and have not been seen in some compromising positions and they still bitch about you to your girl and do not acknowledge your existence, then my friend the answer here is also simple. You must lose these people from your relationship as long as they still carry these attitudes. If you don't, you and your love do not have a chance of surviving.

Hey, I am just being honest here: this is the way it works. I know from the experience of being on both ends. And I tell you unless you have keen judgment like me and you can spot a "Fat Manipulative Whore with 80s Hair" half a mile away, you need to be supportive of your friends. We also have a responsibility to act as a moral barometer to our friends. If you find the people in your life are not living up to the same morals and values as you, then can they really be friends? More on "<u>this</u>" in the chapter on infidelity. Stay tuned! I am sure it will be riveting. You may ask how does one stay tuned, this is a book not a television or radio broadcast. Stay-tuned is actually just being used here as a figure of speech and is not to be taken literally. You could jump ahead to the chapter on Infidelity now but we encourage you to read the book in order. I have included several little gems throughout the book and if you do not read them in the order laid out for you, the whole Infidelity chapter may make no sense whatsoever to you.

At this point I would like to take a moment to make a very important announcement. Actually it is a trivial announcement, however, like everything else I would like to try to make it more than it actually is. When I started writing this book about a year ago, I had my doubts about my ability to write a book on one particular subject. I quite honestly thought it would never come to fruition and it would fizzle out at some point in time and I could just take my place at the bar with all of the other underachievers who have given up on becoming anything in life. But something strange and magical happened during the process. Things that I have periodically shared with you throughout the book. Very personal things about my life and my relationships. Not only my intimate ones, my family relationships as well. I have given you some of my passion and I sincerely hope that you have received some benefit or laughs from what I have shared with you. As for this announcement, you are maybe thinking it is earth shattering. After all, Seed has gone through so much and shared so much with us, in an attempt to help us improve our lives. Maybe he is ill. Maybe his "True Love" has come back. Maybe he has found another and life is great again. Well all of those would be great. By the way: life is good - it always is - even during the challenging times. And just so you know, I would never take my place at the bar with the regular quitters in life. I am not wired that way.

So without any further delay, until the pain and challenges of the past year gave me the motivation to finish the book, the outcome was in doubt. Due to the events of the last year I found the inspiration to carry on and finish this project. And on that note I would like to announce that some 35 or 36 lines ago the highlighted underlined word, yes, "this", is the 100,000th word in the book. That is right: "this". I hope that is not a let down for you, my loyal readers. It would have been nice if the news was about my love life or something more interesting. But I think the simple fact that I have now written 100,000 words on the same subject would be enough of a reason to celebrate. There may even be a parade commemorating the event. Maybe even some fireworks. I know that I now have to change my resume, to inform.... Ok, stop right there.... I am now an author what the hell do I need a resume for anymore? Sure, if I had only written a measly 50,000 words, then I would definitely need to be hitting the pavement looking for unsatisfying menial work, but come on, I have blasted past the 100,000 word plateau like there is no tomorrow. So fuck the resume: I am a writer now. Period. Oh yeah, on a little side note the Vegas odds makers had the word "fuck" as the odds-on-favorite to be the 100,000th word.

Anyway, back to friendship. As we have stressed throughout the book thus far, you probably have far fewer friends than you think. Why is that? I don't know. It probably has something to do with human nature and the fact that our society is a "me"-society, that is, egoism is the highest virtue. Most people are only motivated to help someone, when the answer to the following question is positive: "what's in it for me?" And there you have it: a sign of a true friend is that he or she will do something without expecting anything in return. Yes, a true friend will do something for you because he or she wants you to have some sort of benefit, financial, spiritual or just plain wants to have you around, without expecting any benefit in return. Personal gain is totally immaterial. The only thing that counts is that your friend has been party to a positive experience or you have been able to help them when they needed you. Period.

Unfortunately, although you may not see it right away, most of your so-called friends are a bit different. The scenario is not always plain to see, but often you are involved with certain "friends" in a sort of one-sided competition. That is, you probably weren't even aware that you were taking part in the damn competition anyway. For example, does your "friend" constantly brag about the BMW he's driving, when you drive a Toyota? Or

*Penned By: The Seed & German Seed*

drop subtle yet blunt enough comments about his mega-salary, when you're struggling to make ends meet? Or try to convince you of how hot his girlfriend is, while at the same time attempting to brag about how many chicks he's picked up in the last month? If, when you want to tell someone the "good news" that you have achieved a goal and they just put it down or reply: "Yeah, I could do that too if I didn't have to work so much." I don't think you can classify these people as "friends". This doesn't necessarily mean you shouldn't hang around with them or end your relationship with them. No, the only thing that you should be clear about is, if and how these people fit into your life. If someone always has to compete with you, and I don't mean competition while playing a round of golf for five bucks a hole, rather the types of subtle or less-subtle put-downs listed above, then the chances are that these "friends" are only willing to help you, if there is something for them to gain by it. Maybe not right away, maybe not today or tomorrow but sometime soon they'll be expecting you to pay the piper. Sure, it is normal that a person will help a friend and later that friend will help them in return. However, your "help" or "favor" must not require an immediate reaction or payback. If you are of a different opinion maybe you should provide "friends" with a price list before you help them so that they know how much they "owe" you.

  This process may be a reciprocal one, but not for the sake of: "You owe me a favor." If your friend is worthy of being called a "friend", he or she will return the favor without you having "to call it in". It's more relaxed, that is, what goes around comes around and I know that the person I deem to be a friend, whether I have helped this person or not, will be there for me when I need them. Regardless of what the problem is or what kind of help you need, a friend will always be supportive and more than anything else will simply listen to you, when you have something to say. Often, that is enough. A great man once told me, friendship is like an emotional bank account. It can only exist in a state of balance. If you keep making withdrawals and don't make any deposits, well your bank will only give you money until the balance is zero. After that, you're on your own.

  As a bit of a bonus, I have further broken down this whole friendship thing down to its simplest form. In a sense, a simple rule.

## Seed's Sketchy Relationship Theories - A Guide to the Perils of Dating

That rule is as follows. The other day a friend of mine was having an off day and he was feeling a little bit depressed, so he called me for some support. He was feeling the stress of school as well as some of the corresponding financial issues, which sometimes tag along with the scholastic stress. One of the first points of the simple friendship rule, a point that most people don't get or take a long time to understand is this. My friend was not necessarily phoning me for advice. Rather, he was just phoning me for a friendly "ear". He needed to vent. Friends eventually understand this. If he wanted advice from me he would ask or I will ask him if it is ok if I offer him some, if I think it will be helpful. If I don't ask and still offer, he is likely not open to it and will discount it. So friends quit being so self absorbed. Like relationships, they are not games. Support your friends when they need you. Sometimes just by listening. On occasion that is all they need. This particular friend happens to be in a committed relationship and like the great individual he is, wishes everything would be completed, so life could become just a bit easier. I happened to mention to this friend that it would be great if we could get together, perhaps in New York City and have a few days together not worrying about anything. I offered to pay for his flight. Of course he felt a little more stress about that because he would truly love to pay his own way. I assured him that I wanted to pay his way and he didn't need to worry about it. Sort of my treat and it would benefit me as well seeing him. You may be thinking what the hell are you talking about here, Seed? I thought you were going to share a simple rule with us? I am. The next thing my friend asked me was if it would be ok if his girl came along with him to New York. Here is where the whole friend rule comes in. Of course it is ok. It can be no other way. If you are in a "real relationship", it is a given. "Guys' night out" no longer exists. A real friend will accept this and with every invitation a corresponding attached invitation goes out to his girl as well. If you find yourself still craving the night out with the boys, my friend, you haven't found "True Love". As for your friends, the ones that still try to get you out for the night without your girlfriend, they really aren't your friends. A "True Friend" will never put you in a position where you have to choose. I just hope one day you figure that out for yourself....

(Disclaimer: Seed is much more than just an author, he is also some of the following in no particular order of importance:

*Penned By: The Seed & German Seed*

a man, a pet lover, a cook, a cleaner, a friend, an acquaintance, an athlete, a brother, a sister, an uncle, (disregard the last 3, he thought he was those, but due to some family lies he became an only child and none of those pertain to him anymore), a masturbator, a consumer and last but not least maybe some sort of Saint).

# CHAPTER 25
# Understanding the Roles of Age How The Age Thing Works Between The Sexes. As We Age We Become More Valuable. As They Age Arghh... Run for your life....

*"If you accept the aging process, take care of yourself and live each day to its fullest, you will remain young for the rest of your life."*

-german seed.

*Penned By: The Seed & German Seed*

# THE JUXTAPOSITION OF OLD & NEW

**Scenario:**

You are in your late 30s, but look much younger. You are in great physical condition, have a big heart, a great personality, a great sense of humor, a sense of style and basically you are a well-rounded package. You are in your prime. Somehow you have managed to meet and fall in love with someone who is 25 years old and they tell you that they are in love with you as well. The one catch is that though you are very ambitious, your current career has limitations and provides a great deal of frustration for you. Ultimately, that does not matter because you have the girl of your dreams on your arm and you know that despite of the career challenges, with her support and your effort eventually your earning potential will increase and total bliss will follow. The question is can you count on the girl of your dreams to wait for this to happen?

In this chapter we explore the role of age in the dating world. We explore in detail how, when people are younger, they all want the same thing. Yet they don't know how to accomplish their many goals. When men are young all they really want is a hot girl. They have not yet developed the ability to talk to women or decipher what young women really want. Most of the time the young female may think she has something special to give up and having sex is a special reward for all the gifts and compliments that are thrust upon her. If you know what they want, these women can be yours. Hence, the attractive young women figure out, maybe by accident, that in order to get the material gains they must find older (and as a rule moneyed) guys. That is something Mommy has a big hand in – subtly letting their sweet princesses know which way the wind blows. As you have read in the previous chapters, as a guy ages his "value" on the "relationship market" increases. He becomes more "distinguished". As a rule, he also gains the qualifications for a better job and basically his earning potential rises substantially. Women in most cases, on the other hand, start to gather baggage, kids, wrinkles, short hair and increased sexual desire.

Yet all men do not get better with age, just as all women do not deteriorate. In spite of the fact that many males increase their earning potential, some males don't really develop anything to help their earning or intellectual potentials. Their power is based upon their looks and their bodies. Sure, they can attract the hot young women, but unfortunately for them, the fairer sex realizes that the material potential of these mates is limited and though they provide passionate sexual gratification, that is all they really have to offer. The result of this quite often is a group of men who are fucked up and do not know how to get over rejection. Though they aren't the brightest of the bulbs they do know that, as time goes by, their chances of catching the hot babes is decreasing as without the bling bling to provide the goods, most attractive women will smell the coffee and trade up for the newer model as well.

That is not to say that you can't find someone younger than you who is pure of heart and not interested in the manipulation game. However, just like the biological clock is ticking for the females, the males have a clock ticking as well. Society has told them that they have to be serious and settle down. As a guy ages, if he takes care of himself he can remain desirable. Unfortunately, he may often find the women in his age category to be no longer attractive in most cases. They have acquired extensive baggage and their looks have likely faded, whereas, he still has some prime time ahead of him.

Back to the scenario. Your first challenge is that you are dating a 25 year old. Remember what I have said before, that is before 25 years of age, no one should even consider a committed relationship. Having said that, you are dating someone on the cusp. No matter how much they say they love you, they are likely still to be looking for better offers. The sad thing is that they may actually love you, but they are driven by society, ego and peer pressure and are the prime candidates to look for greener pastures. Or at least to think that they exist. Your second problem here is that you are not yet at ease with your career. It is not mandatory but it sure does help. Money problems and stress will help to deteriorate any good relationship over time and your lack of enthusiasm in any area of life will eventually be a problem. That does not mean that you need to share the minute details of the day to day grind with your mate. But what it does mean, if you despise what you do, your relationship will likely become too important to you. Of course, it should be vitally important, but it definitely cannot seem to be the only thing that gives you a reason for living. You must be well rounded my friend. Having your own solid support network is indeed very key to emotional survival.

So unfortunately right from the start, for the individual in the above scenario, the odds are stacked against him no matter how much love is present. Outside pressures will eventually destroy his relationship. I am afraid that is just the way it works. Now for someone that is that much older than his dream girl, a whole new series of problems arise. He likely feels he knows more about life and that is usually the case. But the problem more likely stems from this, if he truly loved her, he likely is bad at taking this rejection in stride. I in no way suggest taking rejections "in stride", I suggest the opposite. If a relationship is very meaningful to you, it is important to do some self discovery. If not, you are likely to repeat the cycle with your next important relationship. Hell, it is even ok to try to win her back, but only to a point, after a point it becomes futile and pathetic. The real problem for this guy is that because he is probably more mature, he feels that if he just reasons with her and tries to prove his love for her, she will

*Seed's Sketchy Relationship Theories - A Guide to the Perils of Dating*

understand his point. My friends: it just won't happen. You need to slap yourself in the face or take a cold shower and face the facts. No matter how much you loved the individual, the younger mind is not at the same place as you and never will be. It is very sad but you must chalk it up to experience and treat it as a lesson learned. Who knows, maybe someday she will realize how good she had it with you.

# CHAPTER 26
# Connections: Is It Love or Just a Rash

You are seeing her for the second or third time. How is it going? This chapter will help you decide if you should keep banging. Or do you just pull the plug before your already fragile ego and emotions fuck you up for future trips to the plate? We have all been there at some point in our lives. We meet someone. The chemistry goes through the roof so we think. "Fuck, this is the one I know it!" "I want to spend the rest of my life with him or her." Besides making your family and friends truly ill with your gushing or "my-new-date-is-so-perfect attitude", my friends, you are living in a bubble. I do believe in true love and I do believe in the magic that makes every day, every touch, every kiss and every caress better than the last one. That magic is what makes the world and this life worth it. Remember, don't settle – no matter what. Meaning if you find these things subsiding and it is not a just temporary thing which is possibly a result of medical, career or just the temporary blues, then my friend don't hang around because you are comfortable. This is such a sensitive topic: how does one know if it is a temporary lull in passion? How do you make sure that you are not bailing on something good because of your own dysfunction?

Well, if you have learned to be alone and love yourself, if you see the future as bright and not bleak, if you could live without your sweetie but would prefer not to, then it is working. Your relationship is worth some effort. I have said before the grass is not greener elsewhere and if you think it is you likely are going to go through a lifetime of unhappiness. I have some radical opinions here of how to approach new relationships so that your friends, family and colleagues don't have to listen to the annoying stories of the new guy or girl in your life.

First of all, introduce them to as few people as possible. I know how difficult this may be. We want to show off or brag about our new love interests. However, just like sometimes the best thing you can do is to refrain from sex or even kissing on the early dates because it spices things up later, the same goes here for the first introductions. Build some mystery, make your friends anticipate and really look forward to meeting your new love. It will make things go a lot smoother. Spend your time alone with your new date, get to know them a bit and see if the potential is there for something more permanent. Then, and only then, should you start sharing your new sweetie with those you deem important in your life. I know this is a difficult thing to do. We all want to share our new toys or brag, if you will. But if you get into the bragging or showing off too early and then you find out you are dating a drugged-out serial killer who has a fondness for sheep, well, you now will have to go through the drama of explaining what went wrong. Needless to say, any future love interests will be prejudged –do you want that? Unless of course you are also a serial killer with the same wool interests. Anyway, as we mentioned earlier, keep it to yourself for the first little while. Believe me, secrecy in certain cases is often the best policy.

I know it is human nature to share during the initial high of meeting someone new, but please try to wait. It will actually be healthier for the relationship. How many of you have lost relationships because your new date met your family and all of the potential went down the drain because they have now seen what is in store for the future? Or even worse: one of your slimy acquaintances decides he has a shot and succeeds, since your new girl is just as slimy as he is and you didn't know it.

*Penned By: The Seed & German Seed*

      Just like we suggest not rushing into marriage, find some things out about each other before you commit. As for the family I know that this sounds harsh, keep them out of your dating world as long as possible. You know what it was like having dear Mom and Dad impose their morals and values upon you, imagine what it would be like having them impose them on your new love, or still worse, giving you their opinions on a person and a relationship which they don't sufficiently know - unless you can count the first family Thanksgiving dinner (Mom will say: "You know Harry, she's a vegetarian. She's just not good enough for our little Johnny!" Or Dad will just have a major aversion to any man who is sleeping with his dear little Chastity on a regular basis.). The movie "Meet the Parents" comes to mind. So as for the family, I believe it is vital to keep them out of your dating life for, I know this is going to sound really harsh, at least 6 months if possible. If you live in the same town or home as your parents, this may be tough. If you live in the same home as your parents, just get a big L tattooed on your forehead because, Poindexter, you shouldn't be dating in the first place. I don't care what social or economic reasons you have for living at home, you don't have the mental or monetary security even to consider dumping your shit on another human being. That is not to say you are not a good person. There is a chance (ha ha) that you are. Hey, if you are below say 25, it might be OK to still be living at home. Maybe you are still in school or just starting out in the real world. Remember you should not be in a committed relationship at this point anyway. However if you are over 25: "GET A LIFE".

      If you are considering a deeper and more intimate relationship with someone and you have given it time and decided the desire and passion is still there: go for it. Introduce, brag, boast and be proud, as you are taking the right steps necessary in order to enter the world of friends and family. It will be as if you and your new love have sort of become teammates. You have by now let her know how you think and the fact that she is still with you shows that she likely respects who you are. She may even agree with a lot of your opinions and thoughts. If she doesn't even better, as your partner should have their own views and opinions. Since you have taken this time to really build a bond, this will make you better equipped to tackle the challenges of the "family and friend world". Now isn't that better, she is staying by your

*Seed's Sketchy Relationship Theories - A Guide to the Perils of Dating*

side…..You may actually have a connection and not some sort of festering rash. If you have a rash, I don't want to see it. Go to a doctor for God's sake. Go – you are grossing the rest of us out. Get some cream for that unsightly thing. What's that? You're allergic to wool…?

# CHAPTER 27
# Is It Working: The Red Flags?

*"If You Are Not Part Of The Future
Then Get Out Of The Way"*

*-John Cougar (Peaceful World)*

This Chapter will give you the general guidelines to what drama is actually acceptable in a relationship. These points must converge with your values and morals for them to be effective. If in any way you find yourself compromising what you truly believe in or stand for, you have to leave your relationship. That is, unless you are totally not evolved or an individual devoid of morals. Some things should be instant red flags, such as: murder, rape, crimes against children or animals, to name a few. Let's face it, if your mate is involved in any of these activities and you accept it, let us hope that you lost a good portion of your brain in some freak accident, because there is no way certain things should be accepted. Fuck all of those people who say that they love and stand by their family no matter what. There simply has to be some limits based on common decency. If not, then the world would be even more screwed up than it already is. That is not to say that the human race is not capable of some significant mistakes but come on, if the social resume of your new sweetie includes murder or any of the above mentioned criminal or psychological deviations, you must draw the line.

Before you even start to think about the red flags that your new love may be bringing to the table, I would strongly suggest doing a self inventory. If you have now found yourself with the girl of your dreams and you would still prefer to go out 2, 3 or 4 nights a week with your buddies and get knee-walking, bile-puking, floor-licking drunk, then I suggest you just forget it. No girl would see any long term potential in you and you might as well save your sorry little brain the agony of trying to figure out what went wrong later. It is simple: you are an idiot. That is not to say, it is not ok to go do the above occasionally, because it can be. Just pick your spots and keep your debauchery mainly to yourself. Being a jackass in High School or in College may be ok and somewhat intriguing to the opposite sex if they are desperate. Hey, just like us guys, girls know as well that booze increases the chances (Wink, wink).

Another thing: if you have ever hit a girl for any reason, you have a fucking problem. If anyone has ever pushed your buttons to the point where that is even a question, it is time to leave that relationship, because they don't care about you to begin with and they likely know that you are a good soul and that they are not and they need to become the victim to paint you as a bad guy. That is why they are pushing your buttons to begin with. So the point is, if you are being pushed or provoked: dump, don't hit. Using violence to solve a problem, in spite of provocation, is a sign of weakness. And because hearing "Bad boys, what you gonna do" is not really that good of way to get your 15 minutes of fame.

While we are on the topic of 15 minutes of fame, may I give you a little piece of advice? Ok, thank you. I appreciate that. You know I would never volunteer any advice without asking. If you ever witness anything, a plane crash, car crash, train wreck, robbery and I mean anything. If you are ever asked to give an opinion on something political, sporting or newsworthy, and this is important, with regard to any member of the media who puts a camera or microphone in front of your face. Please decline. You are wasting your 15 minutes of fame and you are going to sound stupid. You have watched the news before, haven't you? You are going to sound stupid, really. It will go something like this:

"I saw the plane over there. It seemed to be laboring, and then it crashed right over there. It was disturbing, I feel sorry for those people. I am not an aviation expert..."

Do you get my drift? 15 minutes of fame blown – for that? Help the authorities and tell them what you saw but don't do it for an audience. Unless you ham it up a bit. Make it funny and if it is a tragedy it is not cool to make it funny, so refrain from being a jackass. I hope you get my drift here. And while we are on the subject, if you ever have seen your new love interest do an on camera interview as a witness, well you know what to do....

My friends all I am asking is that you get your own house in order. Figure out the things that you need to improve on yourself, before entering into a relationship. The attributes that you don't like about yourself, they are likely a good indication of what one should not tolerate in a mate. Fix yourself first.

So to simplify this part of the book, we figured it would be best to illustrate in point form whether one should consider pulling the plug on a relationship and moving on. I remind you that this is a decision to be made in the very early stages of a relationship. These pointers may help you in the long run. They will help prevent you from wasting your and your new acquaintances time. Anyway, some food for thought. Are we not all striving to find our "last" long-term relationship all of the time? I know I am, so why would I want to spend too much time with someone who is not compatible? I hope you were not actually expecting any food just now. If you are, may I suggest some pudding?

**You may need to pull the plug on a the relationship if:**

- Your man is prettier than you.
- She insists you meet her family and you have only known her for a couple of hours.
- Most of Her friends are fat single mothers.
- She wears stirrup pants, or leg warmers.
- Your date lives more than 2 hours away by car.

**You more than likely need to pull the plug on a relationship if:**

- She has a criminal record.
- She has an Adam's Apple.
- She doesn't like to travel.
- Any of her family members play the banjo.
- You wake up and she is having sex with another woman beside you.
- Your date does not have a car.
- Your date lives more than 4 hours away by car.

**You pretty much have no choice but to pull the plug on a relationship if:**

- You find out the reason she has an Adam's Apple is because she has a dick also.
- You meet her boyfriend.
- You play the banjo.

*Penned By: The Seed & German Seed*

- Your date lives more than 6 hours away by car.

**You Definitely must pull the plug on a relationship if:**

- You find out here boyfriend is your Father.
- You find any of the following: a crack pipe, a syringe or a shrine consisting pictures of you, in her bedroom.
- You are ever lied to for any reason.
- Any form of violence against you or anyone you know.
- Your new date is constantly trying to get you to defend her honor
- The police show up at your door to inform you that your new date is dead.
- I feel it necessary to soften the last criteria up a bit change that to inform you that your date no longer has a pulse.
- Your new Girl has watched Fatal Attraction 75 times.
- Your date lives more than 6 hours and 1 minute away by car.
- Your date is over 25 and still living with mommy.

I hope you have found this to be helpful. I am just trying to save you a lot of pain and misery. I want your relationships to work. The more categories above that your new date falls into, the more likely it is that you have found yourself an impaired lover and you are not going to make it in the long run, so save yourself some time. It may save your life.

If you find yourself falling into a lot of the categories above, may I suggest taking yourself out of circulation for a while and get some help. There will be a lot of desperate souls waiting for you when you leave the institution. Really there will be.

# SECTION 4
# It's Not Working: Picking Up the Pieces of You

*"When they lose their mates,*
*people need to know that they are still attractive.*
*For a man, this means getting laid.*
*For a woman, it often means being taken out without getting laid*
*Just to prove she's more valuable than that."*

-Unknown

Tears suck. Whether it has been a month or a year, when things stop working, life can really suck. That is, of course, if you have a heart and are not a selfish bastard. If you are a selfish bastard or bitch, I hope you realize that a lot of this book is about you. So could you please change? That's what I thought. There are a lot of theories on the subject of how long it should take to get over the loss of a love. Be it through break-up or some other way. While I am thinking of it, could you people out there, who have been in month-long relationships and are really fucked up by them ending, please grow up? If you were lucky enough to have had a bunch of sex in that time period the relationship was a success, maybe not full of meaning, but a success none the less. So get over yourself.

*Penned By: The Seed & German Seed*

It was not love. When we are talking about picking up the pieces we are talking about at least 6 months. As for the shorter ones, if you are in a lot of grief over it, I am afraid that you need a lot more help than I can provide. Seek a professional. And, if there is any chance that you started collecting little mementos, from every date only to present them a couple months into the relationship in an attempt to show how attentive you are: seriously, get some real help, 'cause you are scaring all of us. Before you get this help which might involve some sort of institutionalization, could you please take out the biggest loan possible and go to *Seed's Fabulous Boutique* at *www.seedenterprises.com* and purchase as many products and books as possible both for your friends and future roommates. It is the least you can do for scaring me!

  This section is to help you get through the inevitable break up. It is here to help you make your way through this period of your life in the quickest and easiest way in an effort to have you come out better and stronger when you do. It will also give you a list of qualities or characteristics that are imperative that you learn to avoid if you actually want to cultivate and nurture a loving, long-term relationship

  I suggest now that you sit back and grab a small bottle of gin or a six pack, recline in your favorite chair and prepare yourself for some laughter and some head nodding. Trust me, it is coming.

## CHAPTER 28
## I Just Want To Be Friends
## "We Have Been Through So Much Together"

*"Our Responsibility In Life Is
Constantly To Keep Changing Direction."*

*-the seed.*

  The love is gone. The girl of your dreams has dumped you or you have dumped her for a newer, more-improved model. But you have decided "to remain friends". You insecure pathetic wimps: what good can come from being friends with someone who does not want you? We have all heard at one time in our lives some of the lies. "It's not you, it's me." "My life is too complicated right now...." Or another gem: "I am probably making a big mistake here ...." "You are the sweetest guy I have ever met but the timing is not right." Or: "Don't you get it, I am a slut." Etc., etc. Oops, that last one just slipped in there and likely is not a lie. If you find that you have been dating a "slut" and have managed to come away disease free, consider yourself lucky. As for the rest, here is the skinny my friends: They are all lies. Your ex-lovers are trying to cover up their feeling of guilt and are trying somehow to feel better about themselves. So you have a couple of choices when this traumatic event happens to you: one is to buy a lot of self-help books and try in as many different ways to tell your ex that you love her. The more different and numerous ways, the better. And of course tell her that after all, you want to be friends because she is an important part of your life (true attention whores might actually go for this because it strokes their ego and just in case their new "fuck" doesn't work out, at least they will have you hanging around giving them attention until they find another – the next – replacement). You sad little sap, are you really that pathetic? Do you truly want to meet with your ex and listen to the stories about whom she is currently spending sack time with?

Your second choice is the one that we recommend. Get away and start healing yourself. If you need to, have some rebound sex, join a gym, learn a new language or find some other activities to fill your time but whatever you do, purge yourself of your ex. As long as you continue to pine for her in any way, you should not have any contact with her. The only exception is if the two of you fucked up and had some children together, then it gets a little more complicated. Even if this is the case, you should limit your contact to brief encounters only for the good of the children. I cannot stress this enough. If you are going to develop into a better and more desirable human being, this time is your time: you need to get your shit together. There is a long road of recovery ahead of you and you need to fix a broken man to have any chance of scoring in the game of life in the future. Fuck guys, did you see "Swingers", don't become pathetic pussies, it won't get you anywhere. Get drunk, get a hooker, feel sorry for yourself, but get your ex out of your mind. If you need therapy, now is the time.

Also, my friends, don't jump right back into something – that is, any old relationship solely for the sake of not being alone. Take this time to learn to like yourself and to learn to be alone. Being alone does not have to mean being lonely. If there happens to be an off chance that you hope that some day you would like to re-connect with your ex, multiply this advice by 2 or even more. If you were going to stop contact for 6 months, make it a year. If you were going to break ties for a year make it two. If it is a true love, this might be your only way to get it back. Face it: you broke up and it was probably for a reason or maybe a bunch of reasons.

In all likelihood one or both of you need to change. That is, of course, unless you want the same relationship again. If that is the case, may I suggest repeatedly banging your head against a wall? A brick wall will do. However, if you want to be a better individual, please follow this advice. You will thank us later....

Before everyone gets all upset with this advice, I will tell you that I had become a case study of this exact point. While I was writing this book, I was with one of the true loves of my life I constantly nurtured the relationship and treated it like gold. We had been through some rough times (very few) and even an infidelity however, somehow, I managed to get past that and because my feelings were so strong, I decided it was worth forgiving. I decided that we were the rare exception. I was convinced that cheaters could change. This seemed to be the right decision as our love bond seemed to be growing stronger every day. The intimate moments were fantastic. Our day to day communication had never been better and despite of some of the shortcomings, I had actually arrived at a place where I was the most content I had ever been. I was being told I was loved every single day. Life was fantastic. Then one Monday morning the alarm went off, and are you ready for it, I got dumped. When I pressed for a reason, I was told: "I am just not as happy as I could be." What the hell does that mean? (just another one of the gutless lies we are told when someone is trying to alleviate their own guilt).

After this traumatic event took place, my life seemed to have lost all meaning. How could someone who claimed to be so in love with me, without any event, forewarning or provocation have dumped me? I was told I was a fantastic man. I was told that she still wanted to be in my life. I was even told that she still wanted to live with me (I know you may be thinking: "The fucking hypocrite"). Minus the hugs, kisses and passion. Can you imagine the torture? So, ask yourself: who did I become after this break-up? You got it, the pathetic wimp I described above. I have actually included some conversations in the outtakes chapter, which painfully illustrate this point. Don't be too harsh on me, I have learned from my mistakes. I continuously expressed my undying love. I continued to do the same little things that I did during the relationship (the gifts, the dinners, etc.). It is ok, I can hear the laughing and the jokes being thrown at me. But I

*Penned By: The Seed & German Seed*

am telling everyone out there that there are few exceptions, if any. When the hammer falls on your relationship – that is usually it. It doesn't matter if the other person is making a monumental mistake or not, no matter how much you love them, you cannot force them to love you back.

My stance on some things has since then softened on this particular point. If you feel that this person is an important part of your life and is making a mistake, it may actually be important to try and find a way to love them back. No matter how much anger and hurt you may feel. If you honestly think you are an exception to the rule, you must get past the hurt and no matter what happens over the next period of time shut up and let them live. You must remove yourself from their life. It will be too painful if you don't. You really do need time apart. If you go on and live your life, work on yourself and work at being happy, even if you feel like you are kidding yourself, then and only then, if it is a true love and you meet again, will you have a chance. If you are living well and happy, you will be desirable, maybe even to your ex. In fact, you will be if it is "true love". So stay away: they are going to date others and they are going to mess around with others. Here is a vital point during this time of suffering as I mentioned in the beginning of this section. It is imperative that you find a way to remove yourself from this situation in order to keep on living and moving forward. That means even if they contact you, say no. Change yourself or give them enough time to change. If you don't, you will start to look pathetic and even if the break was only going to be a temporary thing, the longer that you wallow in self pity the less desirable you will become and the less likely it will be for you to win the love of your life back. If that is at all possible.

# CHAPTER 29
# But I Love Her............Him............

     Let's start off right away with the fact that if you are using the word "but" when you are talking about someone you love, I am very sorry to say that you have likely reached a point in the relationship where you are subconsciously justifying the existence of the relationship. A very difficult subject for me to talk about right now since my relationship ended and I do feel that way. Come on Seed, we know, we know you said your relationship ended several times now. We get it. I know you may get it. That is not the point of the redundancy. The point is to illustrate something and, by the way, I will decide when it is time to stop talking about it. Another thing, this is a book primarily about relationships. Can you tell me a better way to discuss them, than by sharing my own? I did not think so. Back to the chapter at hand, this chapter is all about preserving your mental health so you may function after a breakup and become a better person. It also examines the situation that you have come to the decision that even though you may be in Love, Love may not be enough. This is actually an adult way at looking at separation, breaking up and perhaps even the last option: eventual divorce. Is it worth it, to not be a statistic? A tough question to answer. (Thank you for your above concern on my ability to get over my relationship. It is actually much appreciated. Just so you know I am feeling much better now and really the redundancy is just to illustrate a previous point.

*Penned By: The Seed & German Seed*

If you remember at the start of the book, it was mentioned that each chapter is an essay on its own. Having said that, this is one of the reasons why some points are hammered on so much. Including my relationship. You may now stop worrying about me. I am doing Great!!!!).

You have now invested a year or two, maybe even more, on a relationship that for some reason it has lost all of its sizzle and passion. There seems to be no answer on how to get it back. You are not even sure you want to get it back. Just about everything about the relationship is dull and stale, it has become routine. It may not be horrible, but it just does not send chills down your spine. You are wondering if there is any hope at all for the future. Can you, or more importantly, do you want to give it a chance?

Well, it is time to do some serious soul searching before you go off and do something drastic, like pull the plug on the relationship. Look at everything in your life, your work, your finances, your children, your upbringing and just everything else in general. Has anyone in your family gone through something similar? Is it a family dysfunction that can be worked through, perhaps with some communication or maybe even some counseling? If you are married it is definitely worth some effort. If you are not, it may still be worth some effort to salvage what's left. However, maybe you love this person but you are just only comfortable and that is it. That is no way to live your life. You must, as mentioned in previous chapters, get your own house in order. That means you. If you do and you still have no spark and no magic for the person whom you are with, maybe it is time to seek some outside help. No, not me. Really. But thank you for thinking of me. I mean some professional counseling to see if there are some deep underlying issues hindering your relationship and ultimately your life, which may need to be addressed.

The good and bad news of all of this, is this: if you have honestly given every effort, taken every step possible and looked for solutions to your despair, if you have taken a good, long look in the mirror and you just can't find the passion and happiness coming back into the relationship, if you have turned over every stone, communicated with your partner honestly and the spark for whatever reason is no longer there, then you must leave your lover. This is the bad news, since you have done everything in your power to save a relationship with someone whom you truly love and you know you will always love. Oh yeah, the good news as heartbreaking as it is and it does not matter if you love each other or not (actually it is imperative that you love each other) is that going through the pain, communication and self discovery is a real sign that you actually do love this person. The sad news is that you must leave each other as hard a thing as that may be to do. Your love, my friends, is not your "True Love" and the only way you may ever find your "True Love" is to accept this. Cherish what you had – it will never die. You are getting closer to the land of the exception. Congratulations!

# CHAPTER 30
# "We Have To Talk?" Run, Run, Run. The Myth That You Can Change Someone. We Are Who We Are.

This is an important chapter of the book. Fuck - I say that a lot. It is as though I am trying to place more value on one particular section of the book. When in reality, all sections of this book are very important. The thoughts I have been sharing with you, along with the ones I am going to continue to share with you, represent the thoughts you would find swimming around in my head if you were to cut the top of my skull open. Sort of like a bowl of Alphabet Cereal. These are my thoughts and just like your thoughts, they are important to someone, and damn it, if not to someone else, they are at least important to you. Ok, so some sections are more important than others. I will leave that for you to decide, I just like saying "this is important", that is all. Not that all of the sections of the book are not vitally important to your development into a good, down to earth, hot, red blooded (wo)man. That is right, the staff and management at Seed Enterprises all think that you are hot - "Smoking Hot" if you will - simply due to the fact that you have made it this far and you are still craving more. We understand you may not actually be craving more. Instead, you are just desperately trying to avoid that unavoidable conversation, which you sense has been coming for quite some time. You know the one. The one that starts with these excruciating four words: "You're still away _insert your name here_." Sorry about that. I must be drunk, only moderately drunk though, remember everything in moderation. That is one of the keys to life. Now back to the four words, disregard the last four words, they belong in a different book. The words I am talking about here are, and they are equally excruciating I might add: "We have to talk".

Now listen carefully here, this is crucial my friends and without exception, these are "important" words of advice. If your Sweetie, Spouse, Booty Call or whatever else your girl at the present moment is called, ever mutters these words there is only, and I virtually guarantee only one thing that can come from this. Are you ready for it? I am sure you already know what I am talking about and you have probably experienced this several times in your life. I hope you haven't. That would be too traumatic. Well, I am going to spare you any more agony, you are going to be asked to change or even worse she is about to dump you. "Wow, Seed did not drag that out at all." "Thank you, Seed!" "Hey! Which one of you readers just typed that in my book? Stop that, I am writing this book, not you!" Now that we got that all straightened out, let's get back to the topic at hand. Your sweetie is going to tell you that in some way you are not living up to the expectations and you are being told, you could be a wonderful person, but you need to get with the fucking program to make me happy. The problem with this scenario is pretty fucking universal. Your mate knew what she was getting when she decided that she wanted you in her life, but as mentioned before, *Theory: Women May Fall For the Present But They Stay For The Future.* You have now become a project and the project is based upon what she sees you becoming. Not what you are. Come on Guys, when you hear these words you really have only one choice: it is time to give her the boot. We all know that sure, maybe we do need to change some things in order to become the person we want to be, but fuck, do it on your own schedule and your own terms. If you give in to these demands you may as well snip off your balls and give them to her to put in a jar for safe keeping till the day she dumps your sorry ass, because you are now officially a pussy and eventually, even though she may enjoy you picking up her tampons from the drug store and folding her laundry, in all reality in the end she wants a man and frankly that will not be you.

So my friends you can make your stand now or you can start a life of misery. The choice is yours. My advice is simple, if you hear those words you have but one course of action: *"DUMP HER FIRST."* It may be hard, but you will thank me later. Of course, it must be clearly stated at this point that if you are married with children the stakes are different and dumping will definitely not be an easy thing to do and may not be the correct first course of action to take in this case. So unless you have some hard core behavioral problem, or are abusive, a drunk or a junkie you too, my friend, must stand your ground. Divorce court may not be the way to go, you have to let her know that you are your own man and she signed on for this journey knowing what she was getting and you will change things about yourself when you are damn good and ready.

By the way guys, we should already know this, if you have ever been fired or if you are the boss. How many times in a work situation have the words "we have to have a talk" turned out positive? Give it a little thought here, if you are not fired at that moment, you know you are going to be asked to perform in a matter which is not possible by you or any other human. If this has ever happened to you, do you remember how much fun it was virtually to work your ass off for nothing. Well unfortunately, that is how it CAN work in the wonderful, nurturing world of relationships as well.

Life is full of tests. Fuck, friendship is really just people using each other, and so is romance. Just like your boss tests you to see how much free labor he can get out of you, your sweet girl will do the same. They will test to see how far out of your way you will go to meet their needs regardless of how it impacts you or your day. Sure it is ok to be thoughtful, to do some things, but come on, have a backbone. That is what you are being tested for, it is like a game of chess where they are seeing how far they can push you and believe it or not, they want the occasional "NO". No Girl period, regardless of their level of attractiveness, wants a guy who jumps every time they speak. Tell them occasionally to do things themselves. Your relationship will be better if you do, because if you don't, you are on the road to misery and Dumpsville. I am going to let you in on another little secret here. In the adult world, the world of actually loving another individual fully, do you remember a previous chapter when I talked about being the bad boy? In the adult world, this is all you have to do. Don't be available for every order. That will make you more attractive and desirable. That is all you need to do show that you are not a pussy, rather a man. I am not saying here that you should start being a prick. If you can help out and it does not detract from your day: that is, it does not cause you to make huge detours, to change your time plan and ultimately sacrifice your schedule to bring her "Aspirin", orange juice or yes, tampons (namely, things that she could probably do on her own), then just do it. The gestures are a wonderful thing but not all of the fucking time. I know my friends it is confusing. When is ok to be nice? When should I be an ass? Fuuuccck, Seed!!!

Well you are a man now, decide for yourself. Hey, hopefully your relationship has evolved and it is "True Love" and you can stop doing these little tests and playing along with what can only be called "games". Because frankly, they are annoying. I have also noticed something: I tend to say "frankly" a lot. I am not sure if I am actually being frank when I say it. It just sounds formal. Hell, I don't even know if I like to sound so formal and stern. So if you have any suggestions of what I may use instead, feedback would be appreciated. While I am asking you, do you prefer the term "straight from the shoulder" instead of frankly, that is what the thesaurus suggests. Funny, my thesaurus suggests "phrase book" for thesaurus. Come on, you think that is funny, don't you? At least a little bit...?

# CHAPTER 31
# The Girlfriend With A Lot Of Male Friends

Stay away! Unless her friends are gay. Guys, do you really want your girl to be going out with her "male" friends when you are at work or out of town? I know what a lot of girls are going to say after reading this. You are fuming, you are not interested in your friends that way, and they are not thinking of you in any sexual context. The fact is, it is not possible for guys to think of you in any other way than sexually unless you are a beast. The male friends who may be around for the conversation are really there because they hope some day, if everything lines up right, they will have a shot to get into your pants, especially if these male friends are still single. The only exception I can think of is this scenario, the ex-boyfriend who had a relationship with your girl in her formative years or college which helped her deal with heavy family shit and established some sort of bond, which after their not-so-traumatic break up has evolved into friendship. Even if this "great guy" exists, the point is that he has already slept with your girl, so sexual tension isn't an issue. Been there, done that. Just friendship. However, that is the mega-exception. Otherwise I have to agree with Harry's view in "When Harry met Sally": men and women can't just be friends without some sort of sexual tension or inner desire for their supposed "friend", that is, your girl.

You don't believe this? Well ask them this simple question: "Hey Johnny, if you had a chance to have sex with me right now, would you?" Now listen to the replies, they will either lie or they won't be hanging around you anymore, because the gig is up. You are on to them. Think about this carefully now and try to be honest with yourself. If you actually are a hot or even a not so hot woman and you were to ask your supposed "platonic male friends" the above question, which answer would make you feel better? If he honestly did not want to sleep with you, would that not bother you? Or would it perhaps cause some esteem issues? On the other hand, if he answers that he would seize the opportunity if it should present itself, my God, you are screwed and so is your friendship. So come on people, face reality. If you want a more definitive answer tell them simply: "You know there is no chance of us ever having sex, but you knew that right?" Now let's see who is still your friend. I thought so....

This doesn't mean that your sweet girl cannot have male friends. Of course she can. Some simple rules must be in place. They need to be gay. Ok even gay is not safe if you are dating Madonna, Britney or Kylie. Just about every gay man on the planet will switch teams for an opportunity to sleep with one of these gay icons. I am sure you are not likely dating one of the above, so gay friends would be ok. It would even possibly relieve you of some of the duties you don't like to do, but end up doing just because you love her. Like shopping and make-up, you know the drill. Some other ways that it is likely safe are, if her male friends are your one or two friends that you ultimately trust. You know, your buddies that will admit this to be the actual case; however, they have such strong moral fiber and values that they would never actually cross the boundaries. Unless of course you gave them the invitation yourself. Do these types of friends actually exist? I am not certain whether even these friends, if all the right elements and factors lined up, might not get weak and cross the line. Actually, they do exist I am one of those guys, I will never jeopardize my good friendships. I said "good": so make sure you actually know who your good friends are. The bottom line here is that the girl with a lot of male friends is just keeping her options open. She is always open to a better offer or opportunity if it were to come knocking.

The simple fact is that men and women generally speaking do not have the same interests. What they do periodically have in common are insecurities and the desire for sex. Other than that, be honest with yourself and face the facts. I am not going to list a whole bunch of examples to prove my point. Actually I have decided to include one example. I was working as a bartender and on a day shortly after the events of 9-11 President Bush was addressing the nation on the attacks and about how terrorism would not be tolerated. Any nation who basically was not buying into the "stomp-out-terrorists message" would be considered evil and an enemy. I know it is much more detailed than that, however, a pretty scary time for the world in general. Now here is the thing: the majority of the patrons in the pub were focused on the TV. They were thirsty for what was in store for the world. I myself was very interested in the message. My co-workers on the other hand, three very attractive young women, intelligent and seemingly driven, had different topics to discuss. One of them was in nursing school, one was taking commerce and the other was finishing her education degree. You would think that intelligent women like this would have some strong interest in the fate of the world and mankind, as this could possibly be one of the most significant time periods in their lives. Well, and I kid you not here, as Bush was laying out his agenda, the conversation between these attractive, intelligent and ambitious young women was as follows:

*"Did you get your nails done, I really like that shade on you."*
*"Well, yes I did. Thank you for noticing, I like your hair and shoes."*
*"Really, I think they make my feet look big."*

I wish I was making this up. They showed absolutely no interest in the fate of the world. Life was just moving forward for them with no, for lack of a better word, clue. I felt it was necessary to include one example simply to illustrate the point. I know the men of the world are probably no better and may have been only watching because the game was pre-empted and war is kind of like a game. As for other differences between the sexes and the only true ways we can be friends, I will explain it

*Seed's Sketchy Relationship Theories - A Guide to the Perils of Dating*

in a clearer and perhaps more controversial manner in the next chapter: The only way Men & Women can be Friends. Once again stay tuned. Well actually just turn the page. I am done with this chapter.

# CHAPTER 32
# The Only Way Men & Women Can Be Friends

This is a continuation of the last chapter. Here is a list of the only ways we can be friends with the fairer sex. I hope this simplifies things for you. You may laugh, scoff and shake your head in disbelief, but this is reality my friends.

**1. You are Gay.**

Like I said in the last section, if you are gay, go on – have as many female friends as possible. Imagine the underwear parties and pillow fights. Just do not, no matter what, invite Kylie, Britney or Madonna. Don't you remember the issues you wrestled with when you came to the conclusion that you were gay. Well it won't be any easier if you start playing on the other team. So make sure you don't invite them. Promise me?

**2. You have already had sex with her and have no desire.**

If you dated or already had sex with a girl and decided she is not the girl for you and the sexual desire is completely gone. That means completely. If it is not, you need to be staying away. You are in a real gray area here. At least stay away when alcohol is being served and there is an opportunity to be alone somewhere. Definitely stay away if you haven't had sex for, let's say, 6 months. Hell, if you haven't had sex in the last 6 months and you are not a troll, just face it you are likely gay my friend.

### 3. Enough time has passed and you are both over each other.

This pertains to the actual ex. This is a tough category because if you actually liked someone enough to be in a committed relationship, there is a chance you may have strong feelings for that individual for your entire lifetime. This may lead to all sorts of problems and it is tough to come to the conclusion that no matter what the circumstance you won't cross over the line and enter familiar territory. After all, you spent a great deal of time in that territory and it wasn't that bad. Maybe you have ventured out onto other pastures for awhile thinking that they would be greener to realize that you have made a big, big mistake and would like to reconcile. Well, if this is the case, try to do it for the right reasons. Namely love and the fact you want a future with this individual. Not because you are lonely and she or he will do. You have already fucked each other up emotionally once. Try not to do it again.

### 4. She is fat and undesirable (but come on guys)

If she is fat and undesirable and she is a friend, there is a chance that you are gay. Why are you hanging around a "Fag Hag" if you are not? I know, I have just stepped over the politically correct boundaries in a big way. I will have a lot of fat undesirable women taking offence to what I have just said. "Fag Hags" - they are going to be pissed at me. Perhaps some gay guys and even the odd exception, who happens to have fat and undesirable female friends. How do I get myself out of this mess? I will need to put on my political dancing shoes here that will help me to spin this whole ugly incident into something positive. If I only knew where I left the shoes.

Whew! I found them. Before everyone gets too upset with me, let me try to explain what I mean by this last little bit of writing. First off, very few people are actually that fat and unattractive that no one would want to be their friends. And the ones who are, they know who they are. They are the ones with no friends. Now as for you, do something about it, trade in the stirrup pants, put some product in your hair and "Put Down the Fork". You will feel better about yourself if you do. As for "Fag Hags". Well, honey, if you call yourself a "Fag Hag", you already know that you are not hot.

### 5. You are fat and undesirable

If you, yourself are fat and undesirable you have a different problem at hand. When did you give up? I know for myself personally if I even get a pound or two over my comfortable limit I make sure that I eat better and perhaps get off of the couch and exercise, at least a little. I know you all have excuses. You have a bad back or a bad knee or something. That is all that they are, excuses. It is a sad thing, when did your self-esteem get so low that being a fat undesirable slob was acceptable to you. Learn to like yourself. If you do you will never allow it to happen. Think about it. Do you really want to die an early death due to your love of bacon? That's what I thought. Now go for a walk. Fight for your life.

### 6. Did we say you are gay

You have now been paid a visit by Kylie, Cher and Madonna, yet you were not tempted at all. You are really gay my friend and the female gender is safe from you. For that matter, any hot-blooded American male should feel safe having their girl hang out with you.

So there you have it. A short form, sort of a "Seed's Notes" version of when it is safe for your girl to have a lot of male friends. I hope you have found it helpful and believe me, it works the other way as well. That is: if your man has a lot of female friends. The only difference is if his female friends all play on the same softball team, you won't feel threatened to begin with.

# CHAPTER 33
# Infidelity: Dating or Being Married To Liar & Cheater

*"There Is No Cure For Ugliness."*

*-the seed.*

*Penned By: The Seed & German Seed*

# The Possible Tragic Results of Infidelity

**Scenario 1:**

This topic has impacted a lot of people and usually not in a positive way. To begin with let us make something perfectly clear, nobody cheats by accident, it is never a mistake. Can you just imagine; "Honey I was walking down the street and I tripped and next thing you know I was having sex." "It was an accident". Tripping is an accident, cheating is..........*CHEATING*. It is that cut and dry. Scenario 1 plays out sort of like this: you work at a large corporation and you have struck up a bit of relationship with someone you work with. Every day is filled with a bit of flirting.

The odd touch and maybe even a wink. The two of you anticipate the day when you will actually get a chance to consummate your friendship. One problem: she has a boyfriend. Well, it is not really a problem. You must ask yourself one simple question (ok, two simple questions): do you actually like this person and can you in all honesty imagine having a relationship with her? If the answer is "Yes", then there is no problem at all. You have to let her know that the flirting and everything else must come to a stop. It is not fair to her boyfriend, or for that matter, to you. As long as she is attached you will no longer partake in this behavior. You must make this perfectly clear. If the answer is "No", then go ahead have sex with her. What do you care? But remember this, if you do, she might be a two-timing bitch, but my friend, you are likely the instigator and at any rate simply a bastard. So if the answer is "No", you don't like her, then stop wasting your time. Evolve, for heaven's sake! It is not ok to participate in cheating. Your soul is at stake here....

**Scenario 2:**

This must be a serious topic. Two different scenarios. Of course it is. You or the love of your life has decided for whatever reason to stray and spend some time in someone else's sandbox, toy room or whatever euphemism you choose to use for the infidelity. Maybe your relationship is on the rocks or you are simply a sex addict who can't get enough. Maybe you even truly love the person you are with, but because of your own dysfunctions or complexes, you are afraid or feel trapped or whatever else your lame excuse may be.

There are a few things that may happen here. It may be a one-time thing. Your cheating may be something that your mate stumbles across by accident. Maybe they confront you with it because they have some hard evidence or just instincts and believe me, instincts are usually correct. Or maybe someone you know, a friend, a family member or worst yet, someone who wants to get into your mate's pants, knows and informs you of it. If you are the one doing the cheating, you soulless, spineless bastard or bitch, please take a step back and realize what pain and suffering you are about to inflict on someone you care about and perhaps even love. Why are you about to inflict this pain, trauma and suffering on your loved one. A simple answer: all because of your

*Penned By: The Seed & German Seed*

own selfishness. If you can't keep it in your pants, then get out of your relationship. Or seek help if the relationship is actually important to you.

If you are the one being cheated on, the answer is simple, but it is something that is not often what one wants to hear. There is almost no excuse for the disrespect and if you are to find out, you must initially leave. That is your only option. If you don't, you will never find the respect that you deserve and if you stay, "maybe you don't even deserve that respect." Listen, we must **"FUCK THE CHEATERS"** of this world. After all, they are fucking us in emotional ways.

Is it a bad thing? Yes. Does it happen all of the time? Yes. In the time it took me to right this I am certain that thousands of people have been cheated on by the ones that they love. It is kind of mind boggling isn't it? I am not a supporter of cheating and lying, but, it is almost inevitable. At some point in everyone's life they have either been cheated on or have cheated themselves. People make up every fucking excuse that they can in an attempt to try to eliminate any responsibility for their actions. They say such things as: "The reason I cheated was the relationship wasn't providing me with everything I needed...." Due to their own guilt they sometimes even try to convince their friends that they are justified in having cheated by painting their mates as bad or unloving individuals. They actually believe that "they really deserve better". Let me tell you something: they don't deserve better. They are fucking cheaters and liars. If they do this to the ones they love, I wish that all of their caring friends would realize that it is only a matter of time before they will tell a monumental lie to them.

Better yet: with no regard for the emotions of others or even themselves for that matter. Cheaters either have no conscience or are masters at repressing any feelings of guilt or moral responsibility. They are usually superficial and shallow individuals whose sole purpose in life seems to be seeking self-gratification. They are likely incapable of love. In a sense, they are impaired. We, as a society, have a moral role to police these individuals and to not accept their behavior. Every friend who knows another friend who has cheated has a responsibility to reprimand their friend and to not accept they're behavior. I am not saying people don't make mistakes. They do. However, come on people, do you want to surround yourself with a bunch of friends who are liars and cheaters? Probably not. That is, unless you are one yourself. Think about it. If Johnny worked for you and stole from you and then asked for a job reference would you give him one? Now if Johnny cheated on one of your friends and someone else showed interest in him, could you possibly tell that person Johnny is a good guy? That is what I thought. Of course you couldn't. It is your reputation on the line. Johnny is really no different than the thief.

At this time, I feel it is necessary to include myself as an example in order to illustrate this point. I was dating someone that I truly loved. I would have done anything for her. Then a stranger brought to my attention that my lover might be playing in someone else's sandbox. They sent me some e-mails that had been sent back and forth between my lover and another guy. At this point it was devastating and the evidence was undisputable. I confronted my lover with the "evidence" and was told that the e-mails were forged and that she would never cheat on me. For her, instead of just admitting the mistake, lying about it seemed to be an easier solution. I being stupid and in love, thought that was ok. People are entitled to mistakes and because of my own insecurity I wanted her in my life. So, I decided we should work through this and move on. For me working through it was very emotional. For her it was natural, just lie and say she would never do it again.

So life seemed great until once again, several months later, bang, another e-mail and sure enough she was cheating again. This time it was with someone that she had been talking to during the whole duration of our relationship (remember the section on having a lot of male friends?). Once again I confronted her, once again a lie and once again stupid me gave her another chance. Fuck, was I pathetic. Now, after that, life went along quite swimmingly. Everything seemed great and fuck, I actually believed we loved each other. Then one day bang!!! I was dumped. She still seemed to want me in her life. And I was stupid enough to want her in my life as well. Where did all of my self-respect go? So we worked on being friends. Great! Now she gets to have intimacy with others, with the security of me. A master manipulator. Eventually, she found someone else. Remember, the guy she cheated on me with above (Patrick), well she actually convinced the sucker that he was the only one she cheated on me with and that she actually really wanted to be with him. I found out that she had cheated on me with at least with 5 different people, after the fact. Some friends actually thought that telling me would make me feel better. I only wish they would have told me sooner, it would have saved a lot of pain. By the way, society has terms for someone who sleeps with a lot of different people while in a relationship, correct me if I am wrong, I think the term is *"Slut"*. It is even funnier that during the time she was cheating with this particular guy, she told him she was single and that was the only reason he supposedly showed interest in her in the first place.

As we moved along trying to work on our friendship, I was still a pathetic sucker being available for her and being a true friend. During this time she continued to lie to me. Though, now it was about things that did not even matter. For example, she would be going away for a weekend with her new man, and would ask me to look after her dog. Of course, I said yes. Now get this. When I asked out of curiosity where they were going, she would lie. For what reason? I do not know. Do you get where I am going here, liars and cheaters are exactly that: "liars and cheaters". They will likely never change and they are too self-absorbed and insecure ever to care about anyone but themselves. The fact of the matter is that they really don't care about themselves either. The sad thing for someone like me, who uses the word love sparingly and when I do I want that person to be part of my life from that point on, is that it is very difficult to cut the ties. Even though, ultimately, that is what needs to be done. Should you find yourself in the same situation, for your own health and welfare, you need to get away. No matter how much you love and pine for your former mate, you must give them their walking papers and hopefully some day they will (unlikely) realize the tremendous pain they have inflicted on a special person. Then and only then, can you let them back into your life. Be strong my friends. I know it sucks. If you don't take this advice you are just going to be a continuous doormat and you will be no good to anyone and most importantly you will be no good to yourself.

Having said all of this, there are actually two types of cheaters. There are the malicious, mean and hurtful kind, where cheating is a game. The thrill of the chase is so strong that they play and manipulate their prey into thinking that they are special. That they have a real connection. That is the type of cheater that my ex was. They are so fucking pathological that sometimes they even convince themselves that the next sucker is really the one they should be with. Because, if they are not, they have a tremendous character flaw, namely they are a liar and a cheater. The sad thing is that there are enough suckers out there, especially if the person cheating is good looking, who will buy into this garbage. Moreover, their ego is out of control and they believe that they must be better than the previous love of the cheater. There must be a reason that they cheated. Things must have been awful.

What these sad saps do not realize is that anyone who would cheat on and lie to their past loves, will cheat and lie on the present one. This is especially true if they started their new relationship when they already were in one. These egomaniacal individuals live in glass bubbles. So what I am telling you here is simply: don't fall for it. If your new, potential mate is still in a relationship while they are pursuing you (I don't care if they are fucking 10s): run. It is a game to them and you are not any more special than who they are with now. Not only are you not more special, you are but another sucker, nothing more than a pawn in their game. If you honestly believe you are more special, then you have some serious insecurity issues of your own. The grass is not greener. That is not to say people don't meet their true loves while they are with other people. They just need to settle the score with the person they're with first. Get some time and distance before there is any chance that "next" can work. That means no kissing, groping or anything else until a substantial amount of time has passed. If it is meant to be, you owe it to both of you to give it time.

The other type of cheater basically is the type who gets caught up in the moment, or seizes the "opportunity" and ends up doing something he or she regrets. Maybe on a business trip or at a work "fucktion" and after a few drinks makes an error in judgment. This does not excuse the act. You too are a prick. However, in this case it may be forgivable. This individual is likely to be overwrought with guilt. The mental punishment and anguish that they put themselves through will be far greater than what anyone else can. If you find yourself in this situation, take a deep breath and then go get some counseling or do some soul searching. Find out if it was just a big mistake that will never happen again or if it is a sign that something is missing in your relationship. Just do not be a coward and throw yourself into another relationship for comfort while you are currently in one. No matter what may be wrong with yours, have the decency and balls to sort out matters first. Remember, you supposedly love the person you are with. You owe it to them not to cause them pain. I know this is a serious subject matter, if you come to the conclusion that your relationship is not the right one for you: end it. Just don't be sleeping with someone else when you do. Be a man not a mouse. By the way, the girl who is allowing you to sleep with her, while you are still dating someone else, well, she is an insecure "bitch". And if you hook up with her, good luck.

A final point here: if for whatever reason you have an error in judgment and cheat and then decide that it was a mistake, that is, you "discover" in this process that you are already with your "True Love", then you must deal with the guilt yourself. After all, you're an adult. You made the decision to fuck someone else; you made your bed, now you've got to lie in it. You must live with the guilt and the consequences of YOUR actions. Do not tell another living soul. Deal with it and keep it as your demon. And no matter how tempting it is to come clean and tell your "True Love": don't. Most women say that they want to be told that they've been cheated on: "Honey, whatever happens, promise me you will always be honest and tell me if you get together with someone else." Still, don't do it. The only thing you do by telling her, well two things. First, you have dumped your guilt on her and that is not fair. The guilt is yours to carry as a reminder, not hers. Secondly, you will likely cause your mate immense pain and unhappiness that he or she simply does not deserve. As a result of this pain, even if they forgive you, they will not forget what you've done. They will not be able to trust you anymore, and if they break up with you because of your infidelity, then they will have problems with trust in their next relationships. Not only were you a fucking asshole by cheating, but you've also added to the psychological "baggage" we all carry with us. Good job, prick. The moral here is simple: if you fuck up, and you resolve never to do it again, then shut up.

As I already mentioned, this section is a tough one to talk about. We can't accept this type of behavior in our society. If you are even tempted to cheat please do some soul searching. If you do cheat, you are just slowly destroying your own soul and karma will eventually take care of you. Just like the use of the word Love, your actions can inflict a lot of pain on others. People trust. People love and if you violate this love, they usually have to pick up the pieces. Not you. The only real positive is that they will likely grow. Whereas, you, you will just be the same shallow, superficial, self-absorbed bitch or bastard you have always been. Could you please develop some character? That means you too "Sweetie"!!!!!!!!!!!!!

*Penned By: The Seed & German Seed*

# SECTION 5
# For Better Or Worse You're Staying

    I am going to start off this section by taking a moment and thanking you for spending some time in **Seed's Incredible Boutique** at **www.seedenterprises.com** and purchasing a lot of fine products and books. It is very much appreciated and I am sure you and your friends have received incredible amounts of enjoyment from the wise purchases you have made. I hope that this book has helped you significantly in your relationships along with being able to bounce some of your tough relationship questions off of The Seed. If you have not bounced a question off him yet, you don't have to wait to see him in person to do so. You may send your question to him by e-mailing him at **Ask Seed** at **www.seedenterprises.com**. He promises to reply. For those of you who have purchased some fine products or asked a question already, I commend you and your merit badges are on there way. You guys are really the exceptions and I will show you my appreciation by sending you the badges. Perhaps even one of the Ask Seed Compilation Disks as well. For those of you who haven't gone and purchased anything yet or asked a question: what is wrong with you? Don't you want your relationship to succeed? Are you happy being a clone? No really. What is wrong with you? Now go get your ass in gear find a computer and buy something. I am serious or I

*Penned By: The Seed & German Seed*

am not writing another thing.... I am waiting. You are spoiling it for everyone else.... I am very serious now...............

*Seed's Sketchy Relationship Theories - A Guide to the Perils of Dating*

............................ still waiting – what is taking you ............................?

*Penned By: The Seed & German Seed*

... ok, ok, I am not going to let you spoil it for the rest of the readers, you selfish jerks. You thought I wasn't going to finish the book because of you. My God. Well, I hope in that couple of page break you were able to make some purchases. It will benefit you. But of course you know that. I also apologize to any of you that thought I had pulled the plug on this project and quit just part way in. I am going to let you in on something here. You were reading the book right? Ok, then that means you had purchased it, right? So of course, I finished it silly! I was just having a little bit of fun, that's all.

So, back to the topic at hand. You have been together for several years. Sometimes it has been like going to hell and back. You maybe even have some offspring now. Maybe you are married. Maybe you are not. But the one thing you do know is that you are still in love. Hopefully "True Love", but nonetheless, in love and you want to stay that way and break through any future barriers or jump over any hurdles. Well, Congratulations! I am proud of you. Because of you that eye of mine is welling up again. Man, I am a sap. So the next little bit of the book is on how to stay that way. Together, that is. Get ready, since if you have made it this far you really do not want to spoil it now, do you? Good.... Let us get going then and by the way, grab yourself another gin, beer, wine spritzer, seabreeze, boilermaker or whatever else does it for you.

# CHAPTER 34
# Call It Serious Call It Dead

You have been at work all day dealing with your fuckhead boss and the last thing you want to do is come home to serious talks. The "relationship part" of you life is supposed to be fun. I do not know of one "serious" relationship that succeeded. Come on people, we all need to lighten up. I have been in several serious relationships and guess where they are? In the toilet is the answer. So this chapter explores the importance of keeping it light so you and your partner can help each other through the day to day grind of life instead of dumping another bunch of shit on each other.

Honey, we do care about your day but usually not right when we get home. Hell, if we could just hug, kiss, nurture and love when we greet each other, life would be grand. We do not want to hear what a bitch Marge is or how the kids vomited at lunch. Ok, we do, but let's first have some fun. Go for a walk, have sex or something else before we rehash the nightmare of the day. Save all that other bullshit for the, "by the way, did you know what so and so did...?" It just can't be the main course in a relationship. Your relationship is to be your retreat or oasis of comfort, nurturing and love. Not your place to dump your day to day editorials on each other. As corny as this sounds your relationship is supposed to be your realm of bliss, your "Utopia". I know, I have experienced it. The only problem is that it got serious and ended up in the toilet. I challenge you all to stop having these serious relationships. They will not last. Think about it, how many serious relationships do you have with your friends? I think I know the answer. Sure, you have serious talks. You are there to support each other, bounce your ideas off one another and even to alleviate some of the stress of the day, but even for a friendship to survive it can't always be serious.

So try this: lighten up when you get home from work, no matter how stressful your day was. At least initially keep it to yourself. Shower your mate with affection. She may be resistant to this at first, but it is sure a lot better than dumping your boring day on her. And vice versa, ladies, do the same, whether you are in a career or at home raising the children. Give your man a break from the serious. Send the kids elsewhere once in a while and surprise the crap out of him. All guys like oral sex and it does not have to end with "I do"!!!

Remember in an earlier chapter when it was mentioned to cherish the differences? Well, if you have lived by that rule and are taking the time to get to know fully the love of your life, your life will remain fresh and exciting. If you have been lucky enough to find or stumble across your "True Love", you will have your whole lifetime to get to know everything about them. There will be no rush, because they aren't going to be leaving anytime soon. Perhaps use up your "serious" relationships before the age of 25: have them with your ex's!

# CHAPTER 35
# Honey We're Going To Have a Baby.... Procreation

*"Fuck I Am Going To Make Up For It When This Thing Finally Comes Out"*

-Fiona (6 ½ months pregnant, commenting on the next time she can drink).

Guys, who do you think is in control of whether or not we become fathers? There is no damn way a guy can control whether or not he becomes a father. Well, there is one way... a vasectomy (that may not even be foolproof if your wife is a lying, cheating bitch), other than that, it is out of our hands. If you don't believe me, just ask yourself: do you know anyone who is paying child support for a kid they never wanted? We all think that we participate in this important decision. Single motherhood is rampant all over North America. Sure there are mistakes. Sure there are situations, where the man is a coward and runs away on the family or where the man is an alcoholic/junkie and beats his wife and children, so that getting away from him and entering single motherhood is not a choice but the only option for survival. On the other hand, there are also fantastic loving relationships where a family is a well planned event that both parties take an

*Penned By: The Seed & German Seed*

equal part in and both work at having all the components in place to give the child the greatest chance at success in this big bad world. However, for every planned child, there are many more that are not. A night of passion at the bar turns into a lifetime of grief, smaller pay checks and agony.

We have children for several reasons. We have them to continue on our bloodline. Some want children in order to trap their mates or to keep them from leaving. But the actual decision of when to get pregnant is solely in the hands of the woman. If a girl wants to get pregnant, she will. Period. End of story. That is just the way it works. You have no control. I know this may be upsetting to a lot of people and I am sure a lot may say "Seed, you're an asshole, I am not like that". I am sure a lot of you are not. But tick tick tick goes the biological clock and if that maternal instinct becomes too great, things change. Ladies, you only have so much time before you risk serious complications.

In the old days, families used to be extremely large. In a lot of cases, children were born because the family needed more workers for the farm or as a form of retirement income for the parents. As society changed and urban living became more the norm, the need to have large families decreased. More people had the chance to enjoy a post-secondary education. They started to crave more professional careers and the need and the desire for large families declined. The more intelligent you were, the less children you produced. A pure economical equation. Children cost a lot of money. Sure, there are a lot of large families in the cities, but most of those are in the lower class neighborhoods and a lot of children are unfortunately being raised by single parents.

The whole point of this section is to illustrate that there is a right way to start a family. When you meet the girl of your dreams, don't marry her until you are at least 25 and have acquired some life experience. Spend the next 3 to 5 years really getting to know one another and finding out if you can really make it in the long run. Use this 3 to 5 year period of time to get your financial house in order. If you are mature adults and decide that children are in the future, plan it out together. Start saving for it, so that your wife may preferably stay home in the first, formative years to raise the child (instead of the grandparents or whoever else you hire to assume "your" responsibility). For the feminists out there, if you think that we are misogynist bastards then go work and have your man be Mr. Mom, we don't really care. The point is that a parent and not a "babysitter" or any other "stand-in" should be nurturing YOUR child in its first years. If you can't do this, don't have the child in the first place. It is unfair to the kid and it is unfair to society. I know this may upset some people, but, there is nothing wrong with being a mother and raising a kid. It should be full-time work. Now if your sweet girl starts bitching and claiming she should be paid for her efforts, I am sorry my friend, you likely made a mistake and now you are stuck with her and though you love your kid, you are trapped. Ouch!!!!!!! But since you guys are a great, harmonic and mature team this will never happen, since it was discussed in the first place and you and your dear wife understand each other's roles and the fact that you (or your wife – see above) are working your ass off to feed three mouths should be enough.

The problem with this scenario is that everyone is in a big rush to procreate. If they followed our formula most people would not be having children until they were in their early 30s, and most women cannot wait that long. There is this constant ticking going on. The thought that "if I wait it still might not work out, so fuck it, I am going to reproduce". If you have been paying close attention to the rest of the book we are trying to give you the best possible chance to be with the person that you think you can share your life with: hell, we are trying to provide a valuable service and reduce the divorce rate by a few percentage points and thereby increase the quality of life in North America and the whole world for that matter. Fuck, I think we might be saints!

As mentioned regarding the topic of relationships throughout the book, I am my own case study on single motherhood. Up until September of 2003, I had thought I was the youngest of seven children. I watched my parents both die in my early 20s, very traumatic, only to find out by accident that my dysfunctional upbringing was actually not a mistake. Being treated like I did not belong was not just a case of having mean older brothers and sisters. It was because I truly didn't belong and they were in their own (less than) subtle ways making me aware of it. Childhood was not a cakewalk. I found out on October 21$^{st}$ 2003 that the parents I watched die were not my own and instead of being the youngest of seven, I was an only child. To make matters worse, I am the product of a single mother. In fact my loving mother was 23 when I was born and instead of keeping her son she passed me on to relatives. Also, instead of getting the hell out of my life, she made a point of making sure I knew that I was never good enough. Now imagine that, it was one thing when I thought she was just a bad sister, however, it becomes a whole new ballgame when you find out that the evil sister is actually your mother. As fortunate as I feel for being alive, I have one favor to ask: please plan your families. I am lucky, perhaps instead of a loving and caring family, I have been blessed with truly great friends, who have become my family. I am lucky – I have turned out well. I don't think that most people would be as fortunate. In fact, you might find them as regulars at the "Bar of Regrets".

Let us take the discussion about the procreation process one step further. Here is a brief segment which arose as I answered a friends question on child birth in an exciting venture called "*Ask Seed*":

Q: When a couple is having a child, should they use the phrase "We are having a baby"?

-Anonymous

A: Dear Anonymous:

Well, thank you Anonymous! You have asked the first question of hopefully many in this new and exciting enterprise called "Ask Seed". You may be wondering what makes me qualified to answer these tough questions. Well, there are three things, which are all of equal importance: 1. Experience, 2. I am logical and 3. I am smart. That is it in a nutshell, so he we go with our first exciting question.

Well after some serious thought, it is important to make sure that I am correct in my opinion here, after all this is the first question. So here it is, to summarize my opinion, you just have to ask a simple question: Do "we" look fat in this dress? The answer is a clear and loud "NO". "Honey, you look fat in this dress". And for the sake of this question, let us just assume you are actually a couple who are planning on having a child as opposed to one of those who have them by accident (LOL). First off, last time I checked, the male of the species is not capable of having children and on a little side note, we have no control on when our spouses or dates or one night stands or whatever the hell you may be, gets knocked up. Procreation is totally in control of the woman. Guys, if you believe it is any other way, you are stupid. There are only two ways we can have control, either snip-snip or abstinence.

So, now you and your lovely lady decide it is time to bring a little one into the world. Ok, so you are really just going along for the sex, and a by-product of that is your guys are good swimmers. You now have a couple of choices assuming that you are married. If you are, you likely have already given up a lot of your manhood (shall we say balls). Do you think the wedding was for you? You have likely given up a lot of the freedoms that you used to enjoy. You are now accountable to the Mrs. If your decision to tie the knot was well thought out, it is ok to give up some of your manhood. Nightly drinking with the boys might eventually have killed you anyway and maybe it is time to start a new and better life. Also if you have gotten hitched to the right person, it is worth giving up some things as you now have someone with whom you can share the good times and who will help you get through the day to day crap we face in this fucked up world. But the answer to the question is "no", "we" are not having a baby. Your sweet lady is having a baby and don't let her convince you otherwise. You do have responsibilities and will be giving up more freedom by succumbing to your night of bliss. You now are going to have a lifetime of financial responsibility. The nights with the boys are going to be fewer and farther between. You are going to have to deal with changing diapers, little league, carpools and so on and so on. Oh yeah, I almost forgot you are going have to deal with some of the psychotic hormonal changes that your gal is going to go through. So once again, we are not having a baby but you do both have your roles to play in the raising of your little Johnny or Chastity.

Now ladies, before you get your panties in a bunch. Come on, cut your guy some slack. I am assuming that one of the reasons you hooked up with him in the first place is that you actually liked his balls or the fact that he has some. If you keep asking him to change, eventually he will become an undesirable broken, ball-less wonder. If you two agreed to this whole child adventure,

*Penned By: The Seed & German Seed*

trust him, he is there for the long run and will give you both the financial and emotional support you so desire and on the basis of his "I do" and "Yeah, I want a kid", committed himself to. Come on now, you don't want him doing it out of guilt, do you? Now, if you did not agree on the child experiment, I have one word for you: "BITCH". You will likely get what you deserve and the one who will ultimately pay the price is the child. So my sweet friend, it is you and solely you that is having the baby and if you have really planned this out well and are planning to raise your own child as opposed to some other hired care-giver or worse yet, Granny and Grandpa, kudos to you. You have now entered a phase where you both will play equally important roles; you as the primary caregiver and your man will play the role of the financial provider. So get off his case. He is working for the team here. He needs his sleep, so get up change the kid yourself.

Also guys, just because your girl is pregnant does not mean you have to give up everything in your life. Unless you have a drinking problem or a health reason for not drinking, it is OK for you to still have a few pops with your friends. It may be your only solace from the unpredictable hormonal assaults you will be facing over the next 9 months. If you decide that you need to quit drinking because your lady is not drinking, well I have a saying for you: *MEOW, MEOW, MEOW!!!!!!*

And another thing, my friends, don't give up your balls. In conclusion, here are some other things that do not involve the word "we", the "we's" that annoy, if you will. "We" did not like the movie, the concert, the play, the whatever - you are still an individual so drop the "we". It is ok for you to have your own opinion. It is "I" liked, or "Chastity" and "I" liked the movie. "We" is a trap. Don't use it. Once you start, your balls are gone and the further you go down the path, the harder it will be for you to reclaim them. If you listen, you will be thanking me later.

So there it is answer number 1 of what I hope to be many.

**Remember You Asked....**

**-The Seed**

*Seed's Sketchy Relationship Theories - A Guide to the Perils of Dating*

One last thought on this topic. Please remember the world is over populated now, so please, please, please, no large families. OK!!

# CHAPTER 36
## We All Force It Don't We?

## Seed's Sketchy Relationship Theories - A Guide to the Perils of Dating

Every last one of us on the planet has insecurities and these insecurities lead us sometimes to make horrible decisions. Decisions that we will often deeply regret. These decisions may have some severe consequences which sometimes result in us destroying some of our most cherished relationships. Throughout the book, I have talked about how screwed up the planet is and how everyone is dysfunctional in some way. The way we are raised in the formative years can have a significant impact on how we interact with others later on in life. It may dictate whether we are faced with abandonment issues, whether or not we are forced to grow up faster than necessary in a struggle for survival. Quite often, the kids never actually get to know their parents due to the hectic pace of today's work world. That is, assuming the parents are still around to begin with. And as I have often mentioned, they receive their values and morals from the nanny or grandpa or worse yet, a whole host of people who are raising the kids by committee.

What does this have to do with forcing it? It is simple. These early events have a tendency of instilling the above mentioned insecurities in us. Unfortunately, these insecurities can wreak havoc on the way we interact with our love interests. It does not matter if it is a fairly new relationship or one which has lasted several years, these insecurities have a tendency to eat away at the relationship, to the point where it may unfortunately be too late to save. Just remember, your love has a whole array of day to day challenges and quite often how they are behaving has nothing to do with you. Most people in society, if they are not getting the attention they desire, have a tendency to convince themselves that it is because of them. They internalize. What this does is create some illogical actions. If your love has not called you for a few days, quite often there is an associated overreaction on your part. Or even worse, an overcompensation where you feel you have to talk now or you won't be able to survive. Give your love space, now and then. People sometimes need time to sort things out for themselves and it is very important to give that space. If you are constantly questioning whether or not you are loved, or worthy, eventually your love will tire of the world being about you. Having said that, as tough as it may be, take a deep breath and let them live. If you can, no matter how tough it is, keep your mouth shut and suppress your need to be validated. You will be

*Penned By: The Seed & German Seed*

well on the way to building trust and a nurturing relationship. If your love needs your assistance, you have to trust that they will ask for it.

Please try to remember, if you are an "exception" that is, that this part of life is not a game. No one should be keeping score. If you are truly in love, winning and losing should not matter. You are a team and the only way you move forward and grow is if you remember that. Your interactions need simply to consist of support and trying to find the best ways to co-exist. If you constantly test the relationship and always feel the need to be right: get some help. No one will want to spend their life with a condescending jerk. Unless of course, they have low self-esteem.

# CHAPTER 37
# After All We Are All Human

*"He Has the Staying Power
Of a Buddhist Albino Monk"*

*-the seed.*

We all need to cut each other some slack. We all make mistakes in our life and sometimes a little compassion and caring is all we need to break out of a rut. This chapter is to examine nurturing. It ties in nicely with the previous chapter. If you have evolved enough to have stopped trying to be the winner in your relationship, you will realize that the mistakes we make can be overcome as well. That is of course as long as they are not monumental ones and we will talk about those a bit in the next chapter.

Making mistakes is a big part of being human. Very few of us are perfect. In fact, I know no one who is. Relationships are always testing us. Sometimes they are filled with unreasonable expectations and we get upset over some ridiculous things. Every human being has certain characteristics which a given individual can or cannot accept. If you find you are dating someone who does a lot of things that drive you nuts and you are unable to tolerate them, you need to leave the relationship, or change yourself. That is right. You need to change, not the other individual. If you try to project how you are on another individual, it will be met with resentment and bitterness. As you should have learned earlier in the book, we are who we are and we will change when it is time. If you try to change someone, you don't want an equal loving partner to begin with.

Now that we have gotten that out of the way, let's say that you are now in a relationship that you enjoy and you want to keep. A relationship that you see lasting for a long time. You want to explore the possibilities of a long future together. You have found yourself with perhaps the love of your life. If this is the case, then work on yourself. By this I mean learn to keep an even keel. As corny as this sounds: lead by example. Don't get upset if your love does not do the dishes or laundry. Do it yourself. Don't bitch, harp or nag at them. If it is their turn to make dinner and they don't feel like it, fine. Live with that. Instead of coming down on them, try instead to find out how they are feeling. How has their day been? Maybe they just need some support and maybe they are feeling down. Communicate. Dinner is not that important. Fuck, order a pizza and use the time you saved by not cooking to talk to one another. Remember you are a team and you are in love. Don't impose rules, a cleaning schedule, a cooking schedule or any other anal schedule upon your relationship. You likely have to deal with that crap every day at work. You sure the hell don't want your home life to be a continuation of your work day. Keep things fresh. Frankly, fuck the schedule. As for the cleaning and the chores, if you feel you are doing too many of them, calmly convey this to your love on another day. Not on that day, where you cleaned the bathroom although it was his or her turn and you are ready for a fight. And then shut up. One day, they will start to chip in. If they don't, is it really that important anyway? Above all, look at the big picture. If your mate never takes out the garbage, yet he or she does the laundry and cooks, then you probably really don't have anything to bitch about in the first place.

Life really shouldn't be about who does the dishes. Not if you are in love. If you find yourself bitching about things like that to begin with, whether you are male of female, come clean with yourself. What is the real problem? And remember, you're more than likely not perfect either.

# CHAPTER 38
# Should You Stay Or Should You Go? More Red Flags

*"If two people love each other
There can be no happy end to it."*

-Ernest Hemingway

"IT IS TURNING A LITTLE STORMY

*Penned By: The Seed & German Seed*

    This is when you have decided that it is for life and it still goes south. What things would be so significant to cause you to leave now? Here are a few recommendations on when you should stay or run for the hills. Some of these depend on the timing of the relationship. Something that makes you run for the hills in the first stages of a relationship may be ok after years have gone by.

    Like humans, relationships go through a vast array of changes and cycles throughout our lifetimes. Sometimes the love of your life may have incredible sexual drive and want to ravage you every night. Sometimes you may be the same way, however occasionally you may not be in the mood. It is hard to not take some of these things personally. If you are working on cutting your lover some slack and you realize that we are all human, you are growing. Remember, you are a team and there are going to be significant ups and downs in relationships and in life. It is your goal as a couple to limit the downs and help one another through them and nurture the hell out of each other to make your time on the planet better.

    You have now invested a lot of time in your relationship but for some reason you are not sure if it is going to work out. You know that you love your partner, but that just does not seem to be enough anymore. What do you do? First off that is OK. As for the obvious reasons, where you have very little or no choice on ending the relationship (and we know it becomes harder if you are married and especially if you have children), some of the reasons are as follows: you must leave immediately and likely for good if your partner has committed murder, crimes against children or animals, infidelity or has succumbed to substance or alcohol abuse (where treatment is refused). In addition, if your partner has anger problems (where treatment is refused) and/or has shown the first sign of violence against you (you have absolutely no choice here - you must go - unless you want to fall into the category of being murdered). Those are just a few of the reasons where you have no choice but to run for your life. With some of these reasons for leaving, for example substance abuse or psychological/anger problems, there may be some hope that you can get back together. Maybe with the right treatments and very key time apart, change can occur. However, if you stay, it likely won't. If you do not leave, you are in a sense accepting and indeed reinforcing the behavior. You are setting yourself up to be a victim or worse yet a statistic. As mentioned before, we are not experts and cannot give you advice on what you need to do in your particular situation. Sometimes it just takes common sense and these are a few instances where common sense makes the choice crystal clear. There are some other instances where you may have to leave immediately, you may have to make a decision based on your own values and instincts to determine those, or better still, discuss the situation with a counselor or professional therapist.

That last paragraph was a bit depressing. If you find yourself in any of those situations just remember: it is likely not your fault. You just made an error in judgment. Perhaps a big one, but an error nonetheless. Please cut yourself some slack. You are human.

So where was I? Oh yeah. The passion and the desire seem to have vanished from your relationship. You start finding the stop at the "Bar of Regrets" on the way home to becoming the norm. Life at this moment sucks. You may still love your girlfriend or boyfriend, wife or husband, but the magic just seems to be missing and you don't know what to do about it. Right off, stop going to the bar of regrets, it is not helping the situation. Face reality. Quit giving up. Remember you love this person and hopefully you care for them and respect them. That is, after you have sobered up and realized that the guys at the bar with their collection of useless thoughts are just going through the motions of life and have quit themselves. They would be more than happy to have a new member in "The Life Sucks Club". After all, the more members there are, means more drinks, more recovery time and ultimately it leads to more excuses and inevitably more time in the "Bar of Regrets". It is not pretty. When you take up a stool in these bars, the chances of making it out becomes increasingly difficult the more time you spend there.

At this time, I must take a moment to say that throughout North America and the world there are a lot of wonderful bars, pubs, lounges and clubs that provide a positive atmosphere to share a few pops with friends, both new and old, family members and acquaintances. These bars provide a valuable social environment, where the possibilities are unlimited. In fact, I met a few of my ex's in these bars and proceeded to have serious relationships with them. The bars to be avoided, to which I referred above, well you will be able to spot them. Actually, I think if you read the fine print on the signs it does say: "Bar of Regrets". As for the rest of the bars, keep up the good work. See you soon.

Back to the matter at hand. The passion seems to be gone. What do you do? First off, take another deep breath. Next, grab a gin (ha, ha!). Seriously, try to remove yourself for a moment from the situation. Go for a run, a walk, go to the gym or go do something where you can be alone for a little while to think. Do some soul searching. Maybe the solution is simple. You really don't want to give up on a relationship with someone that you love. Perhaps you or your partner are having some work, health, family or any of a vast array of other problems which may be affecting the relationship. If you remember, we are all full of insecurities and dysfunctions, which sometimes take years to come to terms with. All that might be necessary is some time to sort through the challenges of life. It happens. Remember to cut each other some slack. If you feel that you are not sure if you can get through this alone, then get some counseling. Sometimes we can't work past all of the challenges of life on our own and the people close to us are not equipped or trained to give good advice. They have a host of their own challenges. For the sake of example, I don't know one friend who could have possibly been able to deal with all of the events that took place in my life in the last year. They can listen, but to ask them for the answers is simply not fair.

Hopefully, the soul searching and counseling have helped you to work past some of your issues. While you are working on getting over this funk you are in, I have one simple request. It is the most important aspect of any relationship:

## "Keep the lines of communication open."

This point is so important that I have highlighted it for you. I was going to ask you to get a pen and some paper and write it down. I was going to suggest getting yourself a highlighter and highlighting it yourself. Then a funny thing happened: I realized that if I wanted to keep marching towards sainthood I could simply do it for you. I also didn't want you to stop reading to have to do a menial task at such an important moment. This point is so critical. In fact if you and your mate do not do this, do you really have a relationship? It is even more important when life issues you challenges. It is human nature for us to be self-absorbed. If your love is going through some challenges, you may feel neglected and unloved and force the issues due to your insecurities, which may eventually lead to much greater relationship issues. Stop thinking about yourself. Basically shut up. Don't assume her or his problems pertain to you. Sometimes people just need time and space and not the constant pressure that relationships can place upon them when their significant other is not supportive and nurturing. Trust your partner. They will tell you if their issues pertain to you. If they don't, your decision will become clear. If you don't live with your girlfriend/boyfriend and they don't call you for a few days. Don't sweat it. If you really love them and they do you: give them a break and – once again – trust them. If you don't trust them, what the hell are you doing with them in the first place? Seriously.

If you are the one going through some problems, let them know. Make sure you tell them you just need some time to sort out some things and if your love can be of help you will let them know. This may be tough. Just remember you love this person and have a tough decision ahead of you and it is unfair not to let them know that something is going on. If you communicate, no matter what the end result is, you are definitely growing and evolving my friend. If at the end of this whole process you come to the conclusion the relationship is not the right one and that you both made a mistake, then cherish the good and be honest about it. The love will never go away. Unfortunately it just wasn't true. You owe it to each other to move on. That is only if you have exhausted all other solutions and the passion is definitely gone for good.

That was a bit too intense – even for me. I think it is time to lighten it up a bit and include some other reasons why you may need to pull the plug on a marriage or long-term relationship. Most of these are solely for your reading enjoyment, however, we may have slipped up in a few serious reasons. We will let you judge for yourself.

**You may have to the plug on a relationship if:**

- You find hidden in the "closet" your husband's/boyfriend's figure skates

*Penned By: The Seed & German Seed*

- You have been together for 4 years and you still don't know each other's names

**You more than likely need to pull the plug on a relationship if:**

- Your wife has another husband
- You have had a vasectomy and your wife still becomes pregnant
- Your significant other moves without telling you and does not give you a forwarding address

**You pretty much have no choice but to pull the plug on a relationship if:**

- You don't actually have a pool, but for some reason you have a pool boy
- Your wife loves sushi, yet seems to hate raw fish
- Any form of infidelity occurs
- The Foot Locker promotion never comes
- Somehow your husband becomes pregnant

**You definitely must pull the plug on a relationship if:**

- Your husband/boyfriend has ever won a figure skating medal or any other medal at the Gay Games
- You find your wife in bed with the pool boy
- You find your husband in bed with the pool boy
- In any of the above 2 situations you are not allowed to join in
- Your partner is actually dead.

Other than those and of course the obvious ones. Be kind and fair to one another and work things out. At least try.

# CHAPTER 39
# Finally: The Simple Formula To How It Should Work

*"Moving Forward Using All My Breath
Making Love To You Was Never Second Best"*

-Modern English (I Melt With You)

*Penned By: The Seed & German Seed*

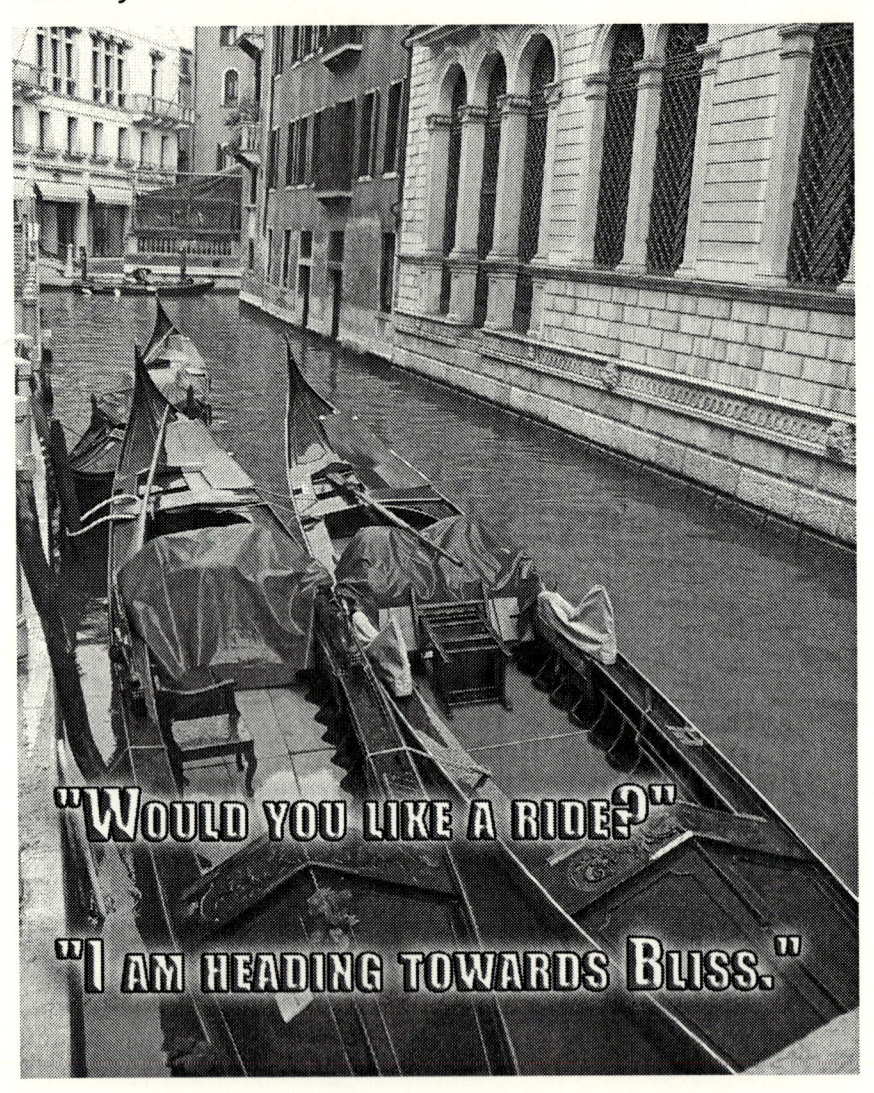

**"Would you like a ride?"**

**"I am heading towards Bliss."**

    Now that we have examined in depth the trials and tribulations of relationships, it is time to simplify things and really, in any relationship in your life, it is indeed quite simple. The problem is that it is difficult to follow the simple rules. As we have said repeatedly in this book, life is a big challenge. There are so many external pressures in everything we do every day of our lives, that half of the time, we don't know if we are coming or going. This gives rise to a lot of different challenges and events in our relationships and affects how we handle them and react to the outside forces that are pulling us in a thousand or so different directions. We stay in fucked-up relationships because of self-esteem issues or a fear of being alone. We throw away great relationships due to a lot of different reasons, such as the fear that this is all there is. Or the messed-up way of thinking that the grass is greener somewhere else and you actually deserve those greener pastures: "I think I am not as happy as I could be." Other challenges, such as peer pressure and the fear of commitment also come into play from time to time. So fuck people, slow down take a deep breath and take some time to examine where you are in your life, where you would like to be and go for it. Anyways, I rant, so let us get to it, the simple formula is as follows:

### 1. Find someone you are attracted to.

A no-brainer here. If you do not have some type of physical attraction to your mate, don't enter the relationship. It is doomed to start with and even if the other person is a great person, do you really want to be the one who destroys their self-esteem for the future? If you are that selfish, why don't you go out and get hit by a bus and spare the great people on this planet some misery. It does not mean to say that you can't spend some time together and enjoy the company the friendship provides. Just be honest.

### 2. Keep the lines of communication open.

This has to be one of the biggest killers of great relationships. Man people, if you find yourself in love with someone, no matter what is going on in your life or what petty little things might be annoying you, for fuck sakes, have the guts to discuss them with your mate. If the relationship is solid and all you really need to be happy is a vacation or dinner cooked for you once in awhile, don't go bitching to your friends about it. Talk to your love. Don't take it for granted that they can read your mind, because unless they are a psychic, it is not going to happen. Too many great relationships come to an end because the bitching to friends takes on a life of its own and instead of a simple conversation you start to believe that things are out of control and there must be something better out there. Well, there simply is not, so please people, talk to each other. You may be pleasantly surprised by the results.

This whole communicating issue has to do with most, but not necessarily all areas of your life. Sure, you don't have to tell each other everything. Some things from your past can stay exactly where they are, in the past. As for other relevant things: talk, talk, talk. You will spare yourself a lot of grief and disappointment. Especially when it comes to giving gifts. The sooner you realize this (and this pertains mostly to the women of the world) the happier you will be. You may show us a thousand bracelets, tell us a hundred times about the trip you would like to go on and you may tell us over and over again that you are a size 5. The problem is: we do love you, however, most of us have a mental block and even if we remember what size, bracelet or hotel you had been thinking of, we will still somehow probably screw it up. It is just the way it is. You have maybe suggested a bracelet and a trip to "Paris", and we end up getting you a toaster oven. We tried. It is the thought that counts. We were probably thinking of baguettes or something, how they come from France, you mentioned Paris and wham: we buy you a toaster oven. We thought we were being thoughtful, when actually we were just being stupid. If there are certain things you need from us and this does pertain to more than gifts: tell us what you are thinking. We can't read minds. If you don't tell us, don't be too upset by the toaster ovens. If your husband/boyfriend happens to be gay, the gifts will be fabulous.

**3. Assess the true value of what each of you have to offer.**

If you dream girl is offering looks and she is a 10, it is nice to think that love will be enough. Be honest with yourself. It is not. If she is a 10, you had better be making or planning to make what a 10 commands in your market area. I know this is upsetting to all of you out there that believe "Love is Enough". I am just being honest: it is not. The more attractive your girlfriend is, love, though important, can't pay for the finer things. The trips, the cars, the furniture and the lavish lifestyle come from ambition, talent and of course luck, to some degree. Unless you are lucky enough to have found an exception. I suggest, strive to be something.

**4. Find someone for whom the small things are just that.**

If you cannot stand the toilet seat being left up and your sweetie does that all the time, guess what: they can no longer be your sweetie. On the other hand, if you don't mind them shitting on the floor, then we know where you live. To carry this thought a step further, try to evolve – yourself. If you are in love, the small things are really just that, small things. Who actually takes the garbage out on what day is not important and if it becomes a real issue for you, look at yourself first.

### 5. Don't project your "will" upon your love.

You can't change them and if you could, do you really want to be with someone who is spineless? When you started dating, you knew what you were getting. When it is time for your love to change, he or she will. You can nurture, support and encourage, that is all. If you want to marry a doctor and Johnny is not cut out for that, you are with the wrong guy, honey. Let Johnny live his own life.

### 6. Find someone that sends chills up and down your spine.

Someone who you look forward to coming home to. Someone with whom you want to share your life. Someone who you feel content being around and just generally having as part of your life.

Find someone with whom, no matter what obstacles you might face, you know it will be worth the journey to make it through these challenges together. You are stronger as a team.

### 7. Embrace each other's differences.

Find someone who compliments you and for whom you have a genuine interest in how they are different than you. This is the spice of life. You have a whole life of discovery ahead of you and if you find someone who fits the description "we have so much in common", why don't you just date yourself? Fuck having things in common, it is boring. Sure, it is ok to have some similar interests, but come on. Embrace new things in life. Think of how fascinating it can be exploring and experiencing new things and situations with someone whom you truly love. Remember the saying: "Opposites attract". The thing about this saying that wasn't explained is that it is not referring to gender.

Another point here is this: "Your greatest strengths are actually your greatest weaknesses" at the same time. Perhaps look for someone who compliments you and maybe you will balance each other out.

**8. Find someone who, even without even thinking about it, you always seem to put first.**

My friends, other than keeping the lines of communication open this may be the most important part of the formula. We all go through a lot of relationships throughout our lifetimes. That is, of course, unless we marry our "High School Sweethearts". Now, in the course of these relationships, I am sure that most of you have experienced a common progression. Starting with infatuation. The other person is perfect. Perhaps he or she is "the One" and can do no wrong. After a period of time, the early excitement wanes a bit and now you start to notice some flaws or imperfections and you enter into a bit of a power struggle, where each of you attempt to see how much you can get the other to do for you. Quite often, if they are too much of a push-over and will do just about anything for you, one loses interest and wants more of a challenge. Perhaps someone who says "no" once in a while. This is all fine and dandy, if we are young and immature and believe that relationships should be a power struggle. Or perhaps, a situation will arise where it is give and take. Stop listening to the propaganda. It is this simple: if you have found someone who you are infatuated with, whose annoying little habits in time turn into being kind of quirky and the attraction and magic does not seem to be subsiding, then my friends, you have found someone who is "worth it". Someone where if they need you to do something and it is not taking you away from something important, it is best just to do it. It is a true sign that you love someone and it does not make you a doormat. It is simply a voluntary gesture out of kindness for the ones we love. With no questions asked. No fanfare. My friend, it is unconditional. Period. And if the one you love feels the same way about you, then you have formed a real partnership and you have found "*True Love*".

There you have it. It is basically that simple. If you are lucky enough to find your "***True Love***" and if you follow the simple rules, your life will be fantastic. Just promise yourself to do each of the following:

## Seed's Sketchy Relationship Theories - A Guide to the Perils of Dating

Promise yourself to *"Live"* life. It is one big never-ending challenge and if you let the day-to-day obstacles get the best of you, you are destined to live a life of regrets. Tackle life head on. Dream and go for your dreams. Don't listen to the negative comments of others. Believe in yourself. While you are at it, let those you love live and shoot for the stars.

Promise yourself to *"Love"*. If you are lucky enough to find your "true love", remove all conditions. Go with your instincts. The love you receive in return will make it all worth it.

Promise yourself to *"Trust"*. Fight through all of your dysfunctions and insecurities. After all, they are products of your upbringing and you are better than that. There is virtually no greater sign of love than trusting another individual. Trust results in respect, which has an end result of greater love.

Promise yourself to *"Grow"*. Basically, do not accept the norm. Don't get trapped into a routine. Change things up now and again and challenge your "True Love" and for that matter, all those important to you. Experience and learn new things. You don't even have to do these things together. You can share your experiences later. This adds spice. Make sure while doing so, you always nurture, love and encourage. The results may be staggering.

Promise yourself to *"Prosper"*. This means in all aspects of life, physical, spiritual, mentally, in your career and by giving something back to the community. If you have been doing the above, you are well on your way, my friend. Your rewards will be much greater than just financial ones.

Promise yourself to *"Cherish"*. Life is short. It is important to cherish the people you love. Treat them like gold. Make sure they know how you feel about them. A kind word and a show of love or affection go along way to make a day better. Don't worry if it is not being reciprocated immediately. Remember you have evolved. The ones you love may still have a way to go.

One last request: can you do it *"With Passion Please!"* Be excited about your life. Don't let others bring you down. If you are working on something that you are excited about and proud of: boast! You have earned it. Don't let others try to take

*Penned By: The Seed & German Seed*

that away from you. People have a tendency to reel you in if you are too excited about your accomplishments. Don't tolerate it. Be excited about your life. Be even more excited about the accomplishments of those whom you love. Be there when they really need you. Just make sure you encourage greatness. I would rather talk about how good my book is, instead of how much my job sucks. Negativity destroys. It suppresses enthusiasm. If you find yourself immersed in it, change your environment and your friends if you must. And as I asked a minute ago, I will ask again: live **"With Passion Please."**

# CHAPTER 40
# Throw Away The Fucking Formula

*"True Love Is Rare*
*It is Too Important*
*Too Fragile*
*There is no Formula*
*It Comes From the Heart"*

*-the seed.*

    Ok, is this Seed guy nuts? He has gone through this whole extensive book, came up with this wonderful formula that seems to make a lot of sense and truly comes from his heart. It could easily be used as a simple guideline for how to live successfully in ones relationship life. But now he simply turns around and says throw the whole fucking thing away. Why the fuck did I read his book in the first place anyway? And hell, I am even saying fuck now. Fuuuck....

    Well, I am not nuts. Life should not be full of formulas. We need to live our own lives and not be told by me or anyone else for that matter, how to be or how to live. Your life is not mine and vice versa. Perhaps, formula was the wrong choice of words. Maybe it should have just been called "The simple relationship suggestions" instead. Like everything else in this book, it is the way things are, as seen through my perspective, as well as the experiences of those who are important me. Along with some general observations on how the world is working. I challenge you to do the same. Every one of the thoughts and observations in the previous chapters comes from the heart and is filled with passion. I know you have hopefully been entertained and thrown for some loops by my off tangent rants. I was just trying to bring a smile to your face and ease the brunt of how things are in the world today. I don't like a lot of the things that I have written about and I truly wish that the world was not the way that it currently is. You may think that this book is just a big load of crap and it is telling you how to play the game of relationships and at the end of it all, you may get laid a lot. But at what expense? If you live your life as if it is a big game, you likely won't be met with a lot of real satisfaction and you probably will end up with a great deal of emptiness and loneliness.

Hell, in a lot of instances in my life, if I would have only read what I had written sometime earlier or had the knowledge that I now have, I might have been able to alter the course of some of my important relationships. I am telling you, if I had to deal with my relationships the way it is being done in the world today, it would make me physically ill. That is not the way I am. I do not want to play the fucking game. It is boring and it tires me out. I am an "exception". In fact, a well meaning friend of mine once told me during a conversation regarding my last relationship that "my problem is, that I don't think like everyone else". Well, honestly, I don't want to think like everyone else. They are fucking puppets, clones and in my opinion they are wrong. The majority is failing and I don't want to be part of that majority.

It is funny that as I write this section I am sitting here waiting for my ex to arrive to pick up some mail. While I write, my heart fills with sadness. This was simply one of the "true loves" of my life and perhaps the one "true love of my life". Life will eventually answer that question. I had given you little snippets of our relationship throughout the book and in a lot of instances, well ok, in just about everyone of them, I did the exact opposite of what I have advised everyone else to do in the book. She cheated, lied, broke my heart and intentionally did things to cause me more pain. She even, at the time of writing this, has been dating one of the guys with which the infidelities took place and is now actually engaged to this guy. And get this, none of the mutual, supposed "good friends" care. They all have this attitude: "Well, she didn't cheat on me." What the fuck is wrong with that? Or should I say: what the fuck is right with that? Is society's moral barometer so low, that people would choose liars and cheaters as friends, over someone who has a good heart and is of strong character? If it is, no wonder divorce rates are so high.

Just like before, if you are a liar and a cheater, I don't want you as a friend and another thing you are fucking up the world. And for those of you who accept that behavior in your friends, you should be ashamed of yourselves. By treating them the same as you did before, you are just condoning the behavior. Hell, a lot of these supposed good friends liked me a lot. Some even told me that they loved me. But guess what: the only one of her friends who has the balls to tell her to slow down and not rush into things is me. I am the only one who really cares. The rest of them are more interested in the rock on her finger. They don't even worry about a situation where someone could possibly be getting married in such a short time frame, when they were supposedly madly in love with someone else just a short time before. Friendship does not mean simply to encourage others all of the time. That is the job of acquaintances. Friends should be able to voice opinions, either good or bad without fear of losing the friendship.

Do I hate her? No. Did I purge myself of her? No. Is she a good person? Unfortunately, probably not. Is it her fault? The answer is probably no to that as well. But that does not excuse her. Her actions were despicable and showed no regard for me or even herself. You may ask: why would Seed not hate her? Well my friends, the only advice that I gave that I did not follow, which I think I failed miserably on, is that I did not break free from her for any period of time. Some of that was due to the other events in my life which I have mentioned throughout this book. My own needs, insecurities and dysfunctions. You see, I was truly in love and if you remember what I said about the use of the word love, it should not be used too frequently. I only love a handful of people on this planet and they know how important they are to me. It should only be used if it is meant from the heart. Never to manipulate or get some sort of gain. And the fact is that I truly loved this individual. I put her first in every situation. Looked forward to every moment that I was to spend with her and the future was nothing but bright. I could trust that it was ok to be human. To make mistakes. To voice my opinion, because we were in the game together and our love was strong. The only problem is that it was not reciprocated. She used the word love frequently. Perhaps prematurely. Sure, maybe she loved me. She told me all the time. I have to believe that for my own sanity. But I am not sure that the love for herself was really there. How could it be? She had gone through her life being beautiful and everyone around told her that. She had to do no work. Hell, the guy she cheated on me with, she had lied to him for a whole year and told him she was single. Guess what? It didn't matter to him because for some reason his ego has allowed him to think that he is better than me and that she would never cheat on him (actually I am sure he doesn't care because she is hot). The point is that a lot of what has happened is not her fault. She is a product of society, her parents, friends and acquaintances.

Should she be in my life? I don't know. Should I hate her? Maybe, but the fact is that I do love her even still. Will that last for ever? That is yet to be determined. I won't give up on her as a person. My chance for growth is crucial here. Moving on does not mean finding the "next" one. Hell, after having moved out of our place for only 3 months she is already engaged. What does that tell you about her? From cheating to engagement in 3 months. Hmmmmmm. My actual growth on the other hand will come from a lot of soul searching and from learning how to love this individual during these extreme moments. I have cried a lot (even the Seed sheds a tear from time to time). I have wished things were different. I have wished bad things upon the person she is with. However, I still get chills when I see her. If there is one thing that I will regret in my life is that it ended. But I am an exception and when I rise from this experience, I will be stronger and capable of giving more to the next person, perhaps THE "true love" of my life. If that person actually exists. If not, I have experienced it and will never, never, never, never, never yes, I said never, settle. Please don't as well. If it is worth it fight for it.

This chapter has turned out to be interactive book writing at its best. She has come and picked up her mail and gone. Perhaps from my life for good. I hope not, but that could be for the best. Was there fighting and a big scene? You may be wondering. No, there wasn't. I can't say that the experience was a pleasant one in any way. I got the chills like normal. You know the ones that I mentioned before. The ones that let me know my love was true. But of course it was not reciprocated. I told her how I felt and how I wish things would be different and that I wished it had worked out between us. I even told her how a year ago she had just moved in and for me that was the test to see if we could get married or not and in my estimation, that was what was next.

So it is a sad time, going into the holiday season without her and with my current family situation, for which she showed absolutely no empathy. She doesn't care. She has a rock on her finger and that is all that matters to her. I know you may be thinking that I should have probably been an ass and told her a few of my opinions. Believe me, it takes a lot of effort not to. Now for the really sad part. The part that I wish would be different. Before I get to that, I want to make something very clear here. I am not pathetic. It may seem that I am. Maybe I could have handled things differently. Played the game perhaps. But that is not who I am. Oh yeah, the sad part, she had moved out of our place just 3 months ago. It is now December 2$^{nd}$ 2003 and here comes the sad part, as I was saying, which has also been illustrated so often in this book and is the part of the book that I ultimately hate the most. That is being right about the state of relationships. I hate living the example. Sure, it gives me some of the knowledge and the ability to write about this. The guy she is dating has money, he is 13 years older than her, not particularly good looking and not in any kind of physical condition. But he has fucking money. Ooooops, that sounded bitter. It was a bit. Of course it was, I am human after all. I have some money but not like this guy. At least not at the present moment. In three months he has bought her a substantial rock (honey, why did you have to be such a shallow bitch?). I asked her if we could get together sometime just before Christmas for lunch or something, to which she replied: "I probably won't be here. Patrick and I are going to Australia." Since she has no cash it surprised me, but this great guy, well he is going to pay the way, so man, she has got it lucky. Honey, I hope your looks hold up and you have learned how not to cheat. I am sure you have matured in the last 3 months and have learned truly how to love. You probably

*Penned By: The Seed & German Seed*

really mean it now. Probably not. Or is it the bling, bling? It makes me very, very sad that some people's definition of love is exactly that: bling, bling.

So even though this is what has transpired in my own life, I wouldn't change how I am going to treat my next love. I can't. I will follow the same program. If I am lucky enough to fall in love again, I will play no games. I will put everything I have into the relationship. I will leave it on the table. I will have lived my life to the fullest. I will use my suggestions, just as they are meant to be used. As suggestions. Next time, I just hope I do not misjudge the character of the one I fall in love with. Next time, I think I will find out more about her mother and her friends. Yes, her friends. They are ultimately a reflection of the individual. My few good friends are some of the best people on this planet, all with exceptional character and depth. Do I hate my ex? No, I feel sorry for her. But I will always love her in some way.

So guys and girls, there you have it. As much as I talked about the big game of relationships and how to compete in the game, I encourage you not to treat your life as if it were a game. Especially this part of your life. It is too important. Be the exception. Don't live like the majority. If you are lucky to find someone who is worth the effort to pursue a life with, then do just that: pursue it. Leave it all on the table. Be spent at the end. Don't use manipulation, formulas or the advice of others who are treating their lives as if it is a game. They are wrong. You know it.

I hope you have learned something. Go out there and **Live-Love-Trust-Grow-Prosper-Cherish-With Passion Please!** Remember to respect and treat each other like gold and if you are lucky enough truly to "fall in love", don't let it destroy you, no matter what the end result is. Cherish it. If you can do that, you are indeed one of the exceptions in our world.

# SECTION 6
# Other Realms

Wow!! 6 sections! I have written 6 sections of a book! Well actually only 5 sections, because technically this is the start of section 6, but that is just a technicality. Actually, in a way I have fooled you. It may appear as though I have written 6 different sections when, in reality, I have basically used the same words over and over again. I have just arranged them in different orders to make the chapters sound different. I am impressed that you have stayed with me this long. I am not sure if I would have. Actually, there is no question that I would have. I may not be the greatest writer of our time, but the one thing I guarantee is that I am open and honest with my opinions and it is just a lucky thing that they are correct *"Most of the Time"*. By this time, I hope you have learned a lot about the messed up world of relationships and, for that matter, about the messed up world in general. I hope you have become more caring, compassionate and have gained an understanding about what is important in your life. I hope mostly that you have become or are becoming an *"Exception"*. If you let me know – maybe we will have a merit badge ceremony in your honor.

I am sure whatever the case may be, you have enjoyed the material presented here to you. Even if it has only been for an odd chuckle from time to time. Since I am fairly sure this is the case.

*Penned By: The Seed & German Seed*

If you have a moment, why don't you encourage some of the talk show hosts of the world, like, I don't know, say David Letterman, Jay Leno, Conan O'Brien, Craig Kilborn and even Oprah to have this Seed fellow be a guest on their shows? Hell, if I am, I promise I will not disappoint. I may wet myself with nervousness, but I guarantee I will be somewhat entertaining.

Now that I have gotten that out of the way, I encourage you to go grab your "Seed Bobble Head" or "Johnny" and "Chastity Action Figures" and go have some fun with your wonderful children that you have done such a magnificent job raising. I commend you. What is that you are saying? You haven't taken the time to purchase any products yet? My God. Do you not listen to the experts? 87% of all pediatricians say that products from **Seeds Wonderful Magnificent Boutique** at **www.seedenterprises.com** will aid in the development of a child by 122%. What that actually means, I do not know. I am not a statistician. But I do know 122% is a very impressive number and that must be a good thing. Think about it: most athletes can give only 110% and this is a full 12% better than that. So if you want your kids to have a better chance in life, that is a full 122% better chance, all you need to do is to visit **www.seedenterprises.com** and your kids will be well on their way. While you are there, do not forget about your under-evolved neighbors, friends and family members. Maybe they need a t-shirt that does not have a beer logo on it. Or maybe just a book so they can gain the valuable insight that you have. As for the percentage of the insight, I am not sure how high it will be. The stats guy has not gotten back to me yet with the figure. Will it be 122%? I don't know. I wouldn't bet on it being less than that. Now that is much better, isn't it? You are helping mankind with your purchases. And perhaps even you may some day be joining me in "Sainthood".

Oh yeah, Section 6. Other Realms. This is basically a big bonus section before the actual bonus sections. Now do you see why they are considering me for Sainthood? Think about it. Not only do you receive more than one bonus section and a Closing Rant, but I am including more paper so that the people who produced this book, all the way down to the loggers, are all receiving a percentage more work. Man, I am helping the economy move forward. Section 6 is going to talk about another two aspects of life which I feel deserve at least some mention now. They, in reality, deserve their own books (which may or may not be in the works!). I just thought it was important to touch on these subjects now. Well, at least briefly. The topics are: the World of Roommates and the Gay World. I know for some of the un-evolved out there, these will be confrontational topics. Well, at least, the Roommates Chapter.

# CHAPTER 41
# Roommates

If you find yourself going down this path and find yourself needing a roommate to afford your pad, well my friend, this may be the most married you ever will be. Your relationship with your roommate will include the following: guilt, passion, fighting, learning to live with one another person, relying on one another, separation, anxiety and eventually splitting up usually without sexual benefits. Marriage in the true sense.

Ah, the roommate. We have all had them from time to time. In college, at the start of our careers and after divorce or separation - or just being dumped by our wonderful girls. Here is the scenario: you and a friend decide it would be fantastic to live together. You are tremendous friends, have a great time partying together, share clothes, drinks and even girls from time to time. How could this not possibly translate in to being a great roommate situation? Fuck, this incredible friend will give you all of the support and encouragement of a girlfriend without the hassle and guilt, right? Well, if it were only that simple.... Unfortunately, if you think that this is how it is, you are wrong. For every single time this situation works out, there are at least 100 times that inevitably it either destroys a friendship or weakens it to the point that it will never be the same again. The reasons for this are many, but one of the prime ones is that it is like being married without the sex bond to help you work through the day to day shit. Just imagine you may be able to tolerate your wife squeezing the toothpaste from the middle or not buying the toilet paper this time. Why? Well, probably because she occasionally performs fellatio. But the 14$^{th}$ time in a row that you buy the toilet paper will start to wear on you when you have just a roommate.

Eventually you will find yourself hoping he/she is not home when you come home. You will start bitching about their habits to others and the eventual result will be the likely deterioration or end of the friendship. This, my friend, can be as hard as divorce or break-up. Simply because this was a person that you felt was going to be there. For life. Like I have said thousands of times, there are always exceptions. But if you value your friendship with another individual never ever become roommates. What do you have to gain from the experience? Saving a few dollars a month is not worth it if you value your friendship. You are much wiser to live with someone you barely know or don't know at all and if you happen to become friends during the process great. If not, nothing has changed. I know you may be saying: "what the fuck does he know?" Well, once again, this comes from life experience. And the life experience of those close to me (very few of whom have been my roommate). I have had several roommates over the years and I am a self-proclaimed excellent roommate. I fucking get it. Buying the toilet paper, milk, toothpaste, etc., does not really matter until it starts to add up to half of the month's rent. Remember, you are living with someone to save money, so if you spend $20 more a month than your loving roomy on common items, don't sweat it. You are still far ahead of the game and to make a big production over it will begin the friendship deterioration process. Another thing that I will tell you is, the fact that roomies, much like dogs, have short attention spans. You may have bought the toilet paper the last 20 times or taken out the garbage the last 50 times, but as soon as they do it once, it is a big deal to them. Once means 50 times to them. That is how they will think. Guaranteed.

So, if you want to save a friendship – no matter how much you think it is utopia – don't become roommates. Unless you are like me and understand how others think. Even then, the special moments friends used to spend together will become less and less and less and less – do you get it yet? You will start to get tired of

*Penned By: The Seed & German Seed*

seeing each other. It will rarely work out any other way. You may still like and care for them, but getting to know every intimate detail of your friend's life can sometimes be very disturbing. So if you really cherish a friendship, I suggest finding someone else to live with. Unless you have no other options. One more thing: if you are over 25, ok maybe 30, what the hell do you have a roommate for anyway? Did you not just move out from mommy's place?

# CHAPTER 42
# The Gay World

This chapter prompted a difficult decision. Do we include it or not? What will it do to book sales? "They have their own bars...Why can't they have their own book?" "Why do they get

*Penned By: The Seed & German Seed*

their own World?" "Don't we give them enough already?" Well, even though the "Gay World" is a whole different ball game, I truly believe that people are people, love is love and relationships are relationships. Therefore, I feel it would be wrong not to include a chapter on gay society.

So let's begin. The gay world, Boys and Girls: fuck, it must not only be hard dealing with your own issues of sexuality and acceptance, but how do you come to terms with the fact that both your intimate partners and friends come from the same gender? If you are like most people in the world, straight or gay or somewhere in between, you try to surround yourself with people who are attractive. So here is a scenario: you are gay and alone with your attractive friend who is also gay or supposedly straight. You have seen his razor in the shower and you are a little tipsy or on some other substance. Hmmmmm....Tough situation, my friend. At least for gays, there seems to be defined roles. Actually, probably more defined than in the straight world. In this world there are tops and bottoms and one partner assumes the more feminine role. The problem here is that most guys are horny all of the time: "Where is the most exotic place you ever have had sex Johnny?" "In the bum." Also, due to the fear and oppression that was faced early on in life, a lot of people in the Gay World unfortunately neglect to develop a lot of areas of their life. There tends to be a lot of drug and alcohol problems and perhaps, in general, a real lack of dealing with emotional problems (substituting sexual encounters for emotional support). The gay world has a tendency constantly to be chasing that perfect high. Whether it might be a chemical high or a new relationship. "New" is a constant motto in this world. Things and people become disposable. The problem is that very few take time to look at themselves first. Another predominant issue in the Gay culture is the "party". For a large portion that is what is important. With no family unit to worry about, there can be a constant search for the perfect party. However, like in the straight world, looks are a commodity and though guys usually hold onto their looks longer, quite often in this world you are washed up in your early to mid thirties. And guess what: the party has sort of ended at this age, but you don't know how to stop.

As for you Lesbians: it must be extremely tough for you. How does guilt work? Who gets to fake it? (Just a little side joke here: Why are Lesbians always so angry? "Sex to them is just foreplay.") When two women are involved, the weapon of the guilt trip likely does not work and there is a constant battle to see who just gets to fake. OK, that was a bit nasty. Just like with every relationship, two individuals in love is a wonderful thing. It is just that in the same sex world, it must take such a tremendous effort. And with two women, it must be especially, difficult. How do two predominately nesters support and provide for each other? This is an area that I can only speculate on. I think I will do my speculating at a women's softball tournament.

This brings us to a little social commentary on how fucked the world is when it comes to the matter of same sex relationships. I was watching the news one day in the Summer of 2003, I saw a report about Gene Robinson. He had recently been elected as Bishop of New Hampshire. The controversy or more precisely the "problem" for a lot of people was the fact that the man is gay. There you have it. The first Anglican gay bishop. The reporters spoke in front of a group of outraged protestors, who rallied together after the decision was made public. What was striking is that a few of the protestors held up signs with the following message: "GOD HATES FAGS". The first question that occurred to me was: Can God hate? The next question that came to mind was: What the fuck is wrong with these people? I wondered whether these particular people consider themselves to be religious, as from my very limited reading of the Bible and from my experience in very few Church services, I have learned that God DOES NOT hate. Period. A message for you: We are ALL God's children, black or white, yellow or red and yes, gay or straight.

Ok, back to Gene Robinson. There were outcries in Church circles, both Catholic and Evangelical, that Robinson's election as Bishop would "shatter" the World Church. Much worse, family values were in danger. One British bishop commented a couple of months later, that homosexuality is, in his opinion, a "psychiatric" disorder. Of course, some people attempted desperately to discredit the man. One person, in particular, accused Robinson of touching him "inappropriately". Robinson had allegedly placed "one hand on his arm" and "another on his back" on two occasions during a conversation at a Church meeting. Grow the fuck up. Have any of you ever patted someone on the back before? Have any of you touched someone's arm in a conversation before? Have you ever watched the NFL? No, you haven't? Do you maybe stand ten feet away from someone and shout during a conversation so that they don't come near you? Who knows, they might, God help us, be gay!!! Don't worry, buddy, I don't think the man was trying to "recruit" you or anything like that, something gay-haters often contend. I touch people on the arm when I talk with them as well, and you know what: surprise, surprise - I'm not gay (I was however in a previous life, and Gay Seed is Gay!).

Unbelievable, right? I find it funny that people come up with such bullshit, and even more appalling that people seriously look into it, rather than examining more closely "other" touching by priests or church functionaries. How many young boys have been molested by priests? How many victims of such sexual abuse have come forward and, what is truly "shattering" is when one thinks of how many victims haven't come forward. Those, who couldn't bear the pain, shame and embarrassment of telling others about the abuse committed by members of and under the guise of the Church. Hmmm. Why did the Catholic Church just keep quiet all those years? Rather than coming clean and dealing with the problem, instead the priest in question would just be transferred to another congregation, and then well, you know what happens then. (Shampoo rinse and repeat). Instead of dealing with real problems, instead of coming to terms with the modern age and dealing with issues that really are important (birth control, the spread of AIDS, same-sex marriages, etc.), people get all riled up about the election of a gay bishop. Instead of looking at what kind of person Gene Robinson is. His credentials. His extensive work with youth groups and above all the hard work he's done to increase AIDS awareness in North America and Africa, people just simply brand him as gay. Get a grip, people. Forget the labels and use your head. We're no longer living in the Middles Ages, however today hypocrisy and stupidity are as accepted and ever-present as they were back then.

I think the key question to all the gay haters sitting in your local pub getting pissed would be: What are you all afraid of? Look deep inside and ask yourself that question. Here's a news flash for you: gay people aren't all members in some evil cult looking to recruit you and they aren't "sick". They're just people.

Why can't homophobes just accept this? A good friend of mine worked as a bartender in a rougher part of town. He had short hair, plays sports and doesn't dress like a fucking hillbilly (meaning his best shirts do not have a beer logo on them), so of course the pub regulars labeled him immediately as a "fag". They asked him where he lives, which was downtown, and they replied: "Oh yeah, by all those 'gay' restaurants and shops." What an amazing brainwave about gay people. Are all you homophobes on crack? Gay people don't eat "gay food" ("Wow, that 'gay steak' was sure tasty. Man, I feel gay now."). They don't live in "gay houses" (they do shop a lot at Ikea though). They also don't drive "gay cars". They just want to live their lives like everyone else. Instead of trying to come up with some sort of pseudo-scientific explanation that homosexuality is "abnormal" or a "sickness", why don't you homophobes out there just leave gay people alone. I'm sure you have enough of your own problems, don't you? (See the paragraph about "family values").

Another time at the same bar my same friend was asked the "where do you live" question again. Same response by the customers: "Oh, so you live in Gayville." To which he quickly replied. "Actually I live in Yaletown. I think the Gayville you would be referring to would be the West End and there is nothing wrong with the West End." To which a big overweight patron whose name will be left out of this (Jamie) said: "Oh, the West End. I don't like it there. Too many faggot weirdos." To which my friend promptly replied: "Well, unlike this area, which is rampant with panhandlers and heroin addicts, the West End is actually very clean and livable. One of the big differences, I guess, is that the people dress a bit better, and oh yeah, I have never seen any rampant gay sex acts breaking out there." "And one more thing Jamie, when the gays come up to you and ask you to have sex with them. You can always say no." To which he replied: "Oh yeah. You're defending them, so you must be one of them." My friend could have continued conversation with this moron at ad absurdum.

The point here is, how can people be so fucking stupid? First off, I was the bartender. And a further little observation on these lovely establishments that are all over North America: have a look around – there are usually between 5 and 10 overweight guys wearing stained beer shirts, listening to Brown Eyed Girl or something like that. There are posters all over the wall and sometimes mirrors and carpeting. There is rarely a girl in the place. Most of these guys can't remember the last time they were on a date or are drowning their sorrows because they don't want to go home to their marginal lives. My anally-retentive, narrow-minded friends, you already are frequenting a gay bar. It's just not a very good one. So, I suggest the next time you are all sitting there and complaining about faggots, may I suggest that you stop for a second and look around. Do a head count. You may be surprised. And one other point here: this is some of the only research I actually did for the book. I looked into it, and guess what? A few blocks from this particular pub is a gay bathhouse. So have fun there Jamie. Life must be tough not having seen your own dick for the last 30 years, or your shoes for that matter.

The point is: "Live and let live". Remember, "normality" is relative. What one person considers to be normal, might be totally abnormal to another. Look at terrorists, or religious fanatics, regardless of whether they are Muslims, Catholics, Protestants or just fucking terrorists. They consider it "normal" to kill innocent people. They think it's even "good" to wreak destruction and death and that their "god" will reward them for murder. How abnormal is that? Normality is relative.

Oh yeah! What about family values? If a gay person is elected as bishop, then the family values will fall apart. Wow! What a statement! I wonder which family values were being referred to. The family values that 40% to 60% of all marriages end in divorce? Man, that's high – and they're not even gay! Or the other family values, in so-called "normal" (= straight) marriages, where Mom gets beaten by Dad every night, because he's had a shitty day and decided to drown his sorrows in vodka? His wife is of course the scapegoat. Good thing she's not a fag. Then he'd probably go get his gun and shoot her because she's not only to blame for everything but on top of that: she's not normal. The kids get a front row seat at the daily beating. Hell, if Dad's on a roll then they also get to have a beating, because, you know, that's the way life is in "normal" families.

Another homophobic statement: "Gays are just promiscuous – they parade around in tight, pink leather outfits and sleep with as many partners as they can". I wonder where they get these pink leather outfits? I have never seen a pink cow. Maybe they breed them in San Francisco or Key West. Straight people, of course, would never do that. Be promiscuous, that is. Did you go to college? Do you remember the first years of going out, picking up and the next morning not remembering his/her name, let alone your own? Sure, maybe you weren't wearing tight, pink leather outfits, but the concept's the same. OK, maybe college was a gong show. Maybe we (straight, normal people) were also somewhat promiscuous. But after we got married that all changed. Hmm.... What about all those business trips? Hotel bars? After the fourth whiskey, you'd do anyone with at least two legs, two breasts who wasn't fast or sober enough to outrun you. Forget the business trips. What about sleeping with the secretary, the intern or the milkman, or hell, in this day and age, the personal trainer? It's OK, after all it's normal. You guys are all straight. If the ref doesn't see it, then it's not a foul. Am I right?

(I hope you readers were able to pick up the hint of sarcasm in the last paragraph, actually in this whole section and throughout the book. I think Seed may have taken a big sarcasm pill just before he wrote it).

Those are the predominant family values of this day and age. The parents don't care and frankly don't have time for the kids. Who, by the way, didn't ask to be born. One story that I recently heard from a buddy of mine, apropos "family values" and "caring parents" is summed up in the following scenario. Grandpa had put aside considerable sums for his grandkids' education, which isn't cheap, and gave this to the parents to take care of until the kids were old enough to go to college. Of course, both kids struggled through school, studied, had day and night jobs, as they didn't have monster scholarships. They were just normal kids trying to get by. Five years of macaroni & cheese because they didn't have cash for food. The parents of course, used the "college money" to go to Hawaii every winter and to pay for their golf memberships. The kids found out after the fact, when they were just about done with college, when Grandpa got suspicious after hearing that the kids couldn't come to visit him at Christmas, as they couldn't afford it and had to work. Grandpa uncovered the lies and the fucked up "values" of his own son. So much for so-called "normal" (= not gay) people and their "normal" marriages.

*Penned By: The Seed & German Seed*

How fucked up is that - you lie, cheat and steal from your own children? Another example of family values in the "me society". Me, me, me. Once again, evil in our society has nothing to do with gay or straight, religious or non-religious, or white or black. Evil lies in human nature, and above all, it is prevalent when money is involved. "Greed: very, very bad".

So someone's gay, does it really matter? It's a free country after all. I saw an interview with some guy on the street in Alabama, who stated, when asked about his definition of the word "freedom", that freedom was basically when the government didn't "meddle in his affairs". The government, "of course", was in any case "controlled by the Jews" and with regards to gay people, they were free to do whatever they want behind "closed doors in their own homes, but they should stay away from his children". Otherwise he would, you know, "grab his shotgun" and put an end to the threat. Wow, not just a homophobe, but an anti-Semite as well! Great! Just because your parents were brother and sister, doesn't mean that your kids also have to be as fucked up as you are. Ever heard of the word "tolerance"? Just because someone is gay, or for that matter Jewish, Catholic, Buddhist or a fucking atheist, doesn't mean that they belong to some secret conspiracy. No, they don't want to control the government, or the world and they probably don't want to have anything at all to do with you, you racist intolerant fuck, let alone your children. I pity your children. You probably preach racism and intolerance at the dinner table.

The horrible effects of racism, and in particular, anti-Semitism, and how far such idiotic concepts as "the Jewish conspiracy" can lead, were evidenced by the Holocaust and the sinister death camps, ghettoes and mass executions of Jews and other groups at the hands of the Nazis and their collaborators in Nazi-Occupied Europe during the Second World War. Simple ideas, which, in the heads of brutal individuals of weak character, led to mass murder on a scale that the world has never seen before or since then. Racists and dictators need and use simple ideas, no matter how irrational, despicable or illogical they might be, which can be repeated by the masses, or better by the sheep. Simple ideas for simple minds.

People that hate others on the basis of their religion, color, ethnicity or their sexual orientation are simply pathetic individuals that don't want to invest any time or thought in solving the real problems of society. They just want a scapegoat. Like the proverb, "you can't teach an old dog new tricks". "You can't teach an old racist tolerance". Yet, if you're a racist and a homophobe then do your kids a favor. Send them away to school, as soon as possible (maybe to a private school or religious school if money's tight) as soon as you can. There, they can learn that there is more to life than the dive bar you spend most of your time in and as well hating others whose only crime seems to be that they are different. A school or place where they can meet people of a different color, ethnic background or religion and learn that they are just like them. Just different. You could give your kids a chance so that they don't grow up to be as simple and intolerant as you are. And by the way, if the person with the sign mentioned at the beginning of the section happens to be reading this, just remember: God doesn't hate anyone. He (or She, who knows?) can't hate. But you know, theoretically, if He or She could hate anyone, then it would probably be you.

Whew!!!!! That was quite a rant. I guess I had a bit of an opinion there. Hey, this is supposed to be about relationships, not a constant political or social commentary. While on this subject, I think it is necessary to make a bit of a statement on the way the world is. The gay culture and gay society has a great opportunity here. They don't live by the same rules and can define where they are heading in the future. Sure, there have always been gay people in the world, it is just that recently, people have been coming out of the woodwork. Is this book for gay people as well? Absolutely. A relationship is a relationship no matter what and the gay culture has a great chance to make some positive changes. Examine the straight world and look at what is happening there. The theories apply here as well, it just takes a little imagination. If you find yourself in a great relationship, follow the sentiment that has been outlined in the "Simple Formula" chapter as well as the "Throw away the Fucking Formula" chapter. Hopefully you will, as well, take the good from the other sections of the book. At least you can derive a lot of pleasure from gaining an understanding of how messed up straight society is. It is not without its own significant problems. Most importantly, strive to be the "exception". Don't

*Penned By: The Seed & German Seed*

accept what has been laid out for you by previous generations. Live your own life. Come on, if you are truly in Love, is there such a thing as an open relationship? And cheating is not acceptable. And could you guys, just a bit, slow down the drug usage? I never said stop. Just slow it down. Though it may be fun for the moment, it is not good for you. You do know that, don't you? Ok, admit it now please. Thank you – I am a little less worried about you.

That is all for now, but if you patiently wait till the tasty, juicy "Gravy" chapter you may be fortunate to get a little bit of banter on same-sex marriages. Only if you behave, though. Now go listen to some Kylie or Madonna or something. And grab yourself a cooler or a cider, while you are at it.

# CHAPTER 43
# Closing Rant

*"The man who follows the crowd will usually get no further than the crowd.*
*The man who walks alone is likely to find himself in places no one has ever been.*
*Creativity in living is not without its attendant difficulties*
*And the unfortunate thing about being ahead of your time is*
*That when people realize you were right, they'll say it was obvious all along."*

*-Unknown*

Well there you have it. We are almost at the end of a work of passion. I would like to thank all of you for reading this and I hope you have received a bit of insight, perhaps some inspiration and at least a few laughs and some entertainment. Most importantly I hope if you take one thing away with you, it is that Seed is a big fan of relationships and wants them to succeed. In no way does he like everything he has written in this book, it is just his way of expressing how it really is right now from his perspective. His main objective is to give you the best chance of succeeding in both your relationship life and your life in general. Seed wants you to be happy.

*Penned By: The Seed & German Seed*

    This brings us to some closing thoughts and one topic in particular. It is a topic that has periodically taken the forefront in the news and other media. This topic is cloning. Medical and Scientific advances have reached the point where they have increased the life expectancy of the human race by about 5 years. They have also reached the point where they have cloned sheep and the debate is on now whether or not it is morally correct to clone human beings (if it has not already happened). Now the medical world is trying to lead us to believe that this will be used primarily for the good of mankind. Allegedly, that it is a wonderful application of science to the preservation of life, where if your liver fails, no problem, we have an exact replica of your healthy liver and we can take out the old and replace it with the new. Basically, for that matter, we can replace every failing organ, limb or whatever else you might require with new genuine parts that come from your own DNA. How fucking wonderful. We can create a spare parts warehouse for our body. Think about it, we are becoming invincible. We can abuse ourselves and basically, no problem. If we injure or damage something, just go down to the shop and have it replaced. Fantastic! We will be able almost to live forever, and to make it even better, both healthy and young.

    The problem is: who are we doing this for? Is it right to play God? Interesting questions. We have roughly 6 billion people inhabiting the planet now and we are currently having trouble feeding them all. At the current pace, this population will double in another 50 years. Just think about it, if we are having trouble feeding people now, what will it be like in 50 years? We now must begin producing genetically-altered "super produce" and "super livestock" in order to have a chance and when we do that, there is an uproar in the population about the effect that these products have, or what is even more unsettling, may have on people in future. We cannot yet gauge the effects, we will have to wait and see. I just hope that it won't be an unpleasant surprise. A real catch 22 – don't you see we have to find ways to produce more food quicker and faster or we don't stand a chance? Also think about this, some are pushing for naturally-produced foods, just as if there were only 3 billion people on this earth. Well, those foods may be far superior, but on the other hand, unless Mother Earth gets on the same fucking program that the human race is on and learns to evolve and shorten the growing season, so the earth can produce more to feed the growing population we are facing some severe problems in the not too distant future. Unfortunately, this is not going to happen and therefore something has to give.

Who out there can afford the healthier, naturally-produced organic foods? The rich. The rest of us have to pollute ourselves with the other crap: that is a fact of life. And to make matters worse, the media (which is controlled by the wealthy) are making us all aware of this fact. They are letting us know part of the story, ultimately for their own good. They do not have the common man's best interests in mind. And by the way, we are already all eating genetically-altered "super foods".

Now something that I would like to ask you, regardless of how you might feel about scientific breakthroughs and at least the theoretical medical usefulness of "manufactured" organs or other "cloned" body parts and gene technology, do you actually think that Johnny, who works at your local Mr. Lube, if he needs a new lung will be able to afford to take a new one out of the spare part and organ storage? Do you think his medical plan is going to cover that? Probably not, and at least for a couple of reasons. First of all, with the world's population going out of control, science can't afford to play God for everyone. The general population can't all live another 10 or 15 years longer than has already been mapped out for them. If they do, it won't be 50 years till we hit 12 billion, it will be 10 and that will double again in another 10 years or so. (Remember these population estimations are just that, they are estimations. The point is just to illustrate that things are out of control.) So unless we get a grip on this whole population thing and slow it down, people have to die when it is their time. I too would love to live another 10 or 20 years, especially if the quality of life I have now could remain close to the same. But not if the price is the destruction of our planet. If we keep treating the earth the way we have been up to now, we are headed for a great deal of trouble. Fuck, if we play God along the way that trouble increases dramatically. My friends, there comes a breaking point and like I said if the Earth does not get with the same program as mankind and find ways to yield more and frankly increase its inhabitable area, as much as I don't like to say this, *"WE ARE LIVING ON BORROWED TIME"*. Something will eventually have to give, and as the Earth cannot change itself, well humankind is heading for a catastrophe. And honestly, I really don't want to be around to see it. Do you? The point here is that these medical advances are not for everyone. They are for a select few. That is, the rich and the elite of this world. Don't kid yourself and think otherwise. So if you want to be on this path, if you are not in the elite, find a way to become one of them. Find something to excel at. Perhaps marry into it.

    I know what you might be thinking, you are likely saying: "hell, where did this all come from?" I thought he was going to talk about cloning. Well, my friends I am, cloning in the non-scientific manner has been going on pretty much for the last 100 years or so. Mankind has lost all sense of originality. Corporations, Entertainment, Education, Religion, Relationships, Sports and just about every other aspect of our lives are not necessarily controlled by others, but we are all being taught how to live. Just think about it, you enter your corporate life (I have spent my time in this area) and you are taught how to sell, how to dress, how to talk, how to kiss ass and most important, how to keep a mediocre and low profile. If you have opinions, you have to be careful as to whether or not you voice them or you may be labeled as a trouble maker or even worse, if you have a low-life superior he may steal them and pretend they are his own. Fuck, the whole corporate world follows the same model. They go to the same seminars, they take the same sales training, they all have virtually copied the same fucking model. They do this all on the premise: "why try new things when somebody else has found an easier way to do it". So what has virtually happened? The corporate world has created (cloned) a whole bunch of un-motivated and above all mediocre sheep. There is no longer any drive to excel. Why bother? Just like in the relationship (divorce) world, if you say the wrong thing some sensitive prick is going to fire you. After all, there are more sheep out there willing to replace you and since no one is outstanding anymore, it really is easy to do. (Of course, just as in other aspects of life and relationships there are also exceptions even in the corporate world).

    Now, regarding the entertainment world, is it really any better? You'd think it would be. After all, these are creative minds at work. Remember this: the entertainment world is also part of the corporate world. Fuck, it is probably the most unimaginative place on the planet. You just need to watch TV to figure that out. Every successful new TV show has several imitators, almost instantly. Once again clones. It is a constant race to produce the same shit, and not even better, just get it out quick. The audiences are stupid anyway. If we can get it on air fast, at least we have a chance at some of those big advertising dollars. Fuck – what is the trend now? Oh yeah, reality shows. Why? They cost nothing to produce, very little paid staff and sure the winner of the show gets a million dollars. Didn't the 6 "Friends" get something like that per episode? Each of them, that is. You figure it out. And we are stupid enough to watch it. As if playing games in some exotic location is reality or dating 10 beautiful women until you narrow it down to 1 on national television is the way we are supposed to find our mates. It doesn't look like the divorce rate is going down any time soon. Hell, how many new ideas are there in the music industry. This industry, just like in the television and film industry, is basically creating more and more clones. Fuck, when did "bling, bling" become a word? And why am I using it?

My God, now that we have taken a look into the corporate and entertainment worlds, there is also the world of education. Everyone is being taught the exact same crap, by the exact same un-motivated teachers. Sure, teachers come out of university motivated, but in time their initial motivation is eroded to the point where just like everyone else they are simply (and sadly) going through the motions. There is very little original thought out there. Just like the regular at the bar who spews back the crap he read in the paper, our children are being taught to spew back the stuff they read in their text books or from their research to show that they know the facts. Rarely are we being asked to form and voice our own opinions or interpretations of this material (just like in the workplace, young people who think critically and go against the grain are considered to be "troublemakers"). There is no reward for doing that anyway. Our educational systems have become factories just to get as many kids out into the corporate and work worlds as possible – to fill our needs to produce and consume, so that our system can continue in future – the rich can prosper and everyone else, well they can serve. Harsh isn't it? Prove to me otherwise if you don't think it is true. Education, though necessary, does not teach original thought. Sure, it is important to know the basics in every aspect. Even more so, it is important

*Penned By: The Seed & German Seed*

to be well rounded in all areas of study. But I believe we need to encourage, nurture and reward our youth by letting them first of all select or define and then pursue their strengths, whatever those may be. We must let them run wild, discover and create. Who the fuck cares if the wheel has been invented? Don't crush the hope of doing it better. Let our youth re-invent it! Maybe we got it wrong the first time around. And I say this to you educators out there, who the fuck cares if Johnny is good at one subject, don't punish him for that, because there is probably something out there Johnny may be phenomenal at. Perhaps even better than everyone else and if you are holding him back at something he will never get the chance to be good at it. All at the expense of his passion. Fuck, then "Shame On You!" It is your job to help him find his passion, not to hold him back with the rest of the sheep.

As for religion. What is it? I have to be careful here, maybe I will refrain from swearing in this paragraph. What purpose does religion hold in our society? Isn't it based upon living good, kind and caring lives and preaches treating people with love and respect. I am not going to get into specific religions here. I don't want to be damned or to have to go to hell anymore than our religious communities already have ordered. Here is my simple formula for how religion would work best: love and care for your family, friends and the people closest to you in your life – fully. Make sure you encourage, nurture and care for these individuals, regardless of the circumstances. Show respect for all living creatures and take time for children and small animals. As for everyone else, regardless of race, sexuality and gender, always treat them with kindness and acceptance. Treat them as you would like to be treated. "Do not judge." It is that simple, treat others well.

Now what religion has us believe is that if we do not attend mass or unconditionally accept the beliefs of one particular religion, we are likely going to burn in hell. Sadly, most religions do not accept others beliefs, in fact they denounce, they judge. Although religions theoretically preach love and tolerance, those individuals who interpret them teach hatred and fear. Some teach that it is "God's will" to blow yourself up and as many innocent bystanders around you as possible. How fucking perverted and sick is that? Some religions teach that if you don't repent your sins before judgment day, you face a life of eternal damnation.

Oh wait, you're dead. Oh well. Hell, every war in the history of mankind has had some sort of religious undertones. So the point is: how can one religion be right to the point of all other religions being wrong? Which god is right? Is it the one that allows us to super-size everything and to consume? I don't know. What is the message? I sure don't feel love when it comes to religion. I feel anger and resentment. I feel bitterness and hate. Should the heads of religion be fondling young boys, but yet at the same time be denouncing same sex relationships? Man, I feel like swearing. In my estimation, if you cannot come up with your own beliefs and sense of what is right or wrong for you in your life (please treat others kindly) then you are definitely nothing more than a weak sheep. Following the rest of the damn flock. Being a good Christian, Buddhist, Muslim or Hindu has nothing to do with how often you've read a given book (except for this one) or how many times you've prayed on a given day. What is much more important is how you conduct your life, how you treat your fellow human beings.

Though the message of organized religion may, on the surface, be a good one, when you break it down to its simplest form, it is really just a major corporation at work. And it costs a lot to get God's message out there, doesn't it? Once again, you have become a clone or a sheep. The mass or "popular" religion of today is to me only for the weak, the masses, which desperately need something or someone to follow. Well, that is of course only as long as you can chip in 10% or more of your hard-earned dollars. If you can't do that, then you're not good enough. Could you please find another religion? All I am saying is just be good to one another. If the church, whichever church you've chosen, gives that to you, great. But don't denounce the beliefs of others. As I have mentioned before, I am already going to hell. Maybe even or probably just because I don't belong to an organized religion. I am ok with that. There are simply a few things that I don't want to see in hell and feel that now would be an appropriate time to put in my requests. For instance, please no polyester in hell. It is going to be hot and it doesn't breathe. Also, while I am making requests, no yard work or gardening. Hell should simply consist of the party, the after effects of the party and recovering for the next party. That is it. Heaven should have all the cleaning, yard work and unnatural fabrics. I want hell to be full of "exceptions"

*Penned By: The Seed & German Seed*

and heaven to be full of clones. Oh yeah, while I am at it, please no Ku Klux Klan or white supremacist groups in hell. They should have their own purgatory, where they can play lawn darts with Hitler. Just keep them away from hell. They are just fucking annoying and frankly boring. If you hated others so much, why did you make them work for you to begin with? The plan sort of backfired, didn't it?

No area illustrates what is wrong with society more than that of the sporting world. Not too long ago, people played sports for the love of the game, for community pride, for entertainment and simply to get laid. There was a pureness to it. Nowhere was creativity more prevalent. We all loved to see the spectacular plays. We watched in disbelief the almost unfathomable plays that the Gretzky's and Jordan's of this world dazzled us with. Then something happened: the corporate world realized that this was big business and the sheep of our society would pay top dollar to see these freaks of nature perform. This led to rapid expansion. Massive stadiums. Huge television contracts and escalating salaries. Corporations were successful at creating another medium to get their message of consumption out to the masses and the athletes and leagues have gone right along with it. Players, now even the marginal ones, are making what a lot of us could only dream of making in our lifetimes. In one year. No longer can the middle class afford to go to the games. Like so much else, it has become accessible only to the rich. The problem is we still support it. We have been told we need it. So we crave it. We have bought into the whole scam. Fuck – we even finance and build the stadiums for the rich owners, and subsidize the teams with lotteries and such, because we are told that our cities will not be world class if we lose our beloved teams. Isn't it nice having a gun held against your head? As for the athletes, they are all now the same player over and over again. Sure some have greater physical skills, that is a given, but now that business has gotten control of our games, creativity is no longer rewarded and at a young age instead of being encouraged to play for fun, systems are being put in place so that one day the athlete, if he is a superior physical specimen, can be ready for the big bucks ahead. Coaches, parents and society are to blame for this. Let the kids have fun. If you do, the games will improve and the entertainment we crave will come back. By

*Seed's Sketchy Relationship Theories - A Guide to the Perils of Dating*

the way, in my estimation the sporting bubble has to burst some time, it can't keep escalating. People are not that stupid.

Relationships. What can I say? Unfortunately it is a by-product of all of that has been mentioned above. We are being mass educated, to act and live as we have been told. We all live the same boring, unfulfilling career-oriented lives and our spirituality, well, what can I say? We are brought up and brainwashed to believe that there is only one way that society will accept you and that is if you follow the formula. The path that our ancestors mapped out for us. Fuck, they tested the waters and found the best and most effective way. In other words, the path of least resistance. We are all supposed to have 2.2 children, drive mini-vans, buy into "freedom 55" or whatever, and eventually die and leave what we have left to our families so they can do it all over again until the end of time. Hopefully that is a long way off. How fucking boring and wrong. Maybe not wrong for everyone. What am I saying? Do what is right for you. Just don't let someone else decide it for you. We all have a responsibility to ourselves to live life to the fullest. If you don't want to be in the family business, don't do it. You will regret it and fuck, who wants to die full of regrets? As for your relationships, the book lays out how it is. Now your challenge is to find out how it is for you. If you don't agree with what I have said that is fine. As long as you have chosen your path for the right reasons. I am in favor of changing how it is. In fact, it is our responsibility to do so, if we want a better world. That is if we want to have a chance. So instead of going down the same fucking path as everyone else before us, live your own life. If you're gay, be gay and don't let anyone tell you what is right for you. Once you have found out who you are and are able to live in your own skin, then and only then can you share your life with someone else. Take the good of the book and use it. Wait to get married. Find out who you are first and when you do find yourself with the love of your life, put them first and communicate. We are all wired differently. Don't assume we know what each other is thinking. Hell, if your mate is doing things and living the same way as you, putting you first, fuck - you guys are unstoppable. You are living the good life, my friend. Hey, before I cracked down hard on religion. I have to give religion props for one thing (ok, amongst other things) they have gotten right and that is this: "Till Death do us part". That is the way it is meant to be, if you have found the person of your dreams and you truly love them. Do not use the term love frivolously. When you find your true love, work on it, grow with him or her and stay with them. Period. The problem with religion is they put too many conditions on this and love is not supposed to have conditions. At least not true love.

So ultimately my friends, the few who control our fortunes – the educators, the employers, the institutions, the entertainers and our predecessors have all done an exceptional job here. They have cloned us. Now do you see why I started talking about cloning? It is not a new thing, sure the applications are different now, but we are all becoming the same person. Aren't we? Fuck – recently I visited Europe for the first time. Fantastic! But the borders have come down and in a lot of ways that is great, but one thing that you can already see is that this freedom of travel and of economies is stripping away identity. We are all becoming the same. Fuck, Europeans, look at what we have done in North America. Every city is the same city. Every mall is the same mall. Please, I beg you, don't follow us. Unfortunately, I see it happening. What the fuck is a fast food restaurant doing next to a cathedral in Italy? Is that progress? We are all now sheep and we have been taught that consumption in every aspect of our lives is good. We all want more, more, more, more, more and more. Do we need it? Hell no! Is it good to want some riches and to live a life with some luxury? Yes. But there has to be a point of excess where we all can say: "I am Ok – I don't need anymore to be happy." Does a baseball player need 25 million a year? I am very serious about this point, to the extent that when this publication and any other that I produce reaches a point where it has provided enough, I will put a percentage of the resulting proceeds towards a worthy cause. As a society, we need to stop buying into the propaganda. We need to go back to a simpler way of life. Can we do it? Frankly I don't know. Things are pretty fucked up in the world. What I do know is that we can all do our small parts and take care of the people and things around us that matter.

I hope you have read this with an open mind and heart. Most important, I would like to thank you for your time. I hope you realize that the message that I am trying to get out there is one of honesty, integrity and love and that it is a positive one. I love people, I love relationships, but having said that, I am selective

*Seed's Sketchy Relationship Theories - A Guide to the Perils of Dating*

in my use of the word. It is too powerful and its meaning is too life altering. I hope you are the same way. In conclusion, well not quite in conclusion of course, there are several chapters which follow and they will explain a bit about me, share some gravy with you, give some much deserved acknowledgements and of course, some gentle encouragement for you to consume some of our quality merchandise.

Once again in conclusion, I would like to issue you a challenge. And that challenge is this: please, please, please be.

*Penned By: The Seed & German Seed*

# "THE EXCEPTION!!!"

\*\*\*\*\*\*\*\*\*\*\*

"When You Love, Nurture and Support
When You Find Yourself No Longer Coming First
You Will Find Something Strange Happening
Your Needs Will Have Been Met
You Can Stop Looking
In Fact You Will Have Stopped Looking Long Ago
Because In Fact My Friend
Something Magical Has Occurred
You Have Become Something Special
You Are The Exception
You Are A Leader
You Are An Original
And

Love Is Enough!!!!!"

-the seed.

\*\*\*\*\*\*\*\*\*\*\*

# CHAPTER 44
# Seed's Wonderful Magnificent Brilliant Succulent Tasty Boutique
# www.seedenterprises.com

*"For some reason
The fluffy pillows of bed,
Are actually just mental stimulants
Which start the wheels turning".*

-the seed.

*Penned By: The Seed & German Seed*

**Merchandise:**

Welcome!

We are so glad you have arrived. If in any way we can be of assistance, please let us know. Please ask. Look at all of this quality stuff. Who doesn't need quality stuff? The store is under construction so be patient. Can you feel the excitement building? Don't go home empty handed now.

Here are some of the exciting products that you will be able to buy:

*Seed's Sketchy Relationship Theories - A Guide to the Perils of Dating*

**Snow Shakers - Everyone needs a snow shaker!!!!**

(Seedville, Johnny and Chastity)

**Board or Interactive Computer Game - "Next Exit Bliss"**

You will enjoy hours upon hours of entertainment trying to wind your way through the streets of Seedville in an attempt to reach your destination Bliss. Every Johnny and Chastity will be born in Seedville General Hospital and jump straight into the Gene Pool to determine their pecking order in life. The one who makes there way over the hurdles and past the obstacles the smoothest will be the eventual winner. Hold on it will be a wicked ride!!!

**T-Shirts**

Look at the fantastic slogans. The first designs will be released soon. We don't think you will need any other shirts. Do you? Slap on one of these shirts and your lonely nights may come to an end.

- (Johnny)
- (Chastity)
- (Who's Harry?)
- (Schmetterling)
- (Attention Whore)
- (Seed)
- ("I'm German Seed")
- ( www.seedenterprises.com )
- (Gravy)

**Coffee Mugs, Hats, Beer Glasses, Frisbees, Greeting Cards, Calendars, Golf Balls & Paraphernalia, Merit Badges & Greeting Cards.**

That is just a small list of the products that the factory is in the process of producing. You won't need to shop anywhere else for you quality stuff. No seriously you won't. No more fighting traffic. Just sit back relax, enjoy and buy!!!

### Condoms

Of course we are going to offer condoms.

### Diapers

Congratulations on your new baby. We know you planned it right? Your little Johnny or Chastity will look smashing in our hot line of diapers. We hope to see your little angels on the fashion runways soon.

### Bobble Heads - Not just for athletes any more.

Seed, Johnny & Chastity and Attention Whore.

### Soundtracks -

We are working on producing some kicking compilation disks for your enjoyment. Watch for them soon.

### The Seed Superhero Comic Book -

A whole action series is being developed. Watch for a new hero soon. We just need to shake the creator a bit harder so the plot lines will start falling out of his head.

### Pudding - (Food & Beverage Department)

Seed's Line of "The Proof is In The Pudding", Pudding.

Watch also for Seed's Superior Gin to be released soon. Who doesn't love gin.

### Books:

This Seed fellow is not going to be a one hit wonder. He has thoughts and opinions on a lot of things and he wants to share them with you. Watch for some of these exciting books in the near future. We know you will enjoy!!! There is something for everyone.

*Seed's Sketchy Relationship Theories - A Guide to the Perils of Dating*

**1. Inside Seed's Head**    In Progress

(A Look @ The Past Few Years In The Life of Seed)

**2. Seed's Identity Tour**    In Progress

(A Fun Roller Coaster Ride. Documenting Seed & His Friend Dave's Journey around Europe).

**3. Ask Seed The Letters**    In Progress

(A Collection of The Ask Seed Letters)

**4. Trish**    In Progress

(A personal look at love)

**5. Letters to The Editor**

(Letters which Seed wrote to the Editor of major papers only never to send)

**6. Put Down The Fork**

(An Exercise & Diet Book)

### 7. Seedisms                    In Progress

(A Book of Quotes and Original Photography)

### 8. Cook Book & A List of Libations

(A fun and light hearted look of some of Seed's favorite meals & drinks. Meals suited for Trailer Park Living all the way to The Penthouse)

### 9. Karma

(A screenplay about you guessed it Karma. Actually much more than that it starts out as a comedy and turns into a suspenseful murder mystery).

### 10. Poutine

(Personal anecdotes taking from the vault of Seed's Life)

### 11. Seed's Top 100 Images

Original Photography (sometimes altered) as seen through the eyes of The Seed Enterprise Entourage).

*Seed's Sketchy Relationship Theories - A Guide to the Perils of Dating*

Watch for the Upcoming Movies and Television Series, Titles To Be Announced!!!!! (Perhaps Seed's Sketchy Relationship Theories).

You Are Very Welcome. We Hope To See You Again Soon!!!

# CHAPTER 45
# Who Is Seed............?

*"It is My Responsibility to be Amazing!!"*

-the seed.

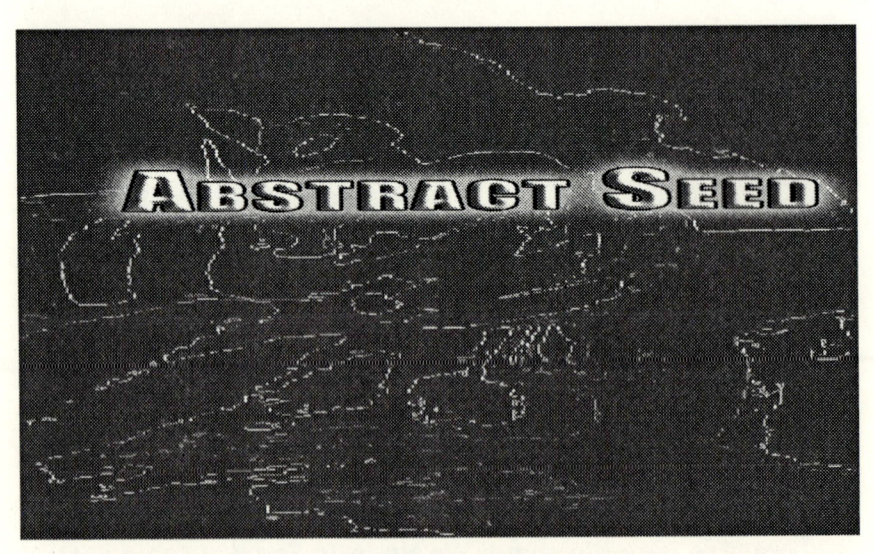

![Abstract Seed]

To begin with, Seed is a trailblazer. If you have noticed, not only has he included "Outtakes" and a bonus chapter called "Gravy", but he has introduced himself several chapters before the end of the book instead of on the back cover. What was he thinking? Let us just say that Seed is so full of depth that he felt it would be appropriate to give some insight and reveal some information about himself. Use this insight wisely. He may ask for it back.

Seed is a lot like James Bond. No one man can personify the true depth of Seed. In a way Seed, is the Exception. He does not march to the same drum as the masses. He charts his own course, makes his own mistakes and is solely responsible for his successes. Well, maybe not solely, he has surrounded himself with some of the best people on the planet and loves and cherishes each friend and interaction dearly. Seed is a simple, yet very complicated man. Actually, he is more than one man he represents the plight of modern man.

He was born in the heartlands of North America, on the West Coast and in the major cities of our nations. He was the youngest of seven and an only child to a single mother at the same time. He was born in the sixties, seventies and even the eighties. He has studied Public Administration on the prairies, History on the West Coast and Law in Munich, Germany. (He just recently found out that he passed his Law exams in Germany).

He was given a unisex name which gave him two options: be witty or get beat up. So he chose to be witty. He did not excel at school, but he did ok and it came to him with great ease. He excelled at sports, yet unfortunately all sports, so he never became focused on any one in particular.

As far as the opposite sex was concerned, he was not stellar in high school, though quite popular he was not the best looking during the early years of his young life. He was a bit of a late bloomer, so he was the guy who got to be friends with a lot of hot girls. However, while he pined, the other guys were getting all of the action. Nonetheless, during this formative period he was watching and observing, he was learning not only how to hang with the guys and cultivate popularity. He was also learning what made the girls tick, especially the attractive ones – and all girls in general. It was during this time he learned how to interact with all different kinds of people, something that bodes well for the future for Seed. His athletic prowess and his wits, charm and developing looks started to help him increase his popularity and quite quickly he began to learn that he was or did not fit in any particular group

*Penned By: The Seed & German Seed*

but was truly an individual who could interact well with all types of people. A skill that is truly rare in the world.

After his High School years, he pursued athletic rather than academic interests. And through this process, he developed his body and increased his exposure because just as in school, in college the athletes were adored. However, unlike most other athletes he did not travel in a pack. Though he was definitely a leader, he had honed many interests and was becoming quite popular. His ability to talk and hold a conversation and not just a beer were opening a lot of intimate doors for him. He also had learned how to be brutally honest with those whom he came in contact with. There was no misleading or telling people what they wanted to hear just so he could get in their pants. Somehow he learned that honesty and good conversation was all you needed to get into someone's pants. Playing games, frankly, is for the followers and the lost souls of society. Seed also learned that the use of the word "Love" is valuable and important and therefore must be applied sparingly.

After a few years, Seed took his athletic endeavors on to University, where by now he had developed many aspects of his personality. He was definitely an individual who had become a very well rounded desirable person. There was rarely a lonely night or weekend for Seed. The others on his athletic teams were constantly trying to figure out how he was doing it and in fact a large portion of his friends were actually tracking his endeavors. The thing they did not realize was that there is no secret. Life is just about treating others well, sharing the occasional smile and having some ambition.

Seed has worked as a dishwasher, gardener, waiter, bartender, hotel manager, bartender, sales representative, gas jockey, coach, bartender, commercial fisherman, an insurance agent, bartender, a hand model, a hair model, a landscaper, a helper monkey, a bartender, a construction worker, a geological core sample tester and a bartender just to name a few. And now he is an Author!!!

He has traveled to at least 17 other countries ranging from Andorra to Panama. He has been a Best Man at least 6 times and a

*Seed's Sketchy Relationship Theories - A Guide to the Perils of Dating*

pallbearer 3 times. He can speak 5 languages, one of which is his own that very few can follow. Did I mention that he is half blind?

**COULD THIS BE A SEED SIGHTING?**

**Hey you may even be Seed................**

# CHAPTER 46
# Gravy

*"Corn Starch, Salt, Caramel, Wheat Starch, Soya Flour, Hydrolyzed Soya, Corn Protein, Torula Yeast, Carrot Powder and Onion Powder."*

*-Bisto (Brown Gravy)*

Now there we have it. The completion of Seeds first book. Yes I said first book. I know that must be hard to imagine. I am sure you are all thinking "Hey this Seed guy what a brilliant writer, he must have won numerous awards. Maybe even a Pulitzer". Well my friends, as hard as it is to believe, this is my first effort. And I hope you feel fortunate to have experienced it. I very much enjoyed going into every crevice of my brain to come up with the valuable information that I have given you in this my first book. Ok, so I did not give it to you. There was a cost, my knowledge, is not free you know. This may have cost you, I don't know $19.95 but every penny was well worth it. I am sure you laughed or at least guffawed at certain parts and at others, disagreed and even got angry at my opinions, but at the end of the day I am hoping and I am pretty sure you spent a lot of time nodding your heads in at least some sort of semi-agreement. And the one thing that I do hope and encourage is that all of the readers are the "exceptions" to the rules and are living prosperous, fulfilling loving lives. I sincerely mean that. Like I said, I am a big fan of relationships and it is a goal of mine to contribute to the straightening out of this messed-up world. At least as much as each of us can do individually. I wrestled with the idea of sharing personal information with you about my life, I decided it was necessary if I was to illustrate why I am so passionate about this subject matter, fuck, reality is painful.

Having said that, I have thus far lived an absolutely remarkable life. It has been challenging, but I hope I have illustrated to you that a positive attitude can lead to some great accomplishment. Hey if you disagree, that is ok, how many of you have written a book? Oh yeah, about writing books, I do have 3 other projects on the go right now. One of them is called "Seed's Identity Tour" which is a mostly lighthearted look at the events and debauchery that took place on a recent one month trip to Europe. I must say that I have read bits of it and it is quite entertaining. Yes, that is right I have read parts of it. You may be thinking, but you wrote it, why would reading it be anything but fascinating to you? Well my friends, thoughts are coming and going so fast that I do not recall most of the things that I think about. At least not in the original form. I don't have Alzheimer's but I am for the most part original and feel that most things and primarily good comedy is really, an "in the moment" sort of thing. So when I wrote the book most things were "in the moment" and when I read them, just like you, it is for the first time and frankly I surprised myself. Oh yeah, the other project is pretty intense and I highly recommend it. It is the story of my life, basically for the year 2003, but it is much more in-depth than that. It looks at a lot of different aspects in Seed's life and it is tentatively called "Inside Seed's Head". It will explain a lot about who I am and it probably will even make some of you cry. Really it will. Expect it some time in 2004. Actually, expect all of these projects in 2004. The third project is a very personal one, it is simply called "Trish" and it is the story of the "Love of My Life" that I have mentioned throughout this book. I promise a lot of passion, maybe even some sex and who knows perhaps even a car chase. Actually, when you go back to the "Stuff" chapter you will note that a lot of books are actually in progress, so I can assure you Seed & Seed Enterprises will be offering you a wide variety of enlightening and entertaining books in the not too distant future. Hey, if you show me a proof of purchase or send a legitimate question to **Ask Seed?** at the *www.seedenterprises.com* web site, we will give you a discount on the purchase of any of these three books. Hell, if you buy a product from the boutique we will also extend a discount on the purchase of a book.

So what was I talking to you about? Oh, I remember you are probably wondering why this section is called Gravy. Well it is simple my friends. If you have French Fries: what makes it a bit better? If you have mashed potatoes, what completes the picture? Turkey: what dresses it up a bit? Do you see where I am going with this, I think I already gave you the answer. That is right it is gravy. Now unlike all other authors before me Seed would like it if when he passes away, on his tombstone reads something like this: "Seed always added a little more to everyone's life, to put it simply Seed was the Gravy of life". So basically, Seed would like to be thought of as the tasty, succulent gravy of life. A great enhancer. I hope you have no problem with that. I am sure you will eventually get used to the thought. So going with the Gravy theme, Seed has decided to give you, our cherished reader a bit more. Sure, you may have thought the book was done a long time ago, maybe even a hundred pages ago. But I will not let that discourage me, so here are some general observations that I have decided to include, sort of as a bonus track and unlike the musical clones out there who release a greatest hits record and include the one bonus track to make you have to buy it. I am giving you this juicy, gooey, good gravy on my first effort. By the way, a lot of these thoughts are the things that were occupying my mind while I was in the process of writing this book. If I would have passed them onto you sooner I would have been finished the book a long time ago. So without any further ado here we go with some tasty gravy....

### The Fear of Success

The other day I was finding myself becoming a bit depressed as the book project is winding down. Why this depression you may ask? You see I have over the last several months asked the opinions of a lot of different individuals on the contents of the work. The results have actually been quite overwhelming. It has not mattered whether the individuals I talked to were friends, acquaintances or strangers. It did not matter whether they were professional or blue collar. After I let them read or I read to them little snippets of the book, the response has been consistent. In fact, there has always been laughter and head nodding. It is as if German Seed and I have hit some buttons with our material. This one particular individual I met with, who happens to be in the publishing industry, after having read several chapters, said to me: "You have a real talent here. I wish I had your talent. You are on to something big". Now you may wonder why that would cause some depression. It is quite simple: it sounds like we have no choice but to succeed. And frankly, that scares me.

I am in no way looking for negative responses, since they could be devastating. But I was looking for something to bring us back down to earth. I decided to take the book out for one more opinion. On the corner where I live is this blind panhandler named Pepe, who hates everything in the world. I figured I would get his opinion. I was sure it would be negative and because of the source I would be able to discount it quickly and get back to the business of succeeding. A small point here, the book is not in braille, so as for his response, well, it should be a good one. On this particular day I approached Pepe. He seemed to be in a rather foul mood. I asked him if he could give me an opinion on my book. He took it into his hands. He carefully went over the pages, gently caressing them and after several minutes he stopped. Next came some unbearable silence. I was eagerly awaiting his tirade that was sure to be ensuing. It had to be. After several more minutes, Pepe finally looked up to me with his blind eyes. Ok, he looked up in my general direction and what he said next stunned me. He softly said: "I really like the paper". That was it. I guess we are doomed to success.

While we are speaking about paper, this whole experience reminded me of the use of paper. I used to have a roommate who loved the use of the sticky note. For this example, we will just say that his name is Kev. While I was living with Kev, he would use these annoying little notes every chance he could. I would leave a cupboard door open and I would find a "Sticky Note". I would leave the toilet seat up. What would I find? A "Sticky Note". If I drank some of his milk, it was inevitable: "Sticky Note". My God, even if I would accidentally sleep with his girlfriend. You guessed it: "Sticky Note". As annoying as this was, there was one set of circumstances where I could never quite understand the use of the sticky note. You see while Kev and I were roomies I was basically living with my girlfriend. There would be times when I would not come home for a week at a time. Now you see I have a cat and she is a bit older, so periodically she would drag the odd deposit from her litter box with her. The funny thing is on occasion I would come home and notice something on the floor. That's right. Another "Sticky Note". So curious, I would pick them up and on them it would say "Cat Shit" with an arrow. The reason I find this funny is that my roomie Kev would rather leave a note, than take the three and a half seconds to clean it up. I guess he liked living in shit.

When I asked my cat about it, she told me that Kev had some bigger problems. Apparently my cat was testing him. She was trying to drive him nuts. She told me that she would put little baggies together filled with cat nip and hang outside of his room. One day she gave him a little sample for free. A couple of days later, sure enough, he was back for more. The deal was a "Little Tuna" for a "Little Nip". It became a daily thing. My cat was becoming one "Fat Cat". When Kev eventually moved out he was up to about 4 baggies a day. I hope the rehab is a success. As for the success of Seed. It is inevitable

## Am I Crazy?

No definitely not. "What's That". "Go Away". "Get Out Of My Head".

Is it alright if I change my answer? If it is. "Maybe".

## Am I even Funny?

There is absolutely no doubt.

*Seed's Sketchy Relationship Theories - A Guide to the Perils of Dating*

## The Pussification of The World the Role of Daytime Talk Shows, The Auto Industry & The Coffee Industry.

"HERE KITTY KITTY"

What the hell is wrong with being a man? Over the last 40 years or so it has almost been a crime to be male. We have been back peddling. Fuck – issues like equality and divorce have sent us into a downward spiral where more and more of us have been losing our balls on a regular basis. Now I know this will be upsetting to a lot of people, but it is a woman's world out there. Fuck - they use their looks to attract us and capture us and once they have us, they have told us that it is our responsibility to take care of them and to give them shelter, food, impregnate them and protect them from the outside world. We have just gone along and done this, but it gets worse. A few women have decided along the way that as much as they want children, they also don't want to leave society and their careers and would really prefer if someone else raised their children. So it is back to work, while the nanny or grandpa or grandma raises the kids (selfish bitches and believe me I know, this one it is a little too close to the heart for me). I know what you may be saying now: "We need 2 incomes to earn a living." Or: "Raising a family is an expensive proposition." Well I am sure that it is, so here are the straight goods. If you can't stay home and raise your kids during the all-important formative years when a mother's nurturing is crucial. Here's the thing: don't have the kid. It is not fair to the kid, to your husband and lastly to yourself. Oh yeah, did I say to the KID. The world already has a population of over six billion. The population boom has to slow down to ensure the survival of the human race. So I beg you not to

*Penned By: The Seed & German Seed*

have anymore children for selfish reasons. The kids of today are already going to have to clean up the mess that we have created for them. Be fair.

Furthermore, this whole goddamn equality debate has fucked up a lot of things. As long as women are the only ones capable of giving birth then there is no such thing as equality between men and women. Are there not Men's and Women's sporting events? We generally have different issues. So women, I know this is a futile plea. You have a couple of choices. You may have a career or you may raise a family. Just don't choose to do both at the same time and if you decide to raise a family and stay at home, then refrain from this selfish bitching about how you work hard all day and deserve a pay check from your husband. Remember, we know Mommy has been lying to us. We survived making our own dinners before you came into the picture and we would survive without you. We are just asking for you to do your part to help out the team. As I write this I feel tremendous despair. Do you remember my friends Wayne and Fiona? I told you that they were having a child, I think somehow in the copy that I give to them, this as well as a few other sections will be omitted, since I do cherish their friendship and Fiona may cut of my b_lls if Wayne follows this advice. Remember kids, that is you "Wayne and Fiona", you guys are the exception here and Wayne should likely do everything. I am not saying this because I fear Fiona more than Wayne. I am just saying it because, sorry to say this Wayne, but Fiona got yours a long time ago. If you understand what I am saying here? Do you find it funny that I have no problem saying the word fuck, but for some strange reason I could not type "b_lls"; what the hell does that say about me?

Back to what I was saying before I was so rudely interrupted by my brain. Do you think he needs the stress of being the sole breadwinner and at the same time needs to hear you bitch about how hard your day is? And another thing, if you are going to be the caregiver, I know this will piss off a lot of people, but accept your fucking role. It should be you getting up to change the baby, it should be you getting up to feed the baby – during the work week this is your responsibility. Your man, if he still is one, has other things to worry about. He needs to be fresh to perform his job to the best of his abilities so he can get the promotions and be able to support his family. Trust me. This is how it should be. I know a lot of people just want to bring babies into this world, what I am suggesting here is, that if you cannot afford to raise them properly, wait, plan for it. You, the kid, your husband and society will thank you for it.

Also worth noting is that a by-product of the whole feminist movement has been to change the scope of the job market. It has made it increasingly difficult for guys to land what used to be predominately male jobs. I am not saying this is necessarily a bad thing, but what I am saying is that unless you are going to focus on your career there is really no equality. Could you imagine if George Bush had to go on maternity leave right now? Who would protect us from the evil-doers of the world? Oprah??? (I think it is very imperative at this time to mention that I think Oprah is actually a very brilliant, kind compassionate and caring human being. As for her protecting us from the worlds evil- doers I believe she would do a significantly better job than the aformentioned president).

Which brings us to the whole issue of Daytime Television. I know the television industry will not listen to my suggestion, but could you guys please stop airing shit during the day? You are fucking up the world. I will not name the show and I am pretty embarrassed to admit that I saw it. I am embarrassed that I even actually had my TV on during the daytime. I swear it was the one and only time that it will ever happen. Ok, on this one particular show some guy (I think his name was "Fatty") was the guest. In this episode, the host showed how "Fatty", who weighed around 390 lbs, went on some radical diet. I think the only thing he was allowed to eat was pocket lint and tree bark or something like that, and was assigned a workout schedule. Somehow this fat bastard was able to drop 210 lbs down to 180 lbs. Now that is fantastic and quite an accomplishment. He should be proud of himself. He should also be proud of the fact that due to his Lard, Mayonnaise and Gravy diet he was able to reach the magic mark of 390lbs in the first place. I personally think getting that obese is far more of an accomplishment than losing the weight. Come on now, think about it: the tricks and lies you would have to tell yourself to gain that type of weight. When did you throw away all the mirrors? Or did you maybe just wallpaper or paint over the mirrors? You must have been telling yourself things like this: "I know that my waist

*Penned By: The Seed & German Seed*

is now 35 inches, but there are these pants that I really like which only come with a 70 inch waste, so I hope you don't mind if I eat out of a fucking trough." You know I think we in this society have an obligation to tell people that they are obese. Except for the 2 or 5 % of you that have a real excuse, for the rest of you there is a simple solution: "PUT DOWN THE FORK". Aren't you getting tired of literally sitting around the house? Or, being fast without the S and having racing stripes on your cutlery? Being obese is not a skill. Actually who am I kidding, maybe it is, not dropping dead from obesity might actually be a great skill.

Back to Fatty, now that he has lost all of that weight, it is a shame that his parents gave him that ridiculous name to begin with. It doesn't suit him anymore. Well anyways, the host of this daytime talk show, if you can believe this, gave him a Porsche to congratulate him for his excellent accomplishment. Can I vomit any more violently than I did when I saw this? Only in America would we reward this type of abusive behavior. So host, you know who you are, if you are reading this, I can't possibly lose 210 lbs because that is 50 lbs more than I weigh. But I am going to try to drop down to, I don't know my birth weight, that is right, 7 lbs 4 ounces and if I succeed I want a house. I think that would only be fair.

While I am at it, the car industry. Cars used to have cool names. Manly names like Matador, Corvette, Nova and so on and so on. Now what do we have? Camry, Previa, Loopy, Grumpy, Sleepy to name just a few. What the hell is going on? You used to sound like you wanted to get somewhere when you got behind the wheel of your car. Now it sounds like, if you can get your fat lazy ass off of the couch long enough to stop watching some program about which stupid moron is the real father of some attention whore who dropped the word attention from her description, to go drive down in your Solara to the coffee shop to order a non-fat, triple caffeinated, mocha enhanced, Hungarian bull milk fortified triple shot extra whipped concoction, you might be clueing into what has gone wrong in the world. Wasn't it much simpler to jump into your Impala drive down to the coffee shop and have a coffee…?

Remember when I have succeeded in reaching my birth weight, I want my house and in a good city. Vancouver, New York, San Francisco or something like that.

## The Politics involved currently in the World of same sex marriages.

This is how fucked up the world is right now. We are all so fucking politically correct and have an opinion on the world of same sex relationships and whether or not same sex marriages are a morally correct thing to allow. First off, who the fuck cares? The whole institution of marriage is failing anyway and if you have read carefully you would realize that society and the world has played a big part and is greatly responsible for this fact. There are opinions on this topic from every facet of society; from the church, to the state to the corporate world and so on. I think we are entirely missing the point here. As for same sex relationships, the only people it should matter to in the first place are the people involved in the relationship. Get out of your fucking bubbles people! It is not a disease nor has it anything to do with social, cultural or upbringing thing. It is just the way a portion of the population is wired and the oppression needs to come to an end. I know that is unlikely to happen in the backward-thinking towns of Butt Fuck (insert state name here). Wow, I think that was an unintentional play on words there. Come on people, if two people are in love, regardless of gender, that is a beautiful thing. Hell, I think I may have just hurt book sales in Butt Fuck, wait a minute, probably not because Butt Fuck still has book burnings so at least a couple of copies will get sold in each town that resembles it. In my estimation that is at least 10 anally-retentive towns in each of the 50 states and if they each purchase the 10 or so books necessary for a good book burning in my estimation that means improved sales. Hell, I must thank the people of these communities for purchasing 5000 copies of my book in protest. It is just too bad I never had a chance to sign them before you burnt them.

Oh, by the way, I thought I would help you out here a bit. I did some research into what is necessary for a good book burning and it came to my attention that it will take at least 5 times that many books to sustain a good fire to make it worth while for the town folk to get into their Matadors to drive into town for the burning. So thank you for improving the count to 25,000 copies! Back to same sex marriages, it is nobody's business what people do in their own bedrooms regardless of what anyone else thinks and relationships and love are tough enough without the intolerant opinions of homophobic asses who think differently.

After all, I think the same sex world is likely making a mistake with the marriage thing anyway and the divorce rate will be substantially higher until they get a handle on what needs to be accepted in their own society. It is true that if you are in a long term relationship, a lot of the legal and social benefits of marriage as well as being recognized by the rest of society is important, but until or shall I say unless you can keep it in your pants and remain monogamous, then what the fuck do you want to get married for? So, my gay friends, the same rules apply for you as in the straight world. Not until you have spent significant amount of time together should you even consider getting married. You will thank me if you do. If you do spend this time together and can honestly say that your search has stopped, then go for it! Be happy but make sure you have waited. Divorce is ugly and it won't be any different in the Gay World.

Let us just all just live in peace without worrying about one another's sexual orientation. So what if your buddy is gay. It is not a reflection on you and only becomes one if you make it that way. Fuck your gay friend has had a hard enough time dealing with oppression, acceptance and fashion issues, to have his supposed good friends rag on him for something he has no choice in. Sexual orientation is pre-determined for us. We have no fucking choice. It is not worth the time and anguish to spend thinking about it. You either are gay or not or you are somewhere in-between those are the simple facts. There is no magical cure for it. I know that this may be upsetting to some of you but that just is the way it is. Face it. Accept it. Embrace it. Gay society has enough already to deal with. It is ridden with insecurity, drug and alcohol abuse, and acceptance issues. In fact, it sounds a bit like the straight world. It is trying to find an identity. Leave it be.

At this point I thought I would be doing women and men a public service if I included a list of the ways that you may tell if you are gay or not and for you women out there, if you notice any of these traits in your man, you perhaps will come home one day and find that you actually have two men and they prefer each others company more than yours. So here we go. The list is broken

*Seed's Sketchy Relationship Theories - A Guide to the Perils of Dating*

down into several categories from: "You may be Gay if:" all the way to "You are definitely Gay if:"

## You may be gay if:

- your razor is in the bath tub or shower
- your magazine selection contains Men's Fitness Magazines
- your magazine selection contains a lot of fashion magazines
- you work in retail
- you do regular facials
- you actually go out because you like to dance
- you choose to spend your Weekend nights in predominately gay establishments
- you don't have a lisp but it sounds like you do
- you ever have had sex with another man
- your music collection contains Christina or Justin
- you are still walking when the treadmill at the gym hits a speed of 6 miles per hour

## You are likely gay if:

- you like gay pornography
- you work as a waiter
- your name is Chad, Jeremy or Josh
- you shave any of your body hair
- you have a dick in your mouth
- you have a dick in your ass
- you call your male friends girlfriend

- you call anything fabulous
- you watch day time television, reality television or any show about cooking or decorating
- you watch Will & Grace
- when you are asked if you are gay, you have to think about your answer and you answer in a politically correct way.
- you have a loofah in the shower
- you work at any of the following The Gap, Old Navy, The Banana Republic.
- you think about having sex with other men
- you are obsessed with body image
- your music collection has a lot of house or techno in it
- you know who Margaret Cho is

## You are more than likely gay if:

- you work as a hairdresser
- you like hardcore supposedly straight pornography, the harder it is the gayer you are
- you have more underwear than your girlfriend
- your diet contains any of the following: E, K, G crystal or poppers on a regular basis
- you spend a lot of time dancing with your shirt off
- you choose to go by Stephen, Patrick or Jonathan
- when you are asked if you are gay, you aggressively answer you are straight
- you use the word fabulous
- you have a dick in both hands one in your mouth and one in your butt at the same time

- you prefer to have sex with other men
- you are a guy and you have a boyfriend
- you say that you are gay
- most of your female friends are overweight
- you are far more attractive than your girlfriend
- you have more girlfriends than guy friends
- your wardrobe consists of a lot of shirts that have Old Navy, Gap, Banana Republic or Abercrombie logos on them
- you watch Friends
- you know what a loofah is
- you move to the city and you continue to drive a pick up truck
- you are a male figure skater
- your music collection has any of the following Madonna, Britney, Kylie, Barbara, Celine, Shania or Cher in it.

## You are definitely gay if:

- you are definitely gay if you have ever been involved in a gay bashing.
- you are not the parent of a male figure skater but yet you like watching figure skating

So there you have it, consider that as Seed's public service to help set people straight on the subject. I want to put a disclaimer in at this point. In no way do I look down upon the gay society. I feel what two or three or more people do in the bedroom or any other secluded location is strictly their own business and no one else should care. It is not our place to decide what is right morally or in any other way for other people. That is their choice. Live your own life, make your own choices and let others do the same. And for all of you bleeding hearts out there, who think that sexual activity is destroying the human race. Fuck, go out and have some sex. Maybe you will enjoy it, then you can shut up. It is good to have free speech and I encourage it but please think before you share your opinions. Because you just sound stupid. As for the last little section, it is primarily a piece of comedy, but it does have some truthful elements to it. Ladies, if you are wondering about your guy, it is simple. The more of these traits that you see, the more likely your man at least ventures or thinks about the other team. You can help him confront his issues. It is sort of like this. If he has one of the traits, probably no need to worry. If he has a couple, hmm... maybe. More than 4, he is likely getting his good sex somewhere else. Don't say I didn't warn you.

## Saddam Hussein or is he really Santa

Wow, this book gets to be somewhat topical on the whole current events front. Congratulations to the free world for finally capturing one of the world's evil doers. Namely, Saddam Hussein. He is truly a monster, so the last little bit of commentary was actually not laced with sarcasm. I just hope we can capture some of the evil doers in our own lands, as they may also be imminent threats to our health, safety and well being. I am not talking about our own politicians here or the corporate giants that are running the free world. I mean the real evil doers of society. Back to Saddam, I just wanted to make a bit of an observation here on his capture. I am sure that unless we are living in a hole in the ground, we have all seen some of the riveting photos of Saddam after his capture. First off Saddam, you were in this small hole living like a rat and your only defense for yourself was a revolver. Come on, you are not doing your nickname any justice. What a weak, candy-assed way to get captured. My God, for someone megalomaniacal, you sure went out with a whimper. You could have at least fired the gun or at least waved a glow stick or something at your capturers. Oh this brings me back to the Town of Butt Fuck (insert your state here). I know that after the same sex rant previously, I had lost a lot of your support and it was unlikely that I would be capable of regaining it. I would like to thank my brain and some of my opinions on the maniacal Saddam for bringing some of your support back to me. It is touching that we can be in agreement on some things. Fortunately the 50 or so of you who have lessened your hate towards my writing, will not affect the sales of my book for the book burning. Anyway, I am not sure if any of you would have read this far into a book to begin with, so what am I concerning myself with. I think this might be a bit of reverse red necking, here I am not entirely sure. Oh yeah, please remember the exception rule here. I am sure a lot of lovely, well-read and intelligent exceptions live in all of these communities.

Back to the maniacal one, Saddam. I was just wondering if it is a coincidence that he got captured around Christmas. After all, doesn't he look like a bit of a disheveled Santa Claus and if that is the case, who is going to deliver all of the presents? I know once again, I said that this was timely. And you are thinking fuck I am reading this in July or August. Well I wrote this bit in December 2003. It is just a shame that my publisher could not get it out in time for you to see the time appropriate reference. I am sure however if you use your imagination you will see the humor. In any case, we can be certain of one more thing: Saddam won't be delivering the presents for Christmas 2004 either. Hopefully before the book is published I will be able to give a riveting social commentary on Osama as well. Dare to dream. Wait, I am not quite done. I just want to add – and this is dedicated to all of the beautiful women of the world – if there is one piece advice that you take seriously from this whole book it is this: no matter and I mean no matter what, regardless of the trips, the quality of material in the Burkahs, do not – no matter how much of an attention whore you are and definitely no matter how much bling, bling the Saddam's and the other crazed dictators of the world have to offer – do not date them. It is not going to end well. Wait, it all depends on how much of a money-craving attention whore you are. If you are in the upper echelon of the category, well then date away. We can't stop you anyway. Certainly, it will be very rewarding for you. Wink, wink!!!!!

## How does one brush their teeth
## When the batteries on the electric tooth brush die.

Here is a dilemma I came across the other day. And I am seeking the advice of my readers. You may send your suggestions to my email at **Ask Seed** and the domain ***www.seedentreprises.com*** and while you are at it if you are interested in some honest hard hitting relationship advice you may ask your relationship questions at the same time. I promise to get back to you with an answer that

*Penned By: The Seed & German Seed*

is honest and at least sort of to the point. Only sort of, because it will all depend on whatever other important information is rattling around in my brain at the time I get around to your question. Don't despair if you get some other info, feel fortunate as I am throwing that in for free. Oh yeah, while you are at the website asking the questions and giving me the suggestion on how to fix my problem, make sure you stop in the Seed Merchandise Boutique, and check out (and purchase) some to the fantastic high quality products that we have on sale there. You will not be disappointed. Ok, onto my dilemma, the other morning, I know they are all other mornings technically, by other morning I mean last Tuesday morning when I got up to brush my teeth with one of those new funky battery operated toothbrushes. A scary thing happened, the batteries died and I did not have any replacement ones on hand so I only got part way through the brushing process. You can imagine how frustrating this was. How do I finish the job? So I ended up going out with half brushed teeth, I felt filthy. At least orally filthy, I did shower after all. So I was unable to fully brush my teeth until later that afternoon when I purchased some new batteries. I was just wondering if any of you have ever experienced a similar dilemma before and if you did, what did you do? Could you please enlighten me? And while you are doing that purchase something.

## Some General observations from my life. Not necessarily proud moments but oh well, I thought I would share them with you anyway.

This one night I met this wonderful girl. This was actually my true love and the only reason that I feel compelled to share it with you now, is because unfortunately that relationship has ended and it seems to have turned sour. If we were still together, you would not be receiving this gem, so feel fortunate or hell maybe unfortunate is the correct term. Anyways, as the night progressed there was a fair bit of kissing and dancing and a real connection has been formed. We both realized that we liked each other greatly and at the risk of all future possibilities the night progressed to the inevitable. Now most of the time, I would suggest waiting for another time, but for some reason everything felt right it seemed like we were supposed to be progressing. So just before we entered the bedroom for some bliss, I, in my best B or C grade porn voice gently placed her hand on my mid section

*Seed's Sketchy Relationship Theories - A Guide to the Perils of Dating*

and looked her deep in the eyes and said: "For the next few hours this will be your toy". It must have been true for love her to stay with me after that. Maybe some of the things she did later in the relationship represented some form of payback.

Once again in my illustrious life, I do think I missed my calling. Just before another sexual encounter, in that same infamous voice filled with passion I said: "You know you want it don't you, don't you?!?" Man, I have matured since those quality moments. I really don't know who that guy is, but I am telling you my friends, that if you can say stuff like that and not spend too many nights alone something weird is happening in the universe. Of course the timing is crucial. If you talk like that too early on in the evening or before the appropriate level of intoxication is reached. SMMMMMAACCCK.......

Now as for this one, I am not proud and it was apparently during an asshole phase of my life. I had met this girl once late at night and quite often, I would visit her on other nights late as well, let us say a 3 or 4 am. I would just drop by knock and spend the evening. Some good harmless fun. However on one of these evenings she decided that it was time to see if there was actually more to the relationship so at 3:30 am one morning she asked:

"Where do you see us going? I am really starting to like you."

To which I replied:

"Well, there is a 7/11 on the corner – did you want to go there sometime?"

Pause....

"Where the hell do you see us going? It's 3:30 am, I am drunk and I have never seen you in the daylight."

Now, though I was being brutally honest in this situation, I do not recommend – no matter what the situation is – treating another human being with that type of disdain. Though funny in the moment, when I think about it, it was just plain mean and I would never do that again. Even though, hell, it was funny.

This is from my post-university work career. I had relocated to another city for a career and knew virtually no one. So, in

*Penned By: The Seed & German Seed*

an attempt to meet people, I started working at a very popular restaurant and bar in order to develop a social life. On one particular night after I was off work for the evening and had partaken in a few beverages, I took my then girlfriend into a storage locker for a little extra-curricular activity. This particular storage room opened onto a full restaurant. So anyways, while with my girl in the storage room, the manager came to open the door to get out some supplies and as the door opens, pants down around the ankles pointing at my crotch I say, in you all remember the voice: "You see what you do to me?!" Another proud moment brought to you from the life and vault of The Seed. I assure you that for the most part I am not that guy. And it was all good harmless fun.

This one is a testament to me that I was actually able to at some point in time find some humor in this. On the day of the breakup of my true love and me. You know, one of those days where nothing matters and if you were to get hit by a bus, so be it. That might actually be an improvement. A day of sheer misery. A seemingly never-ending day. Anyways, I was bartending at this bar, when a customer comes up to the bar and says:

"I am a robber."

My reply back, with no rush of adrenalin, no fear, totally deadpan was: "Well, you're a robber so what is it that you want? Is it the cash drawer? I have an idea here. How about you sit back and relax while I make you a drink or get you a beer. Of course, since you are robbing the place, you will not have to pay, nor will I phone the police and when you are done I will give you the cash drawer and you can be on your way."

He looked at me, quite baffled and said: "My name is Robert. There is supposed to be a meal set aside for me."

One last one which illustrates how self absorbed everyone is. This one particular evening another customer dumps 45 years of life history on me. At the end of 4 or 5 minutes of this, I the bartender, looked at him and said: "You think that you have it bad".

The concerned customer replied "Oh my God, what is going on with you?"

To which I replied: "I caught my cat smoking today."

Now the beauty of this is once again the delivery was totally deadpan. There were 3 guys at the bar behind this guy. Two of them were trying to figure out how a cat could possibly smoke, while the third fell to the floor laughing.

Anyway I hope you enjoyed those little snippets from Seed's life. I am not necessarily proud of them. But I found them to be somewhat entertaining. Not even the best, I have thousands of others and maybe in a future book I will share some more of them with you. Maybe even a book entitled "Seed Snippets".

## Signage

Here are some simple observations on some signs that I have seen around my city. I know this has been done before, but I would like to share a few with you anyway. If you do not like it, I suggest you skip it. Fuck, read it, it will only take you a minute. I have only included a few. For the most part I don't understand what they actually mean. That is what I find funny about them. I wrestled with the idea of actually taking photos of the signs and including them in the book, only to come to the conclusion I would prefer it if you just used your imagination. If you see the pictures, it just means disregard the last sentence and I changed my mind. It must be my call girl past coming out.

### "Watch for moving traffic"

- This is one of my favorites. This is a sign just outside the exit door of a fast food restaurant. Could someone please help me out. What does this mean? Has anyone actually ever been hit by a parked car before. And if you have, how inept are you.

### "2 for 1 barbeque Chicken" on the side of sex shop

- I have virtually no comment here. That is right Seed is shooting blanks. Maybe that is the reason I am not a father yet. I bet you it is yummy chicken. I wonder what they cook it in.

*Penned By: The Seed & German Seed*

## "Buy Sell Exchange and Rental Toys" on the side of a porno shop

- I don't spend my time hanging around Porno shops ok. This is the same shop. I am just wondering who rents toys? The same people who love bowling shoes. Doesn't it make you wonder whether or not any of those toys been used on the chickens? Hmmmm Yummy Chicken!!

## "24 hour door"

- This sign appears above a door at a pharmacy. I won't spend much time with this one. Of course it is a door 24 hours a day. It is a door.

## "Not a door" (on a door)

- This is another sign on a door at the same pharmacy. Fuck the people who operate this pharmacy are confusing. I just hope they label their prescriptions better.

## "Quiet Hospital Zone"

- You guessed it. This sign appears close to a hospital. I just find it humorous to assume that if we are no where near a hospital, it is ok to be as loud and obnoxious as possible. Judging by some members of our society, there may actually be some truth in that.

So there you have it a little bit of "Sign Humor" from the deep and confusing mind of The Seed.

Now back to the scheduled programming. Well at least as mentioned before the thoughts occupying my cranium.

## Old People and power carts, is it a good mix.

Here is perhaps my observation that some of you may likely find to be the most offensive and I swear to you it is not meant to be. I actually did not swear when I said, I swear to you. Kudos to me. If I am wrong here, that is fine. I will accept the shame. I have some experience in this area; my father, grandfather that is, lost his ability to drive as he aged. He could not distinguish between 10 miles per hour and 80 miles per hour, which made city driving a blast. We either go into our Golden Years well cared for, have managed to put a little nest egg aside and have a loving support network to help us with our day to day chores and errands. Or we enter these years broke and bitter, struggling to just make ends meet.

Unfortunately as we age, some of our motor skill deteriorate, our memory, co-ordination as well as a whole host of other ailments start knocking on our doors. It is an unfortunate reality of life. Quite often, we start to lose things like our ability to drive or walk great distances as our strength diminishes. If you are rich and buying up cloned parts maybe you can postpone this process for a while but one day, even your day will come, you genetic freaks! So my observation here is, if you happen to be old and not of great means, is it good for you to have these motorized carts to get around in? I figure if you do not have that loving support network to help you out with things and the Motor Vehicle Department has deemed that you are a danger to yourself and society behind the wheel of an automobile, how can giving you and setting you free on the sidewalks and the malls of the world in these carts be any better? I figure getting hit at 15 miles per hour by some old guy on a cart could likely cause substantial pain and suffering. And by the way, if the old guy does not have someone to help him out he is likely pissed off and cranky to begin with. How can this aid society? Having said that, I hope I have a loving support network when my time comes. If not, watch out! It is going to be "Grand Theft Auto Seniors Edition" on the sidewalks of wherever I live.......

## The Proof is In the Pudding

I personally think I decided to talk about this for 2 reasons. Number 1: I like saying "Pudding". Number 2: I like typing

*Penned By: The Seed & German Seed*

"Pudding". Ok 3 reasons, Number 3: I like eating Pudding. Now as for the proof being in the pudding, what fucking proof are we talking about here? Is this magical pudding, answering the question of the meaning of life? If that is the case, shouldn't we all start eating more pudding? I know speaking for myself, once I started living on my own, my pudding consumption has dropped dramatically, pretty much to zilch. Zilch is a funny looking word, don't you think? I would like all of you out there – actually I insist – you all start using the word zilch more often. Back to the pudding, if the proof really is in the pudding, does that mean all types of proof? If we eat the right batch of pudding will we finally have the definitive answer to O.J.'s innocence or guilt and what about Michael Jackson? If we get the right flavor of chemically-whitened chocolate pudding will we be able to clear him of his charges?

This whole pudding concept is fascinating. If that is where the proof is, I definitely think the law enforcement agencies of the world need to get out of the donut shops and head down to their local pudding shops... "What's that"? "Pudding shops don't exist. "Who am I talking to". "I am so confused". "I get it". "You don't have to tell me twice". I have just been informed, that pudding shops don't exist, so it would be hard for the police or anyone else for that matter to go to a pudding shop to look for the proof. I guess it is up to the supermarkets and granny to provide this valuable proof revealing pudding. That is of course until you start frequenting, "SEED'S DELECTABLE PUDDING SHOP'S" IN YOUR TOWN OR CITY. I promise you a vast array of tasty pudding flavors for your enjoyment. My pudding will be enriched with an extra dose of proof. Don't worry my German pudding loving friends I guarantee you that I will be serving up some scrumptious pork pudding for you.

### Is it really necessary to say dog shit.

You are walking through the park one day and your good friend all of sudden shouts out: "Watch out for the dog shit!" Have you ever wondered if actually saying "dog" is necessary? That fraction of the second that it takes to say "dog" may be the fraction that saves you from stepping in the shit in the first place. Hell, if you are in a park, you may even be bare footed and stepping in shit because your friend says "dog" might even piss you off a bit. And anyway, who does your friend think he is? Is he actually some sort of shit expert? Depending on where you live there are all types of other shit scenarios, it could be horse, cow, bear, bird – or if you live in a big urban center – homeless person shit. These are all equally bad, I might add, to step in. Actually because of the source the homeless guy shit might be the worst. For that matter if your so-called friend is such a "crapologist", perhaps in his efforts to impress maybe he could be more specific, sort of like: "Watch out for the pregnant border collie shit!" or, "Watch out for the "Runny midget homeless guy shit!". My point is: "shit" will suffice. Ok.

## Can one really work, dance or sweat their ass off?

A tad more gravy for you. Have you ever wondered what the above term means? I actually think it is quite stupid and we should not tolerate its use. Just think about it. If we were capable to dance or work our asses off, a lot of things in this life would become useless or just simply things of the past. Say Tad goes down one Friday night to the local club and like a dancing fool does not know when to stop dancing. Well Tad, why are you dancing so much to begin with? Are you gay and you love to dance? Or are you desperately trying to pick someone up? My friend, your dancing prowess is not likely to accomplish your goal anyway. Either way, I suggest that you establish dancing limits. Do not spend the whole evening on the dance floor. Try to sit down and relax periodically to recharge and to make sure that you have not actually danced your ass off. This is vitally important. Especially if you are a suburban white kid, because quite often they don't have a lot of ass to begin with and could very easily exceed their dancing limits and you know the horrific results of that. That is right, you risk becoming ass-less. You may think that that is ok. You may even think that you can survive without an ass just fine. Well I am telling you, that you can't. Think about it. Sitting will become a thing of the past. Without an ass all you are going to have left is standing and lying down. That is why I suggest taking periodic sitting breaks just to make sure you have some ass left and have not pushed yourself too far. By the way, there are other things that your ass is vitally important for, for instance: driving your car. See, once again sitting becomes important and without that ability you may as well say goodbye to your wheels. And what about certain necessary bodily fluid disposal situations? You

*Penned By: The Seed & German Seed*

guessed it. Ass dependent. So please, for your own good, if you ever feel the urge to dance or work your ass off, please don't. Save just a little ass for the future. Fuck, if you are a gay male you will need it. Hey and while we are at it, if your name is Tad - you are likely gay.

## The Wonderful World of Toilets

It is only a coincidence that I have decided to make a commentary on toilets right after the last one. I had no plan on talking about toilets in any manner at all. In fact my fascination only arose after a recent trip to one of the Home Improvement Box retailers with a friend who had just recently purchased a home. I must admit I had no idea of sheer magnitude of comic gems these wonderful retailers provide the world with. Such as products like "Goo Be Gone" along with the toilet creativity I am going to share with you shortly. I will now be spending more time in these establishments. As for the toilets themselves, after spending about 15 minutes in this section I came to realize the comedy and creativity of the people in charge of naming toilets and I would like to share a few with you and a commentary on each. So here we go:

## Seed's Sketchy Relationship Theories - A Guide to the Perils of Dating

| Toilet Name | "My Thoughts" |
|---|---|
| Rough In | Is this toilet meant to be bought by those who eat a lot of spicy foods or perhaps they have hemorrhoids. |
| Champion | This one perhaps indicates the sheer volume the depositor leaves behind |
| Cadet | Perhaps one's stool is to be used to be on the front lines. |
| Patriot | The deposits here are precise powerful and destructive. "Here Comes The Patriot"!!!! |
| Renaissance | Deposits that have been created and stored in the warehouse for an extended period until such time comes that sharing with the masses makes sense. |
| Antiquity | Along the same lines as the renaissance. |
| Memoirs | If your memoirs are what you leave in the bowl. I guess your life has been nothing but crap. |
| Wellworth | A personal favorite. When one looks at the deposit I can just imagine saying out loud: "That was well worth it!!!!!" |
| Leighton | If you pronounce it "Lighten" it makes a bit more sense. |
| Santa Rosa | A place for sophisticated rose-like crap. |
| Rialto | The upper echelons of excrement |
| Devonshire | The Pinnacle of crap-I am sure it flushes itself. |

*Penned By: The Seed & German Seed*

So there you have it a bit of a commentary on the world of waste and waste management for that manner. I am sure you have enjoyed.

## Here are 25 words which will not be seen in this book.

Gossamer, graminivorous, quokka, rapturous, Bossy boots, reimbursement, antependium, perspicacity, omphalos, meticulous, necrophilia, achromatic, popinjay, caucuses, posse, chazzan, jodhpurs, Mars, Jupiter, Pluto, Uranus, Scooby, leprechaun, gadget and entrails.

## The fine line between genius and just plain nuts

What is a genius? A person with extraordinary intelligence or exceptional abilities. In short: an exception. Who isn't a genius? Probably the surest sign that you're not a genius is if you feel you have to convince everyone that you are. And what is the difference between being a genius and being just plain nuts? I think it is incredibly difficult to differentiate between being nuts and a genius. A genius will be labeled as crazy, because he or she doesn't "fit" into "normal" society and will often be faced by an alliance of idiots which will attempt to discount all that they do.

Most geniuses are off the wall as otherwise they would just be like the sheep of this world. Maybe a different color though. This color may be affected by drug or alcohol consumption. Many geniuses in our history were avid users of opium, absinthe and other mind-altering substances. This chemical influence may very probably have brought them over the fine line into Nutsville, yet it only enhanced their creativity.

Genius lies in how one approaches and lives one's life. Anyone can work. You don't have to be a genius to work hard, hard work requires discipline. Yet the genius possesses more than that: creativity, lust for life and above all passion. Are you a genius? I don't know. All I know is that if you're not holding that gun, we're not having this conversation. Wait a second, who are you talking to? Who am I talking to? And why do you need a weapon in the first place? Anyway to answer your question, if you regularly smoke opium, sniff glue or consume absinthe, and your apartment isn't decorated with your works of art, or your shelves aren't filled with your literary gems, then perhaps you have more pressing issues than whether or not you are a genius.

# CHAPTER 47
# Outtakes:

*"Eyi Eyi Yikie Yi Yhoni"*
*Yappa Poni*
*Alla Calla Whiskey*
*Chineese Chump*
*Beep! Beep!"*

*-the seed.*

    Well, we are almost done. This has been quite a wicked ride. For your reading pleasure, here is one of the bonus sections and what I think is a literary first. I have decided to include some outtakes. I know what you might thinking: "How could one have an outtakes section of a book? That just sounds ridiculous." Well kids, what I have decided to share with you are a few things. I decided that in the writing process, it would be necessary to have a co-author. A second Seed if you will, to bounce some of the ideas off and to help with editing and flow. Just to make sure that my medications were having a positive impact on what I was writing and not just a bunch of inane drivel.

    So, for your pleasure, we have decided to include some of the correspondence via email and internet conversations for your viewing and reading enjoyment. All we ask of you is when

## Seed's Sketchy Relationship Theories - A Guide to the Perils of Dating

you view the words you actually process them. If you just look at them, they really will not do you much good. So please do us and yourself a big favor and actually read them. Preferably in the order they appear on the page. If you do not do that, you will still be reading a book but not the one that we wrote.

I have even included some conversations which took place between me and my true love after the breakup. These conversations illustrate a couple of things, such as how pathetic we can become at times, along with proving sometimes there really are no "exceptions". The names have been changed to protect the identities of the parties involved. Also, Second Seed and I used a lot of aliases in our messages, by doing this we were just having a bit of fun. There really were only two of us working on the book. Ok, maybe a lot of our other personalities and alter egos were involved as well. You can decide for yourself. Some of the outtakes have a bit of a commentary added, as a way to help you to understand the context of the conversation. So sit back relax and enjoy a literary first. I think Saint Seed has a nice ring to it. Don't You...?

The following outtakes are in no particular order. The outtakes themselves have not been edited with the exception of some of the names. They are in their raw, original form. We thought it wouldn't be appropriate to edit and spell check outtakes. Don't you agree? So sit on your most comfortable chair and once again grab another gin. Enjoy!!! One last thing for fun we decided to shrink the outtakes to a size 10 font instead of 11 to conserve a little bit of space.

### Outtake 1

This outtake is just a simple conversation between Seed and European Seed. It illustrates some of the thought process involved in the writing of such a classic work as this. It also illustrates some of the possible Seed Spin Off ideas and marketing possibilities that you will find in **The Tasty Boutique** at **www.seedenterprises.com** . Who knows if you have some creative juices flowing maybe you can join the Seed Juggernaut. Watch for employment opportunities. Please continue to take your medications.

*Penned By: The Seed & German Seed*

**Hey Sky,**

I'm studying right now and an idea for the book just occurred to me. Tell me if you think this makes any sense.

What would you think about a "soundtrack" for the book? I thought maybe we could include a CD with tracks appropriate for each section, I have a few ideas and I know you'd have a ton of musical input. Either to be listened to while reading, or simply to emphasize the points we're making (Breakups, fucked-up dysfunctional families, the gay world, etc.). I think this might be a good thing. Of course, there will be extra work involved to get the licenses from the record companies, but I think it would be worth it.

This is just a first brainstorming - maybe we could include the CD with the first 1,000 copies or so, then sell it separately, or see how the mood of the public is.

Let me know what you think about this.

**Love ya, Brother,**

**German Seed**


## Outtake 2

This outtake is a bit dry and basically was written near the start of the whole process. It just shows how monumental the task of organizing a project like this can be. It also shows that German Seed may actually be some sort of control freak. You will also notice, that German Seed is one of the first people to start to recognize the untapped brilliance of the Seed. Seed only has one concern though if you look at the last line of this outtake, was German Seed getting ready to ask Seed to marry him. The answer would have been "No". Now raise your glass "Prost"!!

**Dear Seed:**

Thank-you for sending me the manuscript. So far it's fucking great!

<u>Material:</u> As always, when we chat on the phone, I have to howl. The material in the book so far is no exception. Some parts were totally

hilarious, others made me think, which I feel is the point of the book in the first place.

I find the idea of "Theories" good. I think that this is a better breakdown/structure than "Chapters". Whatever, we can discuss this further. The main thing is to gather material.

I will write regularly and send you the bits once a week (is Sunday OK for you?).

Format: I copied the text from your mail and saved it on my PC as a Word document. When we get a bit further, I can format the text as a .pdf-document, so that the format always stays the same when the document is sent back and forth. To read it, all you need is Acrobat Reader (can be downloaded from the Adobe website free of charge). Until then, I would suggest that we stay with the Word format and simply add the text as an attachment to our respective e-mails.

Formulation/Style: Every text, like a raw diamond, has to be polished. Yet I agree with you that the formulation will take shape over time and that the priority has to be, at this time, the material itself.

Suggestions: If it is OK with you, I would work in my material with yours (I will write in a different color, so we can tell the contributions apart). If it's OK with you, I would go over the text you sent and make style changes, punctuation changes, etc. Let me know what you think about this.

I don't want you to think that I am sitting here with a red pen and that the point is to make tight-assed grammatical changes. Your work is fantastic. We need to agree on a style and, of course, to correct minor errors that occur. Sooner or later this will happen, either we do it ourselves or the publisher/lector from the publishing house will do so.

Organization: As this is just the beginning of the project, it is relatively easy to have an overview of the material. This will change fast as we proceed with our contributions. I believe we need a simple system to keep track of the versions, otherwise we will have serious problems later.

Simply create a new folder on your PC: "Complete Texts" (or whatever you find better or easier).

*Penned By: The Seed & German Seed*

I would suggest that we save the texts under the following system:

"Date_Text x"

I have saved your text on my PC under the folder "Complete Texts" as a Word document with the file name: "2003-01-20_Text 1". This text version is saved on my PC and will not be changed. It is the basis of our joint work. Before I write anything, I will make a copy of this file and name it (for example: "2003-01-22_Text 2". Any changes I make will be made on this new copy of your text, so that the original version (and eventual versions) will remain unchanged for future reference (also handy for the section "Outtakes").

When I send you my text on Sunday, I would ask you first of all to save it (if you agree with the system, of course) as "2003-01-xx_Text 2". This way we have the next version in our archive. Then when you want to make changes, copy it as "2003-01-xx_Text 3".

If we save our texts and they are sorted after the date and text number, it will make organization later a lot easier. These texts should not be changed and will serve as a library of our texts for easy future reference.

Does this sound OK or have I been living in Germany too long?

Please give me your suggestions, criticism and feedback so that we can create the best work possible.

I'll give you a ring at the end of the week.

**Greetings from Munich,**

**German Seed**

### Outtake 3

Some more on the early organization of the book. A little more of German Seed realizing that if he plays his cards right he maybe able to hop onto the Seed gravy train. Also a little insight into the whole world of friendship. Perhaps the use of the word friend was a little premature.

*Seed's Sketchy Relationship Theories - A Guide to the Perils of Dating*

**Dear Seed,**

Thanks for your mail. I have to agree with you - we're on the way to something big.

I was sitting in the train today and I thought of something. The text you sent me on Monday (20.01.2003) is the basis of our work. On Tuesday I wrote a couple of pages - I'll send it to you on Sunday, take a critical look at it. If it sucks, then tell me and/or edit it. I need your feedback, Brother.

My contributions are in a blue font. The problem is (that's what I was thinking about in the train) as we both continue to write and write, the changes will become difficult to keep track of.

Here's my suggestion: any and all new contributions that we write (of course in our "own colors") should be (in addition) highlighted. When you write a bit and when I write a bit we should use the highlight function in Word. I will highlight my text in yellow. Simply pick a color. At first, this may seem superfluous, but as time goes by our texts will grow and it will be difficult to differentiate between our various contributions.

If it's OK with you, I could administrate the complete texts and work in our bits, so that we don't lose track of our texts and good ideas.

As I said in my last mail, I look forward to seeing you in March. I am not 100% sure that I will come, but 90%. My boss (and former good friend) promised it, but we'll have to wait and see. He has promised quite a bit in the last year and a half and very little has proven to be true. A long story.

**Take care, and hopefully I'll see you soon!**

**German Seed**


**Outtake 4**

This is outtake is a very beautiful one. It represents the light going on in German Seed's head. He shows that he has actually bought into the whole project. Joined the Seed Cult if you will. The other reason it was included is this. It is simply, "Fucking Kicking".

*Penned By: The Seed & German Seed*

**German Seed:**

Your suggestions are very much appreciated and whatever you feel is appropriate for organization is fine with me and any material that you want to add to any section that is fantastic as well. It may take me a little while to comprehend the text and archive stuff but with your assistance I don't think it will be too difficult. I think this could be a smashing fucking success and whether it is in the comedy or relationship sections of the stores or both it will be kicking (who the fuck am I when did I start saying kicking). I also think as we always said one day we would write something together well this is the start brother and who knows where we can go from this. Man when this is the success it is going to be, we will look back and say what the fuck took us so long to get started (working for others really does lick). Also I think it is very important to keep it pretty raw, soliciting a few opinions from others but at the same time not letting them influence our thoughts remember people are dysfunctional. And finally when writing it we should be looking at possible spin-offs T-shirts with the Theory Slogans on them, interactive stuff, perhaps a game etc., just other avenues for exposure.

Let us go World Wide brother.

**Respectfully Yours,**

**(The Seed)**


**Outtake 5**

This one is included simply because: "We'll make up some "business" reason to come to Vancouver, so that we can write off the trip". This quote will be used extensively when Seed negotiates percentages with German Seed. I heard German prisons are a lot of fun Fraulien.

**Hey Seed!**

I completely forgot to tell you. The chances are very good that I will be in Vancouver either in mid-March or the last week of March this year.

I will be coming over with Jens my boss, as he wants to establish some business contacts on the East Coast of the USA and needs me to break the ice in English. We'll make up some "business" reason to come to Vancouver, so that he can write off the trip.

I've just been working on the manuscript. Have a few ideas about the chapters/theories and how we can structure the book. These are just the first ideas/suggestions which we can change and refine.

At some points in the book I can see the critique from people: "Those arrogant fucks, who do they think they are". However, I don't think that's our problem. You can't please all the people, all the time.

**Take care, my Brother!**

**German Seed**

## Outtake 6

This is a messenger conversation that we saved between the two Seed's. A lot of it will not make any sense to you, the readers. I guess it shows some of the human side of the Seed's. It might even show how messed up our brains are. At least the German portion of our brains. It comes complete with typo's. It is in the original form, no spell check or anything. I am not sure why German Seed noticed the picture of my bed. Hmmm disturbing. If you notice Seed made a comment about the size of his dick. After he made that comment he actually measured it and it only takes up 38 pages. Sorry for the misinformation. "I am not your mother". The character Silvia is German Seed's loving girlfriend. I know you may be questioning that with the dick comments. I checked she has no Adams apple.

The character Dave is a friend that has included a quote in the book and also Dave took part in Seed's European Adventure. He will also be a co-author on Seed's Identity Tour. Look for it in **Seed's Delectable Boutique** at **www.seedenterprises.com**. Basically this outtake is a lot of witty banter and positive vibes between two friends and up and coming authors. One last thing notice the tremendous scope of friendship.

Dave is a friend, however, if he gives up the ghost before Seed can write him the cheque mentioned in this outtake. Seed's heart would not be broken (of course he would be very sad). Ahhh true friendship.

German Seed says: Hey Seed!

Seed Says: Hey German Seed!

*Penned By: The Seed & German Seed*

Seed Says: That is how the home looks now sort of not with the light trails though they only happen when your drunk

German Seed says: Wow, the apartment looks fucking great!!!

Seed Says: It is amazing how the camera knows when you are drunk

German Seed says: did the camera share a bottle of vodka with peer?

Seed Says: I think so

German Seed says: Looks good, brother - great colors

Seed Says: You don't have to keep the pics

German Seed says: nice bed

Seed Says: Thanks it is so lonely

German Seed says: but I want the pics

Seed Says: just kidding

Seed Says: i can be a tramp when nec . But it is no longer fulfilling

German Seed says: what is nec?

Seed Says: I am working on the book now and some more CD's

Seed Says: necessary

Seed Says: don't know why I abbreviated

German Seed says: you're kooky

Seed Says: I guess I was afraid to spell it wrong

German Seed says: you spelled it right

Seed Says: Book is 109 pages now goal is 250ish

Seed Says: Some is a bit weak but some tweaking and angst will help fix that

*Seed's Sketchy Relationship Theories - A Guide to the Perils of Dating*

Seed Says: I figure about 300 odd pages with pics and illustrations

German Seed says: hey, that's fantastic. have about 30 pages, maybe more.

Seed Says: I am also going to start on The Identity story of Seed.

German Seed says: 300 is realistic - it shouldn't be "war and peace"

Seed Says: about 250 text and about 50 of shots of my dick

Seed Says: actually it will take about 50 for the one shot

German Seed says: do you want to see a picture of mine?

Seed Says: it is really big

Seed Says: no

German Seed says: how bout now?

Seed Says: by the way I am going to save some of these conversations as possible outtakes

German Seed says: since when do you smoke - I just made out the Gauloises on your dresser, you bastard!

Seed Says: those are certs you fucker

Seed Says: I don't smoke

German Seed says: well if you're gonna smoke anything tonight, make it hog, to quote an old poet

Seed Says: what was the song with the cat drawings that Sylvia liked

German Seed says: music is the key, I think by "Cool-T"

Seed Says: Merchandise Snow Shakers, Board or Interactive Computer Game, T-Shirts, Coffee Mugs, Hats , Beer Glasses, Condoms, Frisbee's, Cook Book, Diapers, Bobble Heads, etc. Items that need to be addressed: The Role of Friends, (Who can and Who Can't be in your

*Penned By: The Seed & German Seed*

relationship if you want it to succeed). The Politics involved currently in the World of same sex marriages.

Seed Says: these are two sections that if you get an idea of other things jot them down so we don't forget

German Seed says: OK, just copied and pasted it - will add to it

Seed Says: Cool are you sure it is not Sarah Connor

Seed Says: or is the song the Magic Key

German Seed says: No, it's not Sarah Connor

German Seed says: Maybe it is the magic key

German Seed says: I don't know, you guys killed the last functioning brain cells I had

Seed Says: Did I tell you I found a lounge in Sitges that is exactly the way I want Seed's to look

German Seed says: no, where was it in Sitges (I'm assuming on the beach)

Seed Says: No it was in the village

Seed Says: fantastic place

German Seed says: ok, love to see it

Seed Says: It will be part of Seed's Empire one day

German Seed says: photos?

German Seed says: I hope I can be part of your Empire

Seed Says: there will be Seed's in Vancouver, New York, Negril and Spain

Seed Says: German Seed you are in on one of the projects already

German Seed says: If you need a bar porter in Negril, I'm your man

Seed Says: Just don't cheat on me

## Seed's Sketchy Relationship Theories - A Guide to the Perils of Dating

Seed Says: Fuck you set your sights high

Seed Says: where are you now

Seed Says: fuck I can type fast

Seed Says: fuck I say fuck a lot

Seed Says: fuck

German Seed says: No problem, cheating's for idiots

German Seed says: at home - moosemaus is giving me the evil eye because "I'm neglecting her". Women!

German Seed says: fuck's ok.

Seed Says: tell her to go for a walk

Seed Says: Hey here is the thing

German Seed says: where should she go for walk?

Seed Says: I was in this relationship once and the person I was with was on the computer a lot and I used to git pissed because I wanted some attention. But then I realized that hell I had other things to do and in which world is it that when you are together you must always give undivided attention. I don't think it exists and people will be sadly mistaken if they think it does

Seed Says: I bought some stuff with Daves Credit Card Today on line do you think he will be mad or do you think I should tell him

German Seed says: Well, seeing as it's Dave's card, you probably should tell him. Did you buy porn?

Seed Says: Ok actually just bought the Software I was using to make CD covers. I had mentioned I was going to do it, he said Ok and actually next time I talk to him I will let him know

Seed Says: But I can turn it into porn.

German Seed says: Then it's no problem.

Seed Says: It is me German Seed of course not

*Penned By: The Seed & German Seed*

German Seed says: Yes, I know, I saw the rest of your cds and I can see the trend.

German Seed says: Of course, I know it's not a problem. I just know how some people can react, but I don't think that Dave's uptight

Seed Says: that is just the beginning now that I am somewhat European

German Seed says: oh no

Seed Says: I am giving him the bling bling

Seed Says: I have to right him a big cheque for the rooms from the trip

Seed Says: Unless he dies before he gets the bill

German Seed says: what is the bling bling?

Seed Says: $$$$$$$$$$

German Seed says: aha, kaching, the cashier sound

Seed Says: Well at least what the kids call it

Seed Says: that is the biggest song in Amsterdam Sylvia may like it

German Seed says: wayne looks somewhat not thrilled - I'm assuming that's Thai

Seed Says: No that is Fiona on a bad day

German Seed says: Unfortunately, I can't hear the song right now (my speakers are fucked)

German Seed says: I understand.

Seed Says: ahh should I turn mine up

German Seed says: seed, gonna go to bed - gotta get up early. will call you on the weekend. by the way, who won grey cup?

Seed Says: Edmonton 32 Montreal 24

German Seed says: fuck. was hoping for Mtl

*Seed's Sketchy Relationship Theories - A Guide to the Perils of Dating*

Seed Says: piss off

Seed Says: good night

Seed Says: I need to make a new birth certificate illustrating my new bday

German Seed says: eat aself. the birth certificate sounds good. looking forward to celebrating your birthday with you next year.

Seed Says: for sure good night talk to you soon.

German Seed says: good night brother

**Outtake 7**

The next two outtakes are extremely personal. They represent two conversations which my ex and I had regarding me looking after her dog on a weekend she was going to be out of town. A recurring theme in the conversations is that they both started out with me trying to act as if everything was really positive, when she was simply using me because she needed something from me. She was treating me as if there had never been any intimacy and it was a real inconvenience for her to have to deal with me at all. I was being pathetic, with a desire to try to salvage some friendship, basically come across very weak and for lack of a better term a bit pathetic. I remind you that she had cheated on me repeatedly and had lied to me. The cheating had been brought to my attention by others. She also had rubbed it in my face that her new relationship was significantly better (Patrick her new man and her had cheated the whole length of our relationship). The reason I included it is it really illustrates just about everything you should not do. I should have kicked her to the curb but love can be blind. I am responsible for what I accepted, actually I trusted her. She showed no remorse for her actions and as you can likely tell, has developed no character of her own. My weakness was love. It was also my need to be accepted, my insecurities showed through in these conversations. I trusted her because she told me that she loved me almost every day. We all make mistakes.

These two conversations were not enjoyable for me. They are however, some very strong examples of why separation is very important. It is nearly impossible to accomplish anything if you stay in contact. When I read these conversations, I realize as much as I was trying to stay positive and non confrontational I was still trying to convince her

*Penned By: The Seed & German Seed*

how great I am. The facts of the matter is that she was cheating on me repeatedly without remorse. Regardless of my character, my accepting this behavior showed a real lack of self respect. I won't take my love away, but I was definitely handling the situation wrong.

Seed Says: Hello how are you feeling today

The Big 26 says: fine

Seed Says: the cold is ok

Seed Says: did you get the messages last night

Seed Says: Did you get the one about me changing my name.

The Big 26 says: no

The Big 26 says: but i heard bout it

Seed Says: Oh I sent that the pic of you with your dog and also I was thinking of changing my name. What do you think of Sky Pepin? That was a suggestion of Danielle

Seed Says: Do you have any suggestions>

The Big 26 says: no

Seed Says: Well try to think of some

Seed Says: Maybe I could change my name to Patrick? LOL.

The Big 26 says: so can you watch my dog Thursday. We get back from SF on Monday evening

Seed Says: See (LOL) if you would marry me I could change it to a last name that you actually liked.

Seed Says: Only if you are willing to talk to me a bit.

The Big 26 says: what's to talk about

Seed Says: I am just kidding of course I will

Seed Says: there is lots to talk about we didn't spend all that time together with nothing to talk about

Seed Says: If we don't talk we both end up big losers

## Seed's Sketchy Relationship Theories - A Guide to the Perils of Dating

Seed Says: we can talk about how life is going. How my family stuff is going and what postitve can come from it.

Seed Says: We can talk about how beautiful you are.

Seed Says: There is a pic of me and Waynes dog Thai.

Seed Says: Sweetie things don't have to be so screwed up between us.

The Big 26 says: I know what wayne's dog looks like

Seed Says: t is a good pic. If someone else sent you a pic you would accept it.

Seed Says: Sometimes it seems like (just seems like) others are telling you how to treat me.

The Big 26 says: I have my own mind...I don't need people to tell me how to be

Seed Says: Please try to remember why you Loved me. I am still that same guy.

Seed Says: I am not arguing I just said that is how it feels.

Seed Says: Look I would do absolutely anything if I thought it could repair things, despite of what others tell me. I feel that we are the exceptions to a lot of rules at least I hope we are. But, I know that at the present moment whatever I do has no effect. But at the same time I am very consistent, I love and I care and that will never change. And I do this from my heart not with manipulation or

Seed Says: anything else in mind.

The Big 26 says: I'm going to go now...

Seed Says: it is all good

Seed Says: Hey I will talk to you a bit later

Seed Says: Have a great day. I do miss your companionship. It is all positive.

Seed Says: And I really miss your Bonita Sandrissa

Seed Says: probably spelled incorrectly.

*Penned By: The Seed & German Seed*

**Thursday Morning.**

Seed Says: Morning. Hey I am just trying to be helpful and I did think you were leaving today. The offer for lunch or dinner is an open one. Please just let me know OK!!!!!

Seed Says: Oh by the way, the bank keeps calling I am sure it is just a Credit Card offer or something like that. I keep telling them I am not sure when you will be back. Do you want me to give them your cell #?

The Big 26 says: just tell them I don't live there any more and you don't know what my new number is.

Seed Says: ok will do.

Seed Says: have a great day I hope you are feeling a bit better. I am off to the gym now and like I said if you would like to go for lunch or dinner it would be my plessure just let me know.

Seed Says: The book is down to less than 100 pages to completion. Wish me luck with it. It actually might be good. In fact I know it is good.

The Big 26 says: I told you I'm too busy for lunch or dinner

Seed Says: OK

Seed Says: All I can do is offer it is a girls perogative to change her mind

The Big 26 says: I will however still like to ask if you would take my dog again tomorrow

Seed Says: Of course I will, you know that is no problem

Seed Says: I would like to be able to sit down with you for awhile but my offers are pure.

Seed Says: Hopefully you know that

Seed Says: So you have to let me know the schedule and when you need me and what for

The Big 26 says: I will drop him off tommorow before I go to work at 1

The Big 26 says: I will come by at around 3:30 to drop off the car and head off to the airport

Seed Says: How are you getting to the airport

Seed Says: Hey how about lunch tomorrow I would really appreciate it.

The Big 26 says: probably airporter or my friend Cheryl

Seed Says: What about your friend Seed

The Big 26 says: I don't have time I told you

The Big 26 says: stop asking

Seed Says: You have to eat JERK LOL

Seed Says: I can give you a ride

The Big 26 says: I don't think that would be appropriate seeing as Patrick will be waiting for me when I get there

Seed Says: man you have a nasty tone with me even when you type the hatred shows and I don't deserve it.

Seed Says: So what if Patrick is waiting. I am just dropping you off

The Big 26 says: how was what I wrote being nasty?

The Big 26 says: essentially that's what it is

Seed Says: you are short with me, there is not an ounce of lightheartedness and it is like I have done something awful to you

Seed Says: You would not talk to another human the way you talk to me.

Seed Says: You express zero interest or compassion.

Seed Says: It is like it is a fucking business arrangement and the feelings of the parties involved are not important

Seed Says: I just offer kindness

The Big 26 says: how you interpret things is not my problem

*Penned By: The Seed & German Seed*

Seed Says: You serve up hatred

Seed Says: exactly my point look what you just wrote

Seed Says: not, I don't mean to give you that impression

The Big 26 says: you know what...forget it

Seed Says: Or How is your Day?

The Big 26 says: forget the whole deal

Seed Says: no

Seed Says: I don't mind I am just being honest with you

The Big 26 says: if this is the hassel I have to go through I'd rather not have to deal with it

Seed Says: I will take Kingsley I don't mind and if you need a ride

Seed Says: ok

Seed Says: Hey I am just asking for you to be courteous

Seed Says: that is all

Seed Says: I don't mind doing things for you, you know that. Just treat me like, I don't know a friend maybe

The Big 26 says: I am being courteous...I'm giving you advance notice and I'm giving you the opportunity to say no. What more do you want

Seed Says: Just a little kindness and appreciation. That is not much. Perhaps to know that in the slightest of ways I matter.

Seed Says: Read everything I write or say it is all positive and it is all met with coldness. ask how you are, you show no interest. I let you know about things and you disregard them.

The Big 26 says: well I'm sorry to say this but your track record isn't that great. I mean every single time I've come close to putting all the stuff behind me you do something else to try to fuck things up so I'm sorry if I seem to be a bit cautious

## Seed's Sketchy Relationship Theories - A Guide to the Perils of Dating

Seed Says: treat someone how you want them to be and you have a better chance of getting the results you want

The Big 26 says: I don't know if I can ever forget all your actions during our break up and your latest attempt...that e-mail you sent

Seed Says: You know I am a great person full of passion and compassion and love.

Seed Says: The last email was a product of something you did. It was the truth, perhaps wrong to send, but fuck the painting me as a bad guy

Seed Says: we both have responsibility in everything that happens. here are things I am ashamed of, maybe there should be some things you are as well. but they are done I don't believe for a second that you or I are those people. And you know that.

The Big 26 says: the point is you are still doing these things

The Big 26 says: I am not

Seed Says: What am I doing

Seed Says: you are cold to me

The Big 26 says: and you are judgemental

Seed Says: In public not you, but there has been an attempt to hurt

Seed Says: Judgmental of who?

Seed Says: The email you sent was 17 days into my trip it devestated me.

The Big 26 says: what i am doing...of Patrick especially

Seed Says: No you are wrong

Seed Says: I give you my honest opinion

Seed Says: and I don't think it is good

Seed Says: You will make the ultimate choice

*Penned By: The Seed & German Seed*

The Big 26 says: well the e-mail that I read from you was just as bad. You were the one who put me on the defensive

Seed Says: my opinion is out of genuine caring

Seed Says: Sorry for that

Seed Says: You cheated at least 5 times and then put his pic up with no regard for the impact it would have on me. You cheated.

The Big 26 says: yes but you keep forcing your opinion

Seed Says: anyway let us move forward forget this shit

The Big 26 says: once is never enough

Seed Says: I know that given time we would have been great, we were and it is a lost opportunity.

Seed Says: I want us to move forward

Seed Says: let us not argue I don't want to win anything here

Seed Says: I just want us to be happy together, as friends and to be able to share good times

The Big 26 says: it's not that simple....you've taken your time to sort through your stuff and I didn't press a time limit on you

Seed Says: sorry what do you mean by that?

The Big 26 says: you kept saying during our breakup it's gonna take me more than x amount of months to get over this

The Big 26 says: well it's gonna take twice as long or even longer for me....whenever I am ready

Seed Says: please do not take this for anything other than shat it is. I do truly Love You and when I say that please realize that all of my intentions are pure and what I feel are for the best. Sometimes I should not say anything but I do care. You know you can count on me and you know I am not just saying this. I want you to be in my life. I don't give that to many people. I hope one day you realize that. I believe in you with everything in my heart.

### Seed's Sketchy Relationship Theories - A Guide to the Perils of Dating

Seed Says: Try not to shut me out. If you can't be there for the good ahead as my girlfriend at least you can be there as one of my best friends. Remember I lost a lot when I lost you. Lover, Girlfriend , Best Friend, my Soulmate. You, I left it all on the table for.

Seed Says: Hey I still have a lot of things to sort out as well the family stuff is incredibly heavy

The Big 26 says: well you can do that for someone else

The Big 26 says: there is someone else out there

Seed Says: Sweetie I don't think it happens often and I was lucky

The Big 26 says: well it can happen more than once

Seed Says: As much as an optimist as I am maybe not.

Seed Says: Not the same. and I will never settle.

The Big 26 says: well I am sorry you feel that way

Seed Says: it is not negative I cherish it

The Big 26 says: so is that supposed to be some cheap shot at me?

The Big 26 says: I am not settling

Seed Says: NO god, no not at all

Seed Says: I never said you were

Seed Says: I just know, that is all.

Seed Says: You did at one time as well it just got messed up by a loss of focus

Seed Says: Sweetie I wish our time was now

The Big 26 says: I have to go now

Seed Says: I will never take cheap shots.

Seed Says: So tomorrow

The Big 26 says: tomorrow at 12:45

*Penned By: The Seed & German Seed*

Seed Says: ok that would be great. If you can break down give a call and say hello later. I would appreciate it. I don't expect it but it would make me feel good. Sweetie try, slowly if you must I know it will be worth it. Fuck I get the odd tear in my eye when I type this. Take care. Hugs Seed

If you are worried about me, don't be. Once I regained sanity and found my balls, I had the big "L" tattoo removed from my forehead.

### Outtake 8

A little more conversation between the 2 Seed's on editing content. Nothing earth shattering or even funny here. After the last outtake it seemed like a good time to change the mood a bit.

**Hey Seed,**

Here is the text for the Opening Rant. New version is not quite correct, as I said, I didn't change much — just a once over for grammar, spelling. Here and there I added a few words and rounded off a few sentences. I added some material, have a look at it and maybe we can chat on the weekend about it. We talked about death, tragedies, disease and war. At the end, I found that talking about fun doesn't really fit in with this. I changed the end from "fun" to "a different perspective", working with the general message in the text of "positive thinking". What do you think about this?

**Talk to you soon, Brother.**

**German Seed**

### Outtake 9

More lights are going on in German Seeds head. He is starting to think about the marketing possibilities. This one also shows the start of the alter egos being represented. It is also the point where Seed realizes the book has to be a success, since German Seed is starting to work on the book more and perhaps neglecting some of his studying. Feel proud of yourselves for buying the book. You have saved Seed and given German Seed something to fall back on. Thanks to all of you. We very much appreciate it.

*Seed's Sketchy Relationship Theories - A Guide to the Perils of Dating*

**Hey Sky,**

I'm studying right now and an idea for the book just occurred to me. Tell me if you think this makes any sense.

What would you think about a "soundtrack" for the book?

I thought maybe we could include a CD with tracks appropriate for each section, I have a few ideas and I know you'd have a ton of musical input. Either to be listened to while reading, or simply to emphasize the points we're making (Breakups, fucked-up dysfunctional families, the gay world, etc.). I think this might be a good thing. Of course, there will be extra work involved to get the licenses from the record companies, but I think it would be worth it.

This is just a first brainstorming - maybe we could include the CD with the first 1,000 copies or so, then sell it separately, or see how the mood of the public is.

Let me know what you think about this.

**Love ya, Brother,**

**German Seed**


## Outtake 10

There is only one possible answer, yet simple answer here German Seed. "Yes you are drunk". "Remember moderation".

Hey Seed,

here is chapter 2 - I used the new copy you sent me. Am I drunk, why are my words red? And centred?

Didn't add much, just a little bit of punctuation. Shortened some sentences and added a word here or there, but there simply wasn't anything to add. Good work, my friend.

Will call you on Sunday, Brother. Take care, and sleep well.

**Love**

**German Seed**

*Penned By: The Seed & German Seed*

## Outtake 11

This outtake is just funny. It represents German Seed getting in touch with his feminine side. When I visited him and his girlfriend Sylvia in Munich, I do recall her mentioning seeing his figure skates tucked away in the closet.

**Hey Seed,**

Thanks for your mail with section 1.

Near the end of the chapter 4, where you talk about music and love I added in poetry - please take it out.

Maybe I am gay.

**Maybe Gay German Seed**


## Outtake 12

German Seed is here showing a weak moment he seems to be loosing his edge a bit. But like the great author he is, he quickly realizes his error.

**Seed,**

I think sucker's a good word and probably, no definitely, better than candidate, which is more neutral and lastly watered down. That doesn't fit in with the tenor of the book. I suggested "candidate" because in the sentence after sucker we use the word "sucks" and that bothers me. I am not sure why, but it does. I'll get over it.


## Outtake 13

This simply represents Seed being hard on German Seed for wanting to use the word candidate instead of sucker. As you can see by Seed's gentle nurturing, he is calmly encouraging German Seed he might be losing his edge. He is also showing off his ability to spew out useless information. Really it is nurturing and not sarcasm. Ha. Ha. Ha. Pumpkin is German Seed if you were wondering.

## Seed's Sketchy Relationship Theories - A Guide to the Perils of Dating

**Hey Pumpkin:**

I see what you mean about sucker and sucks right after each other. Guess what I did. I went into the big thesaurus in my brain and changed sucks to bites the big one. Way to go candidate. LOL, LOL ha-ha. On a side not do you know what ha-ha actually means. It actually is a deep ditch or a sudden change in levels. Go figure. But why do I know that. I must get rid of some of this stuff so I can replace it with new thoughts.

**Yabba Seed**

### Outtake 14

Some more alias's are created here. I believe personally all books should make references both to Webster's Dictionary as well as Webster the one time child star. In fact it should probably be a law. Maggy is a possible new name for German Seed.

**You like Maggy.**

We could substitute the long definitions for the Webster's definitions. However they may be too short and not complicated enough. I also am not sure where Webster is hanging out these days.

**Hugs**

**Seedy Your Over Lord.**

**P.S. Flow on this. Ha Ha Ha............**

### Outtake 15

This is a flashback to one of the earlier correspondence between the two of us. Of course not in the true sense of a flash back. We don't know how to add smoke or clouds to represent a dream sequence. If we figure it out we will definitely include it. A few points worth mentioning here are the following. German Seed is really getting the possibilities here about merchandising. Though our book is basically intended for an adult audience, I have no problem with their children using their lunch money and allowance to purchase copies for themselves to get a head start on their future dating lives. Perhaps if their parents are clueless

## Penned By: The Seed & German Seed

they could give a copy to them. I am also not opposed to the book being read out loud in churches, if the organist has a copy she may edit out the profanities with organ music. I do have to draw a line in pre-schools. Fuck, what the hell, it is not like the kids haven't heard mommy and daddy using the word. Finally do you readers think it is fair that German Seed made fun of my blind eye. I don't think it is.....

"YOU ARE NOW ENTERING A FLASHBACK"

**Wow those are some powerful special effects.**

**Hey Seed,**

I think the idea of Ask Seed? is great. Also the idea of publicizing the book through this medium is very good. Merchandising is also a good idea, an Emperor Seed action figure, coffee mugs, calendars (especially with New Year's Resolutions for our readers) would also be, I think, a good idea. The idea for the second book is food for thought.

I found your answer to the first ever question for Ask Seed? good, maybe somewhat misogynous at times, but I think the readers have to take the answers, as well as our book with a grain of salt. They're old

## Seed's Sketchy Relationship Theories - A Guide to the Perils of Dating

enough and nobody forced them to read it: so ask an honest question get an honest answer.

Perhaps we should include a disclaimer with the book (along the lines of the one in Ask Seed?). I must admit that at first, I found the use of the word "fuck" a bit heavy. However, after a bit of thought I think you're right. With the word "fuck" one can express all emotions and it is fitting in almost every situation or mood. After all, I don't expect that the book will be read out loud in church or in preschools. The people/readers are old enough (or should be) to realize this.

Questions:

1. Can I be of any help with Ask Seed?

2. Would you have anything against me proofreading the answers to Ask Seed? Often two pairs of eyes are better than one, especially considering that in proofreading one's own work, we often oversee spelling or typographical errors.

Take care, give me a ring when you get a chance. I'll be in Nuremberg Thursday and Friday, otherwise you can reach me at home on the weekend.

**German Seed**

### Outtake 16

The creative effects of insomnia are starting to take effect during these two. We both seemed to have forgotten who we are as the alias's are beginning to fly freely.

**Hey Maggo**

I challenge you to come up with one short antidote for the Gravy section. I challenge you.

**Bussing**

**Spunky**

*Smacky:*

I can't sleep brain won't stop. So in my deprivation I came up with this for the inside cover. If you think of some more gems let me know.

*Penned By: The Seed & German Seed*

I think we can do a few pages of them before the Table of Contents. Let me know what you think.

**Hugs Seed**

### Outtake 17

A series of outtakes that once again show the smashing creativity of our new names. Come on Goo, Vinkie don't get to critical this is a bonus section after all. Feel fortunate to be reading it. Ok, so maybe fortunate may not be the right word. It is once again good to see how affectionate German Seed is. "Cupcake". I prefer."Kitten".

**Goo:**

Here is the acknowledgements section. Don't edit my stuff yet but if you think of other things to add send them to me and I will insert them in the appropriate areas. Remember, this is mostly light and funny k.

**Hugs**

**The Emperor**

**Vinkie,**

So you made me laugh yet again. Who's Harry, very good! Not sure I can add anything right now, will do so when something occurs to me.

Before I went to bed last night, I surfed a bit looking for domains. I searched for *www.seedproductions.com* at ICANN, the über-controllers of the internet world, and couldn't find any entries for "seed productions", which is a good thing. I placed an general inquiry at an internet service provider regarding reserving a domain and am awaiting their response.

**Take care, cupcake and we'll talk tomorrow.**

**Smacko**

*Seed's Sketchy Relationship Theories - A Guide to the Perils of Dating*

## Outtake 18

This trilogy of outtakes shows once again German Seeds acknowledgement of Seed's potential comic brilliance. It also shows that we realize some of the material may offend some of the readers. We also point out that the child's raising takes the efforts of both parents. We are also showing 2 of the critics comments which were not good enough to be in the book. Oops! I guess they made it in after all. I also wish one of my alias's was "Goo Daddy".

**Hey Seed,**

I've just read the Acknowledgements. As always after your mails, I am laughing right now - thank-you.

**Sticky regards,**

**Goo Daddy**

**Sky Hookan,**

How was your weekend? Here is the edited version of Chapter 5. Two short notes:

1. "By the way, Seed has expert knowledge on this subject, because in a previous life he was a call girl." Fantastic.

2. "Also, I am not trying to say that the father has no role in the raising of the child. Like I mentioned before, he plays a very vital role and that is to bring home the income that allows you to raise the child yourself in the best possible environment".

Have the feeling that we are going to get a lot of flak on this point. This can be very easily construed as chauvinistic ("Man works, while the woman cooks") - do you know what I mean? It comes across as though we're denying women the right or privilege of working, going out or having fun.

That said, I agree with you that for the formative years, the first few years till Kindergarten, that the mother should primarily take care of the kid(s), yet we have to somehow make clear to the reader that the father also has an important role in supporting the mother (fuck I don't know, I'm not a father yet - I suppose changing diapers, cooking, cleaning and taking the kid when Mom wants to go out - we'll have to do a case study with Big Daddy Wayne). This is all the more important as

*Penned By: The Seed & German Seed*

we are trying to be honest and to an extent liberal (see the Gay World, etc.) and if we are construed as being chauvinists then no one will take us seriously.

**Anyway, very good work, my Brother.**

**kisses Kaja GooGoo**

**Hey Affenschwanz!**

Thanks for the mail with the critics' comments. As yet only two have occurred to me:

"If only I had taken my own advice."

—Leroy in Exile (member of the Seed editing team)

"After reading this informative work I have decided to learn from my parents' mistakes and start using birth control".

—Chastity

By the way, the German word for Seed is "Saat" (pronounced "saht" . It might just be a rumor, but I heard somewhere that Saat really likes pork.

Hey Cupcake, if I don't talk to you before Thursday then have a great time in Seattle. Don't think about anything else and enjoy the break and just have some fun - you've earned it, Brother!

**Fuckfully yours,**

**Spacko**

### Outtake 19

We figured 19 outtakes were going to be enough. 20 just seemed like too many. We had hundreds to choose from. Hey, maybe a book of outtakes is in the cards.... Ok, so some of them are not so fantastic. We were just trying to emphasize a point. Putting a book together is not an easy task. Especially on such a difficult topic. This series once again illustrates the amount of work, the goofiness and the friendship involved in the process. I hope you can see how we actually attempt to stay positive while taking the odd shot at each other. They are all in good fun.

## Seed's Sketchy Relationship Theories - A Guide to the Perils of Dating

You may think we are a little nuts. We probably are. We did however, write this book from the heart and like we said before, we hope that it has helped you at least in some way in your relationship adventures.

We also believe that humor is an important gift to give and hope that some of this work actually comes across as some sort of comedy. It may be a bit abstract at times. However, it is definitely original. We hope you have enjoyed this section. If you notice that the commentary has been a bit one sided. German Seed was so overwhelmed with the originality of this idea that he allowed me to write it myself. Trust is a beautiful thing. He knows I would never take any uncalled shots at him. After all he did call me "Cupcake".

Back to this series of outtakes, other than the mention of the work that was involved in this project, we also have here a reference to my new Birth Date. I found out who my actual mother and father were on October 21$^{st}$ 2003 in Munich Germany. I am sure you can imagine the emotion involved. I am glad German Seed was there to offer me some support.

The second last update is simply another sign of the effects of the insomnia. And the final one. It is simply my favorite one. Who wouldn't enjoy being called "Rat Bastard". Once again thank you we hope you enjoyed our creativity.

**Hey Seed,**

Thanks for the birth certificate - it looks cool. I will never forget your birth and am honored that I had the privilege to be with you at such a fucked up yet important time.

The table of contents is great - fuck, when I read the section titles I have to laugh. This book is fucking great!

**Gotta go, talk to you soon, Brother Saat**

**P.S. Hi, I'm German Seed.**

**Gaucho,**

The photo is overwhelming - I think it reflects the urban jungle and being lost in it.

The font is good, on the screen it's a little bit unclear with the shadows. I printed it out in color and it's better, but still it needs to be a

*Penned By: The Seed & German Seed*

bit clearer. I find that the yellow font is clearer, maybe it has to do with orange. Perhaps it is clearer without the shadows, although I find that the shadows are a good idea.

**Talk to you soon.**

**Ciao Brother,**

**Wimmerl**

**Bongo:**

Updated version. I may be stupid. Ok I am stupid. Could you please explain, your quotes to me. Hey also when you get to the outtakes section I am pretty sure you will penetrate it, it is so yummy. The creativity started to flow and bang……..

The space represents how much room we have left for quotes. I have included one actual serious one. Kind of from your emails I hope you don't mind. I am going to solicit one from Wayne or Fiona or Dave or someone as well. No one knows who this Greg fellow is.

**Lumpster:**

I can't shut off my brain. Is that a good thing? Here is the begining of the game development. Don't spend much time thinking about it. I can't help myself.

**The Big Guy**

**Cuba:**

Just so you know we are up to 306 pages.

**Hugs,**

**Rat Bastard**

Oh one final note. There were actually 28 outtakes in total. But, who was counting. I guess I might have been.

**We hope you thoroughly enjoyed the flashback sequence.**

# ACKNOWLEDGEMENTS

*"There Is a Fine Line
Between
Creativity and Being Drunk"*

*-the seed.*

What – is this Seed guy fucking drunk? Why are the acknowledgements at the back of the book? Well, it is simple: how could they possibly be at the front of the book? I had not written it yet and if my editor and publisher never got it together to have the guts to put something so relevant instead of the same cloned crap into the bookstores, then there really is no need for me to get all mushy and start thanking a bunch of people for their inspiration and support on this project. Actually, another reason is that I want to revolutionize the publishing industry by putting the acknowledgements where they belong. The one thing that I am not going to attempt to change about the publishing industry is that I am going to have a lot of positive critiques at the start of the book. Maybe even some from some famous, well-respected people. Hopefully that is what enticed you to purchase the book in the first place. Ok, wait a minute, if you are reading this, you have purchased the book and the reason, it really is not that important.

On a side note, I wonder if any of you out there are like me and have ever wondered how all of these influential people were able to submit comments of how much they enjoyed a book in order to persuade the reader to buy it. Wouldn't that have meant they read it before it was published? Is it fair that all of the inspirational people get a copy before the rest of the general public? And how do these people find the time to read all of these new books? I hope they are at least paying for them. If not, it just simply is not fair. Nobody has ever sent me a copy of their book to read. Have they you? So as for my critiques, my people are going to write them before actually reading the book based on my opinions. Then just like the rest of the public they are going to purchase their own copies. Seriously!!! And no fucking discounts, I am putting your name in the book, that should be enough for you.

Having gotten that out of the way, I would first off, like to thank you, the reading public for purchasing this wonderful book. Without you, I would have to consider that management job at Foot Locker. I would even like to extend this "thank-you" to all of the book burners out there. Thank you for keeping the capitalist system rolling along so smoothly. Sorry editor and publisher, I know in a big way you should come first. And in a big way you should, for having faith in this project, but part of the reason for that faith is that you had a hunch that the reading public would eat this up and hopefully we were both correct in our estimations (my estimation is it will be a best seller and sell well over 2 million copies: "DARE TO DREAM"). So big kudos to both my editor and publisher, I will thank you more when I pick up my Pulitzer.

This brings me to some of my very wonderful and supportive friends. Primarily Wayne and Fiona whose inspiration and drunken times spent together were imperative for this project. If you guys read carefully and understand my feelings on certain topics, I do consider you great friends and love you both dearly and that will never be taken away. Well, that is, unless of course you don't buy a copy of the book and that means each of you. Actually 3 copies: one for your child "Little Seed" as well. Hold on, I have just been informed that Fiona has given birth to a wonderful baby boy. What, his name is not "Little Seed"? It is Aidan? Aidan, listen closely, when you grow up – don't worry you can always change your name. Anyway, congratulations Fiona & Wayne. Aidan is lucky to have you as parents. Now where was I?

Oh yeah, of course I will give you a discount of each purchase as long as you buy something from **Seed's Outstanding Boutique** at <u>www.seeedenterprises.com</u>. While thanking Wayne, I must remove some of my gratitude. You see I owed him a bit of cash and when I paid him back he said he would be my business manager and literary agent for $100. He assured me I needed one and without his assistance I would be a miserable failure. Maybe he is my mother, that type of encouragement sounds a bit too familiar. Anyway Wayne, I don't really think you did anything for me, sure you supported and encouraged me. You even told me some of your stories on marriage and pregnancy, for which I am grateful. But other than your occasional call to see if I was a published success, I am not seeing any evidence of actual work. Hmmm... maybe "The Proof will be in the Pudding"? If it isn't, I want my $100 back. A little more on Wayne here, I bet you he just really wanted the book to be done. I asked him to give me a quote, an original that I can put at the start of one of the chapters. Are you ready for it? Here is one of his suggestions: "Love has no seasons." (Insert vomit here).

I feel it is also very important to thank my ex and her new man Patrick. Without you two fucking up the love of my life by your selfish cheating and lying ways, I am not sure I would have had an understanding, nor the angst necessary to accomplish such a project. Nor could I have been such a case study for my own book. Hey, I just want to say despite of all of your selfish, bitchy pettiness: Sweetie, you eventually will get what you deserve. Although I wish nothing bad upon you, I just know that karma will take care of you in the long run. And Patrick, sorry my friend, you are just a fool. The next sucker if you will. Oh, and Paddy, if I may call you that, just because you don't know that someone is dating someone else when they cheat with you, does not remove you from the responsibility. The fact that you accepted that person's lies and started to date them shows your incredible lack of character. And the fact that after a few months you would ask them to marry you shows what a pathetic insecure individual you are. For your information, my Sweetie... – ooops! – your Sweetie told me she loved me almost every day. She would never lie to you now, would she? That is right – you have more money (when the above estimations on sales come true, that past statement will automatically change to "you had more money"). Your "bling, bling" will never be enough. Let's just hope for the sake of your relationship it never runs out. As for you, well I can't tell you what I wish for you, it would not be politically correct....

I would also like to thank my loving family, which once again without your neglect, lack of nurturing and 40 some odd years of lying to me, I would not have experienced the angst and pain necessary to develop the guts to share my experiences and to do the soul searching necessary to gain an understanding of how fucked up the world is. Thank you for being my role models. I know some of you may even care about me, maybe even love me. Quite honestly though, I do not want to hear or accept your reasons or try to understand your guilt. Just know you have devastated me and stay away. Especially you, Mommy.

Those last two acknowledgements may have seemed a bit harsh, bitter and jaded. Well they are. But like everything else they do come from the heart. I truly hope no one has to experience the type of pain that has come from these two experiences and if you are unfortunate enough to experience it: Have strength and courage my friends. There are people out there who do love you and will offer you the support that you need. Just don't give up. You are worth it and it really is not your fault. As for my sweet ex, in some strange way I hope she gets her stuff sorted out and experiences some pain herself and becomes the amazing person that I saw her some day becoming. Nothing would make me happier. I am sincere when I say that. As for discounts on the books.... For the family? God, no. For my ex? Probably not. For Paddy? I will give you a copy or two.

Others, whom I think it is very important to thank at this moment, are my good friends: Vodka, Beer and Wine. Without you, life though healthier, may not have been filled with so many inspirational life-altering experiences. Not only did these friends sometimes make 5's appear to be 7's, but they led to many highly educational conversations about, oh, I don't know, cheese. These substances throughout life have been some of the greatest nurturers and supporters during some trying times. At this point, if you find yourself in a situation where these friends are a constant companion and you are living in a box or in an alley somewhere, please seek out the appropriate professional help. For the rest of us, moderation is the key. But my friends, "thank-you". Without you, I would not have become as well rounded as I am and I would not have met so many interesting and fascinating people. Sure there were a lot of annoying slurring idiots along the way, but even amongst the crowd of clouded, mind-altered illusions there were a few gems that provided some inspiration.

I would like to take at least a line or two to thank the following: Tits, the clitoris, the vagina and my father's sperm.

Since I have taken the time out to thank some of my favorite spirits, I believe it is necessary to thank some of the foods which I have consumed over the years. I know that you cannot hear or acknowledge the fact that I have thanked you, as you have likely been processed as some sort of waste material by now. If you haven't. "Get the fuck out of my arteries I am trying to live here."

I would also like to thank toilets and toilet paper. Without you I wouldn't want to imagine what life would be like.

Thank you once again alcohol, without your influence I almost had forgot to thank the person who was easily the most important in the whole process of writing this book. That is right: **"ME"**. Without me, this would have never happened or come to fruition, if you will. Without me, a lot of lives would have not have been enriched. Life taught me valuable lessons and without life I would have never been able to share them with you. So big props must be extended to **"Me"**.

While we are on the subject of me, I think it is important to thank a very important part of me. My hands. My hands have helped me in a lot of areas of my life. First off, I typed this book myself, and without my hands that would have been much more difficult. Without my hands I do not think I would have had as many dating opportunities throughout my life. Come on, face it, a guy without hands may have a killer personality and he may have developed other skills, but without hands it's not going to be easy for him. Yet, in reality, a lot of girls who are after the bulge in the back pocket look for hands second. Ok, I may have made that up, I am sure there are no actual statistics on what appendages are necessary. I am just thinking if a girl looks at you and you are handless, she might just keep on looking for the next guy. So as I was saying, thank you hands. Without you, the lonely nights may have been a bit more painful. If you remember from earlier on in the book, I am actually blind in one of my eyes, which brings me back to my mother. Ahhh... Mommy, whoever you may or not be. I am sure in a few years I will find out that the person, who as I have just been informed supposedly was my actual birth mother, actually is not and that is a lie as well. I have been working on interrogating one of my pets. I am sure they are going to break soon and tell me the truth. Oh yeah, back to my hands and my supposed mother. She would like to have me believe that the reason I am blind in one eye, is because of my hands....

    I would also like to thank insomnia. Without you, the voices in my head would not be so clear. Due to insomnia, I am convinced that the bed is really at times hell and the only place to get any real sleep is behind the wheel of a car after sleep deprivation. For some reason, the fluffy pillows of bed are actually just mental stimulants which start the wheels turning. Without these endless nights of tossing and turning and trying to trick myself to sleep, the creative juices which are constantly flowing in my brain may have not come out to the forefront to the extent that they have. Sort of like hot steamy molten lava. Without these sleepless nights, though I would be much closer to sanity, I would lack some of the comedic touches that I have shared with you. "What's that?" "Huh...?" "Who are you...? Anyway thank you insomnia, you are a true pal.

    Well folks, that is just about all she wrote. Actually in this case all he wrote. Before I leave you though, I feel I must send out some heartfelt thank-you messages to some people. I have really appreciated their help and support throughout the years. First I must send a big Thank-You out to my friends Corrie and Vern. Corrie was my longest-term girlfriend and Vern (he may actually be the one who coined "Seed") is her loving, doting husband and one of my best friends. I have known them for a long time and have shared many fantastic experiences with the two of them. They have always been there to share the good times and give support during the challenging periods. The love we have for each other is a prime example of how it is meant to be and can never be taken away. It is a pleasure having them in my life.

I must also thank my great friend Whitey and his wife Rhonda. They are also dear friends that go back to my High School days. Whitey and I have shared a lot of fantastic times together including some drunken debauchery. He has first-hand knowledge on some of the mad skills I have and I wish we could spend more time together.

Also big props out to Kleo and Barb and their husbands Victor and John. As well as to Joe Sabbagh (Eoj) and Kim. Not to forget Scott and Patti Berg, we have known each other for quite some time and I think we have always provided one another with some priceless entertainment, and never ending support. And of course, how could I not thank Homer and his dysfunctional family. Thanks, you truly inspire.

Other Buddies that need to be mentioned from my youth are my friends Tony Gagnon, Chris Arnold, Bart Arnold, Jase EAEE and Bernie Hrapchak to name a few. We had a blast growing up together and have some stories that need to remain in the vault.

A little later in life, some friends that also deserve some mention are Rick Gillis and his brother Ken. The only challenge with these two is my memory from the time from hanging out with this pair is a bit foggy: "Seed, ask for more Napshkins".

I must also thank my great friend Danielle. She epitomizes what a real friend is. I am lucky to have her in my life. Andy, you are truly a lucky man.

I also must thank Wally or "Sticky Note". We have been through a lot together and I am sure we will share a lot more good times in the future. Pat Murphy where ever you may be you have been a great friend over the years and "I think your fries may be ready."

I must also thank Fuzzy, Kingsley and Thai, you have no idea how much you have helped with your occasional licks and purring. Kingsley, I miss you.

I know I am just touching on a few here and I will miss a lot of people who have touched me, such as coaches (Mr. Mantyka), teachers (Mr. Mantyka) and bosses (Glenn Stewart and Rick Lumby) you guys are all first class. However, in an attempt to keep this reasonably short here is a list of people who in the last year helped me through some very tough times. Jerimiah and Roland, thank you for not bailing on me when my relationship ended. It is quite refreshing to see some people still have some depth. Dale MacCalder, you are a fantastic man. Toni Walker, sweetie you are a real gem and something good that was a result of my relationship. Stephen Castle, well what can I say now that I am British as well. Kevin Guthrie, Carol Jamison (you know how I feel), Dale, Gio Branco, Keith, Stuart, Shantall (you make me smile) & Wayne and David – you guys have all restored my faith in human nature. I must thank you for your kind ears during a difficult time and not running when you saw me coming. You guys are all gold and I look forward to the future. Michael, I can't tell you how much I appreciated the day at the park when you asked me if I was ok. You were a complete stranger and you extended an olive branch to me, thank you. Gestures like that sometimes save lives.

Scotty (my bartender) – thank you, I am searching for domesticity, you are a true friend. Colin my other bartender, that is right I have two, you are a fantastic guy and I wish you the best. It will come, keep plugging away. Nikorn your kindness does not go unnoticed. I have only known you for a few months and you have saved me from being a starving author. It is strange that some people I barely know take better care of me than my blood relatives. Thanks to the wonderful people of Europe for embracing me and letting me know it is ok for life to screw you up sometimes.

Thank you to my friend Ben, you are a "wicked" man. It has been my pleasure getting to know you. Thanks for making me feel good about myself I can't tell you how much that means to me.

Second to last and definitely not least. I do not know how to truly express my love and thanks for my late (Great) Aunt & Uncle Priscilla and Roy. I learned during the writing of this book that you took me in for my first two years of existence and for some reason we remained in touch. You seemed to understand our bond did not require physical presence. You were the only members of my family who would phone me to just say "I Love You". I miss you dearly.

And finally a big thank-you to David Slater, his girlfriend Kirsten, Greg (German Seed), & Silvia and Wayne & Fiona once again. David, I can't tell you how much I appreciate you chaperoning me through Europe. I think it shows that you have some huge character. Kirsten you are just sweet. Greg, you just know brother, it has been a treat writing this together. Silvia (Moosemaus) thanks for your hospitality and taking care of me on a tough night. Wayne and Fiona, I am out of words.

---

That is all for now my friends. I truly do hope that I have in some way provided you with the panacea to all of your relationship woe's. At least I hope I have been able to bring an occasional smile to your face. Remember to:

**"Live-Love-Trust-Grow-Prosper-Cherish-With Passion Please!"**

**-the seed.**

**Thanks for Reading. We Truly Appreciated It.**

I HOPE EVERYTHING IS A LITTLE CLEARER NOW

"Ahh True Love"

RELAX SIT BACK YOU MADE IT HOME

"Everybody Loves Puppies."
-The seed.

Life is Fantastic

# The Last Page

## Seed's Sketchy Relationship Theories
### A Guide to the Perils of Dating

**Welcome to Bliss!!!!**

**Congratulations you have made it!!!**

As for the book. It is a journey that will take you through the confusing world of dating from the first date to the eventual "I do". And everything in between. It Encourages you to become an "Exception" an "Original". If you accept the challenge. We commend you. Either way enjoy the ride!!!

-THE SEED.

## ABOUT THE AUTHORS

Seed is a lot like James Bond. No one man can personify the true depth of Seed. In a way Seed is the **"Exception"**. He does not march to the same drum as the masses. He charts his own course, makes his own mistakes and is solely responsible for his successes. Well, maybe not solely, he has surrounded himself with some of the best people on the planet and loves and cherishes each friend and interaction dearly. Seed is a simple, yet very complicated man. Actually, he is more than one man, he represents the plight of the modern man.

Seed has worked as a dishwasher, gardener, waiter, bartender, hotel manager, bartender, sales representative, gas jockey, coach, bartender, commercial fisherman, insurance agent, bartender, hand model, hair model, landscaper, helper monkey, bartender, construction worker, geological core sample tester, and a bartender just to name a few. These experiences gave him the wisdom necessary to be what he is today. **An Author!!!!**

Printed in the United States
25216LVS00002B/108